The American Social Experience Series

GENERAL EDITOR: JAMES KIRBY MARTIN

EDITORS: PAULA S. FASS, STEVEN H. MINTZ,
CARL PRINCE, JAMES W. REED & PETER N. STEARNS

The pupil becomes an individual, *American School Board Journal* (1922). (Reprinted by permission of the Department of Special Collections and University Archives, Stanford University Libraries.)

SCHOOLS AS SORTERS

Lewis M. Terman, Applied Psychology, and the Intelligence Testing Movement, 1890-1930

———————

PAUL DAVIS CHAPMAN

NEW YORK UNIVERSITY PRESS

NEW YORK AND LONDON

1988

LIBRARY OF CONGRESS
Library of Congress Cataloging-in-Publication Data
Chapman, Paul Davis.
Schools as sorters : Lewis M. Terman, applied psychology, and the
intelligence testing movement, 1890–1930 / Paul Davis Chapman.
p.   cm.—(The American social experience series ; 11)
Bibliography: p.
Includes index.
ISBN 0-8147-1420-X (alk. paper)
1. School children—United States—Psychological testing—History.
2. Intelligence tests—United States—History.   3. Terman, Lewis
Madison, 1877–1956.   I. Title.   II. Series.
LB1131.C447 1988
371.2'6'0973—dc19   88-15382
                                                        CIP

New York University Press books are Smyth-sewn
and printed on permanent and durable acid-free paper.

For Helen

Contents

Illustrations

Tables

Preface

During the past 150 years American education has been transformed from decentralized common schools and academies to a highly complex and differentiated system. Midway through that evolution the intelligence test was invented. At the same time schools created numerous means to classify students and channel them through their education. These two developments combined to make the American school a powerful mechanism for sorting students and shaping their futures.

For some time we have needed a careful study of the rise of intelligence testing and classification in American education. Much recent scholarship has consisted of emotionally charged attacks on tests and classification systems. The testing establishment has contributed countless studies, many of them defending the value of tests. Historical studies of testing have concentrated extensively on leadership and ideology. Few have examined how and why intelligence tests and classification systems were actually introduced into the schools and what difference they made in the lives of students. This book seeks to address these needs by providing a comprehensive understanding of how testing and classification became a permanent part of the American educational system.

This work was initiated in the 1970s, a time marked by heated debate and sharp controversy about the uses and consequences of ability testing and tracking. In the years since, tests have been part of my daily life, as a teacher, counselor, college admissions officer, consultant, and school principal. I have used tests for selection, guidance, diagnosis, and planning and know that when properly administered, interpreted, and explained they can be of real value. It is also clear to me that there is significant potential for the misuse of tests. All too often administrators, teachers, students, and parents alike misconstrue the meaning of tests and their implications for individual growth and academic achievement. Nationwide a debate continues about appropriate policies for ability testing and classification of students. For practitioners and policymakers alike this book is intended to provide a historical perspective on the role of schools as sorters.

Many people have helped me prepare this study, and I owe them an enormous debt. David Tyack gave me wise counsel and the inspiration for this book during my graduate study in the history of education at Stanford University. Several other people have taken a special interest in the project: Daniel Resnick of Carnegie-Mellon University; Lee Cronbach of Stanford University; Bernard Gifford of the University of California, Berkeley; and Tom James of Brown University. Each has read the entire manuscript and has provided valuable suggestions for its improvement. Fellow students shaped the study, among them Toby Edson of the University of Oregon, Michael Katz of the University of Nebraska, and Eric Bredo of the University of Virginia. Others have read and made helpful comments on all or portions of the manuscript; Decker Walker and David Kennedy of Stanford University, Michael Holt of the University of Virginia, and Peter Stearns of Carnegie-Mellon University. Those who have assisted my study have saved me from many errors; any that remain are, of course, entirely my own responsbility.

Many provided institutional support for the project. I am thankful for the Research Traineeship awarded to me by Stanford University using funds from the U.S. Office of Education. In addition, the Carnegie Corporation provided funds to support my research during two summers. Release time from my work at Reed College, San Francisco University High School, and the Head-Royce School allowed me to complete the project.

Every historical study requires careful detective work, and I am grateful to several library staffs who aided my search for information. Ralph Hansen, Roxanne-Louise Nilan, Margaret Coesfeld, Juanita McKinley, and Robin Chandler at Stanford University, and Sonia

Kaufman and Suzanne Gallup at the University of California, Berkeley, were steadfast. The manuscript was prepared by Charlotte Can-
ning, Cynthia Hagen and Amy Kaplan, whose expertise was greatly
appreciated.

This book was completed only with the encouragement of my entire
extended family. Most of all I give my thanks to Helen and my
children, Will, Peter, and Lesley, for their support and their patience.

Introduction

Testing: Past and Present

In April 1917 the United States declared war on Germany, and a month later Stanford University professor of psychology Lewis M. Terman answered the call of the American Psychological Association to aid the war effort. Over the next two years, the United States Army used group intelligence tests developed by Terman and other psychologists to test and classify 1.7 million recruits. Shortly after the war's end, Terman observed that the army tests "demonstrated beyond question that the methods of mental measurement are capable of making a contribution of great value to army efficiency. . . . That their universal use in the schoolroom is necessary to educational efficiency will doubtless soon be accepted as a matter of course." Terman's prophecy was accurate, for in the next decade intelligence testing spread throughout the public school system with astonishing swiftness. Under the auspices of the National Academy of Sciences, Terman helped transform the army tests into the National Intelligence Tests for schoolchildren in 1919, and within a year over 400,000 copies of the examination had been sold. By 1925 psychologists had developed over seventy-five tests of general mental ability; according to some estimates yearly intelligence test sales approached four million by mid-decade.[1]

During these same years the practice of ability grouping became widespread. Although American schools had begun sorting students early in the nineteenth century, the first quarter of the twentieth century witnessed a dramatic change in the means by which students were classified for instruction. Increasingly after the turn of the century, schools fashioned a variety of curricular sequences for students with different backgrounds, ability levels, and aspirations. In the 1920s the terms "ability grouping," "homogeneous grouping," and "tracking" became familiar words in the educational lexicon. A survey conducted by the U.S. Bureau of Education in 1926, for example, revealed that a large majority of urban schools classified students according to ability. This same study also showed that 86 percent of the cities in the sample used intelligence tests as one basis of classification.[2]

In the nearly seventy-five years since Lewis Terman began his work on intelligence tests, the practice of testing and grouping students has become a permanent fixture in American education. The use of tests has also elicited sharp controversy. When testing and tracking first became widespread in the twenties, psychologists, educators, and journalists engaged in a furious debate about intelligence tests. The publication of *The Tyranny of Testing* by Banesh Hoffman in 1962 reignited public controversy, fueled by the civil rights movement and a climate of dissent in the sixties.[3]

In the seventies and eighties, the debate on testing policy has continued unabated. One of the most public controversies swirled around the Educational Testing Service (ETS) and the Scholastic Aptitude Test (SAT). Critics such as Ralph Nader and Allan Nairn in *The Reign of ETS* (1980) and David Owen in *None of the Above* (1985) charged that the SAT has "victimized" countless individuals and groups in American society, assertions which have evoked strong rejoinders from ETS. Psychologist Arthur Jensen in *Bias in Mental Testing* (1980) identified numerous criticisms of intelligence tests, including:

That they are culturally biased against minorities; that the test items appear schoolish, defective, or trivial; that psychologists cannot define intelligence and therefore cannot measure it; that the tests measure nothing but the ability to do well on similar tests; that the tests fail to measure innate capacity; that the norms are unsuitable for minorities; that the IQ is a measure only of specific knowledge and skills acquired in school or a cultural home; that the IQ is inconstant from early childhood to maturity; that test scores are lowered when the tester is of a different race; and that tests and test results have been misused.[4]

Such considerations have prompted several national assessments of testing policy in the 1980s, among them the study on the role of testing in American life conducted by the Committee on Ability Testing of the National Academy of Sciences. Many of the studies in the educational reform movement of the eighties have also focused on national issues in testing such as score declines, minimum competency testing to raise standards, truth in testing to protect consumers, and teacher tests to strengthen instruction. In 1987 the Commission on Testing and Public Policy, established by Bernard Gifford, dean of the School of Education at the University of California, Berkeley, launched a three-year investigation of how tests affect educational, social, and economic opportunity in American life. As Gifford has noted: "The controversy over testing is fundamentally a dispute about politics, about what means and measures will be utilized to determine who gets what, when and how!" And another recent analysis of the IQ controversy observed:

Ultimately, the war over testing will be won or lost on the issue of test use. Intelligence and aptitude tests only matter to the extent that they are used, and therefore the most important question one can ask of these tests is: "What good are they?" Are they the efficient decision-making tools they are purported to be, or are they biased, invalid instruments and therefore undesirable selection tools?

The continuing debate about test use in American society suggests that we greatly need a more thorough understanding of the history of the testing movement.[5]

The Scope of the Study

This study explores the origins of the use of intelligence tests to classify students into ability groups. The study focuses on Lewis Terman, a leading figure in the intelligence testing movement, and his prescriptions for the use of tests to classify students. Two related questions are examined. First, why was this educational innovation— the intelligence test—adopted so rapidly in the public schools? Were the tests incorporated, as some have argued, as a great contribution of applied psychology to social and educational progress? Or were the tests foisted upon the schools, as others have claimed, by groups seeking to promote their own social philosophy and to protect their own self-interest? Second, what was the historical relation between testing and ability grouping, or tracking? Did the adoption of intelligence testing lead directly to a comprehensive system of ability grouping? Or did schools develop a systematic means of treating students differently at an earlier time? If so, how were students evaluated and by what means were they placed in different curricular tracks? Was the historical relation between testing and tracking more complex, perhaps, than is suggested by these conflicting and mutually exclusive interpretations? This study also offers some tentative answers to questions about the role of the school in promoting social opportunity. What were the consequences of the rise of intelligence testing and ability grouping for equity both within the school and beyond? To what degree did the tests and ability grouping increase opportunity by providing new ways of discovering and cultivating talent? And to what degree did these innovations stifle opportunity by creating a segmented curriculum and by sorting students with methods which reinforced social class and race differences?

Three models help to explain the rapid emergence of intelligence testing and ability grouping. First, a network of newly emergent professionals—university professors of psychology and public school administrators—advocated the widespread use of tests to classify students. They were supported in their efforts by philanthropic foundations, educational publishers, and such organizations as the National Education Association, the National Society for the Study of Education, the National Research Council, and the U.S. Bureau of Education. To a large degree the adoption of intelligence testing and ability grouping was a "top-down" reform emanating from university departments of psychology and supported by school administrators.

Second, intelligence tests were adopted by schools—administrators and teachers—in response to a vast array of problems they faced around the turn of the century. Urban school enrollments mushroomed because of massive immigration, the shift in population from the country to the city, and the newly enforced compulsory education laws. School populations represented an increasingly diverse patchwork of ethnic groups. Responding to this new constituency, schools developed new objectives during this same time. The largely college-preparatory common school curriculum of the nineteenth century gradually gave way by the time of the First World War to "social efficiency." According to one national educational commission in 1917, schools were to prepare students for life, including citizenship, the working world, and the use of leisure time.[6] School administrators' lives were complicated further by soaring costs and a drive by reformers to make the schools more efficient. In response to these problems —increasing size, diversity, changing objectives, and rising costs—the school curriculum became much more differentiated. School administrators needed a means to classify students and assign them to different curricular tracks. While student achievement and teachers' judgments aided in that task, intelligence tests gave school administrators a more efficient and more scientific means of sorting students.

Third, intelligence tests were adopted in the public schools because the tests reflected widely shared values of the Progressive Era. University professors and school people alike saw the tests as a logical outgrowth of the progressive quest for efficiency, conservation, and order. The tests were welcomed by people who placed their trust in the authority of science and the expert. For psychologists like Terman, the hierarchical order of intelligence portrayed by the tests reinforced, as well, a hereditarian interpretation of individual development and group differences. Finally, relatively low test scores for recent immigrants, blacks, and the poor seemed to validate widespread assumptions about certain ethnic groups and the superiority of Nordic Americans. The publication of group intelligence test scores fanned nativistic fears, fueled a drive for immigration restriction, and provided schools with a new way to explain poor performance among certain immigrant groups—lack of ability.[7]

Because the subject of testing and classification is vast, this study has been defined and limited in several ways. The investigation focuses on the years between 1890 and 1930, a period that saw the emergence and waning of the progressive movement[8] as well as the rise of the testing movement.[9] The 1890s marked the origin of the progressive movement as well as some of the earliest attempts to develop mental tests. The 1890s also witnessed the rapid emergence of a new set of problems for schools and of new attempts to solve those problems. By

1930 both intelligence testing and ability grouping had become central features of the educational system.

As the title of this book suggests, the experience of one man, Lewis Terman, illuminates the adoption of intelligence tests. Although there were other important figures in the early testing movement—Edward L. Thorndike, James McKeen Cattell, and Robert M. Yerkes, to name a few—Terman was probably the individual most responsible for developing and promoting intelligence tests for use in the schools. This work is not a biography of Terman, nor is it merely a study of his ideology, for these studies have been done. Rather it is an analysis of the relation between Terman—a leader in the psychological measurement community—and the schools that adopted intelligence tests. By prescribing the use of intelligence tests, Terman played a major role in the schools' adoption of tests for sorting students.[10]

This book focuses on tests of intelligence. These instruments have exerted significant influence on the classification of students, and their use has sparked great controversy within the psychological profession and among the public. The rise of intelligence testing, however, was part of the broader measurement movement. Achievement tests, developed during the same period, were used in later years to accomplish some of the same sorting and classification functions as intelligence tests. Because this study refers often to complex phenomena—such as intelligence, the tests that attempt to measure ability, aptitude, and achievement—a discussion of terms is contained in the appendix.

To describe the way IQ tests were first used, the study examines the adoption of testing in three case studies. These cities were among the earliest and most comprehensive experiments with testing and tracking. Each had a direct link to Terman and Stanford University. Together they represent a spectrum of settings, from a large, diverse city to a small, homogeneous town. Elsewhere in the study, discussions of the adoption of tests typically refer to urban schools.

This study does not attempt to resolve some of the more disputed elements in the historical controversy over intelligence tests, such as the nature-nurture question, test validity, and cultural bias. These issues have been examined in great detail elsewhere and are part of the continuing debate about testing.[11] This work seeks to show how contemporaries at the turn of the century saw these issues and to assess the impact of the debates on the adoption of tests by schools.

Historical Perspectives

This study has built upon the work of those who in recent years have probed the history of intelligence testing. After a long period of widespread approval, the testing industry came under fire from a variety of critics in the 1960s. During this decade, several historical studies explored the origins of the movement. Typically these studies of testing were relatively brief and were contained in social and intellectual histories of America. In *The Transformation of the School* (1961), for example, Lawrence Cremin briefly discussed the origins of the testing movement at the turn of the century, the use of the tests in the army, and the controversies surrounding test interpretation in the twenties. Willis Rudy's thematic study of American education in the twentieth century, *Schools in an Age of Mass Culture* (1965), linked the testing movement with the rise of "science in education," describing the evolution of testing from Francis Galton's studies of intelligence in the late nineteenth century to the present. Taking a biographical approach, Geraldine Joncich's account of the life of Edward Thorndike, *The Sane Positivist* (1968), examined the man who was perhaps the central figure in the development of educational psychology in the early twentieth century. In *Education and the Cult of Efficiency* (1962), Raymond Callahan showed how business community pressure for efficiency, combined with the vulnerability of school administrators to outside influence, led to attempts to measure student achievement and teaching effectiveness with standardized tests in the first quarter of the twentieth century.[12]

Several studies in the 1960s viewed the testing movement as an illustration of the relationship between scientists and public policy. Loren Baritz's *The Servants of Power* (1965) focused on the "industrial use of social scientists and their sciences," but concentrated on the business use of psychological tests for personnel selection rather than on the experience of the schools. Daniel Kevles's article, "Testing the Army's Intelligence" (1968), explored the role of psychologists in the military during World War I. Like Baritz, he argued that the marriage of scientists and the military was an unhappy one, noting that professional army men "resented the professional psychologists as a threat to military autonomy."[13] Mark Haller's *Eugenics* (1963) examined hereditarian attitudes in American thought and the impact on public policy.

Eugenics—defined by contemporaries as "the science of improving the human race by better breeding"—arose in part from a growing concern in the late nineteenth century about society's misfits. The movement was in large part directed by superintendents of asylums for the feebleminded, insane, and alcoholic, by prison wardens and prison physicians, and by sociologists and social workers. After the turn of the century, the development and use of intelligence tests in asylums, schools, and the army contributed to a pervasive myth that the feebleminded were a "menace" to society, a myth that fueled moves to sterilize the unfit and restrict immigration. Although Haller touched only briefly on the use of intelligence tests in the eugenics movement, his searching analysis of the social consequences of hereditarian thought proved to be a stimulus for several further studies of intelligence testing.[14]

In the 1970s the historical debate about testing intensified and was frequently polarized. Revisionist educational historians attacked intelligence tests as an instrument of social control. In "Testing for Order and Control in the Liberal Corporate State," Clarence Karier argued that intelligence tests were part of a reform movement whose purpose was to solve for large-scale corporate capitalists some of the problems resulting from urbanization, industrialization, and immigration. Specifically the tests were designed to rationalize and stabilize the society for efficient production and consumption of goods and services. According to Karier:

The roots of the American testing movement lie deeply imbedded in the American progressive temper which combined its belief in progress, its racial attitudes, and its faith in the scientific expert working through the state authority to ameliorate and control the evolutionary progress of the race.

The tests, he argued, were biased in terms of social class, economic, cultural, and racial background. Their use in schools served to block opportunity for the lower classes and immigrants. To the intelligence tests and to Lewis Terman, he attributed responsibility for fashioning a system of tracking in the schools that reinforced social inequality.[15]

Karier's student Russell Marks conducted a more in-depth study of Terman and the ideology of the testing movement and found the deliberate effort of a scholar to maintain his favored position in society:

In attempting to preserve the status-quo through scientific evidence derived from testing, Terman sacrificed objectivity for expediency, individuality for industrial efficiency, and freedom for social control. . . . As a result Terman promoted social control and industrial efficiency at the expense of the freedom of the feebleminded, the soldier, the parent, the child, the poor, the immigrant, the alien, the worker, and the Black.

Like Karier, Marks blamed Terman for the rise of tracking: "Terman perceived the public school as the most effective institution for molding and controlling society."[16] With a similar orientation Joel Spring analyzed the "meaning of intelligence" in the army tests. He argued that the ideas of the early test developers were elitist and hereditarian, and that their definition of "intelligence" was merely "an indication of the ability to function in modern corporate forms of activity, such as the army, the factory, and the school." The meaning of intelligence, said Spring, was culturally derived, subject to change, and an instrument for social control.[17]

Other revisionist historians criticized the rise of testing from an economic perspective. Samuel Bowles and Herbert Gintis in *Schooling in Capitalist America* (1976), for example, sought to explain the historic failure of educational reform movements to reduce inequality. They concluded that schools in America were created not to promote equality but to meet the demand of employers for a trained labor force and to serve as a vehicle for social control and stability. Schooling, in other words, served to reinforce and reproduce the inequality of classes in a capitalist society. Analyzing the period of reform around the turn of the century, they observed: "The essence of Progressivism in education was the rationalization of the process of reproducing the social classes of modern industrial life." Turning specifically to the history of testing, they noted that as large numbers of immigrant and working-class children began to attend schools, reformers pushed to dismantle the common school curriculum of the nineteenth century and within the secondary schools to propose a system of stratification. Curricular tracking, they claimed, both symbolized and reinforced racial, ethnic, and class divisions in the larger society. In this context intelligence tests were introduced into schools: "Particularly after World War I, the capitulation of the schools to business values and the concept of efficiency led to the increased use of 'intelligence' and scholastic-achievement testing as an ostensibly unbiased means of measuring the product of schooling and classifying students." The rise of testing and tracking, they claimed, faced little organized opposition either from labor or from "idealistic Progressives who worked in vain for a humanistic and egalitarian education." Rather, the adoption of testing "proceeded smoothly" and "seems in retrospect to have been almost inevitable."[18]

An analysis of "Education and the Corporate Order" (1972) by David K. Cohen and Marvin Lazerson reached similar conclusions. They, too, adopted an economic interpretation of the rise of testing and tracking. Arguing that the history of education in the twentieth century must be seen in the context of the "schools' adaptation to large-scale corporate capitalism," they observed: "Education was fashioned into an increasingly refined training and selection mechanism for the labor force." They concluded that "the tests quickly came to be seen as the surest way to classify students and to organize schools for their work in occupational pre-selection." Importantly, they noted that curricular differentiation preceded testing, but that "testing provided a powerful reinforcement and rationale for it." Although they argued that the adaptation of the schools to capitalism often engendered conflict, they found in the origins of classification and testing few who could pose realistic alternatives. In fact, they said, it was "hardly surprising that differentiated educational 'equality' met with such rapid acceptance."[19]

At various points psychologists themselves entered the debate about the origins of intelligence testing, oftentimes in response to the controversy stirred up by Arthur Jensen when he reasserted a strongly genetic, hereditarian interpretation of race differences in intelligence in an article entitled "How Much Can We Boost IQ and Scholastic Achievement?" (1969). One study by Leon Kamin, *The Science and Politics of I.Q.* (1974), flatly rejected Jensen's claims. Reviewing the work of the pioneers in intelligence testing, as well as the immigration restriction legislation in the twenties, Kamin concluded:

The I.Q. test in America, and the way in which we think about it, has been fostered by men committed to a particular social view. That view includes the belief that those on the bottom are genetically inferior victims of their own immutable defects. The consequence has been that the I.Q. test has served as an instrument of oppression against the poor—dressed in the trappings of science, rather than politics.

Kamin's judgment approximated that of the revisionist historians.[20]

In another article spurred by the heated Jensen controversy, Lee J. Cronbach explored the "difficulties that arise when the scholar enters the arena of policy." Reviewing "five decades of public controversy over mental testing" (1975), Cronbach argued that the controversies have served to distort both the intentions and findings of social scientists. Journalists eager to make headlines and a public hungry for sensational news have helped to distort the process of scientific inquiry. Scholars have often fared poorly when discussing their work in emotionally charged times. And scholars have also, in their desire to be of public service, occasionally failed to gauge the political impact of their work. The controversy over testing in the twenties was a case in point. Critics attacked the mental tests as racist, elitist, and deterministic, charges that elicited a furious response from the testers themselves. Yet for Cronbach the significant point about the controversy in the twenties was that it was relatively short-lived and had little impact on the trend of public policy: "Virtually everyone favored testing in schools; the controversies arose because of incautious interpretations made by the testers and, even more, by popular writers."[21]

David Tyack's *The One Best System* (1974), an excellent survey of American public education, viewed testing from the vantage point of social history and the participants in the testing movement. Describing an educational system recently centralized, bureaucratized, and under pressure to adapt to the demands of the twentieth century, Tyack observed:

Intelligence testing and other forms of measurement provided the technology for classifying children. Nature-nurture controversies might pepper the scientific periodicals and magazines of the intelligentsia, but schoolmen found IQ tests invaluable means of channeling children; by the very act of channeling pupils, they helped to make the IQ prophecies self-fulfilling. Likewise, the differentiation of secondary education into tracks and the rise of vocational schooling represented a profound shift in the conception of the functions of universal education.

Pointing to the consequences of the testing movement, he observed that "the notion of great and measurable differences in intellectual capacity became part of the conventional wisdom not only of school people but of the public."[22]

By the late seventies it was clear that inquiry into the history of testing had only begun to reconstruct the past. Franz Samelson advanced our understanding with his study, "Putting Psychology on the Map: Ideology and Intelligence Testing" (1979). Analyzing the war experience, for example, he discovered that the actual contribution made by psychologists was less significant than previously thought due to "administrative roadblocks" and internal, political squabbles within the army. Contrary to the testers' claims for objectivity, he demonstrated the clear influence of ideology in the conception of the tests and plans for their use in schools. Most importantly, Samelson argued that the rise of testing changed the way Americans viewed intelligence: "Mental testing produced a change in the conceptual landscape; it transformed the idea of intelligence, itself a descendant of the idea of reason, from an amorphous, creative force to an 'objective' yet clearly value-laden dimension of individual differences consisting essentially, or 'operationally,' of getting the right answer on more or less clever little problems."[23]

During the eighties there has been sustained interest in the history of testing as policy questions about the use of tests in schools continue. In *The Mismeasure of Man* (1981), Harvard paleontologist Stephen J. Gould captured national attention with a book "about the abstraction of intelligence as a single entity, its location within the brain, its quantification as one number for each individual, and the use of these numbers to rank people in a single series of worthiness, invariably to find that oppressed and disadvantaged groups—races, classes, or sexes —are innately inferior and deserve their status." Gould surveyed two centuries of effort to measure human ability, from Paul Brocca's craniology to Arthur Jensen's reassertion of a strong hereditarian interpretation of intelligence. The science of mental measurement, he argued, has fallen prey to two fallacies—reification, or the "tendency to convert abstract concepts into entities," and ranking, or an effort to order complex phenomena in a single scale. He devoted considerable attention to the rise of the intelligence testing movement and to Lewis Terman as the leader of "mass marketing of the innate IQ." Gould criticized Terman and other psychometricians for not recognizing that their work, and science in general, is a "socially imbedded activity."

The ideology of Terman, and other pioneers in mental testing, served to limit social opportunity and to solidify the existing socioeconomic order.[24]

In the eighties historians also continued the quest for the origins of the testing movement. For Paula Fass, in "The IQ: A Cultural and Historical Framework" (1980), the testing movement reflected the culture of turn-of-the-century America and the need for social control. Importantly she recognized the connection between the testing and sorting functions of schools. So strongly imbedded in the culture was the concept of the IQ, she argued, that "it was almost inevitable that it be adopted by the schools."[25] While not addressing the history of intelligence testing specifically, John O'Donnell's study of American psychology, *The Origins of Behaviorism* (1985), illustrates how the transformation of academic psychology from "the science of consciousness to the science of behavior" provided an impetus for the testing movement. In the half-century from 1870 to 1920, American society and the psychological profession increasingly focused on objective measurement. As the nation responded to the experience of the First World War, the stage was set for the widespread acceptance of the testing movement and an application of the newly emergent psychological profession.[26]

Studies of the history of testing in the eighties have reflected a more balanced approach and an emerging consensus viewpoint on the origins of the testing movement. Of special note is Daniel Resnick's study, "History of Educational Testing," prepared as part of a major analysis of ability testing by the National Research Council in 1982. Resnick argues that the testing movement has been supported by many important groups—psychologists, school administrators, and publishers—who have nurtured test development, as well as local, state, and federal agencies eager to hold schools accountable through measurement. Acknowledging recent criticism of testing, he observed: "The present wave of controversy would have to wash very high to erode a base of use and support that has grown considerably in size and character over the past three quarters of a century."[27]

Of all contemporary studies of the history of intelligence testing, among the most impressive are those completed by Michael Sokal and other scholars associated with Cheiron, the International Society for the History of the Behavioral and Social Sciences. In *Psychological*

Testing and American Society (1987), Sokal has assembled important recent studies of the pioneers in intelligence testing—James McKeen Cattell, Henry H. Goddard, Robert M. Yerkes, and Lewis M. Terman. Henry L. Minton's analysis of Terman examined the role of political ideology in shaping the testing movement. He appropriately character-ized Terman as a liberal reformer whose zeal for applied psychology was very much part of the broader progressive movement. Yet Min-ton, like other students of Terman, had to confront the fact that "Terman's democratic ideal of a meritocracy based on innate ability was not, in the context of his own times, a bona fide democratic ideal. His legacy of mass intelligence testing served to perpetuate an unjust social order."[28]

Sokal has written extensively in the history of American psychol-ogy, and his most significant contribution perhaps is his suggestive article, "Approaches to the History of Psychological Testing" (1984). Here he offers guidelines to shape future histories of the testing move-ment. These studies should be: empirical, firmly grounded in primary source material; detailed, explaining "precisely just which specific tests were used at which times for what purposes"; contextual, in relation to society such as progressive America and in relation to "disciplinary origins" such as the rise of applied psychology; personal, relying on biographical background; broadly conceived in terms of subject, whether it be the range of testing or the many applications of tests in society; broadly conceived in terms of period, to describe the full sweep of the movement's development; and dispassionate, to avoid the polarization that has characterized much of the scholarship to date. It is hoped that this present study meets at least a few of these vital criteria.[29]

The Plan

The three principal themes of this book—the professional network, the schools' needs, and progressive values—are explored in several ways. The first chapter examines the emergence of intelligence testing in the Progressive Era from 1890 to 1917, especially Terman's role in developing the tests, the rise of applied psychology in Europe and America, and the development of an educational measurement move-ment that forged a network of individuals and institutions interested in testing. The second chapter discusses this same period from the vantage point of the schools, the problems they faced, and their initial attempts to solve them through new classification plans. This chapter also describes some of the first experiments using intelligence tests to classify students in Oakland immediately prior to the First World War. In the third chapter a detailed examination of Terman's role in the war shows how the tests were developed and used, and why they were adapted for school use. The fourth chapter explores Terman's rapid rise to national prominence in the intelligence testing community after the war, his prescriptions for school reform, and the way he helped to shape the national movement for testing and classification. A fifth chapter examines the early adoption of testing and grouping plans in three California case studies—Oakland, San Jose, and Palo Alto—each of which had a direct, personal link to Terman and Stanford University. The initial programs in testing and classification, in California and across the nation, sparked a vigorous dissent within the psychological community and in the public forum, a controversy that is evaluated in chapter 6. In the last chapter some national patterns in the use of intelligence tests in schools during the twenties are described. Finally, the study concludes by evaluating the adoption of intelligence tests, the relation between testing and tracking, and the implications of this history for current policy.

It is the purpose of this study to analyze in detail how and why intelligence testing became part of the "conventional wisdom" in schools. A close investigation of the adoption of tests will provide an opportunity to evaluate the historical interpretations which have been advanced and will offer a valuable perspective on current policy on testing. By addressing two specific questions—why intelligence tests were adopted and what their relation was to tracking—this study will expand our knowledge about the role played by schools as sorters.

CHAPTER I

Solutions in Search of Problems: The Emergence of Intelligence Testing in the Progressive Era, 1890–1917

In 1916 Lewis Terman published the Stanford-Binet intelligence test, an event that prompted Ellwood P. Cubberley, dean of the Stanford School of Education, to observe confidently: "The educational significance of the results to be obtained from careful measurements of the intelligence of children can hardly be overestimated."[1] Both Terman's contribution and Cubberley's comment forecast the rapid emergence of intelligence testing in the Progressive Era. The publication of the Stanford-Binet culminated over twenty-five years of intensive research in America and in Europe on the nature of intelligence and how to measure it. For what purposes were intelligence tests created? How and why were they first used in schools?

There were three principal reasons why intelligence tests were developed and used in American schools during the Progressive Era. First, the young profession of psychology, curious about the theoretical nature of intelligence, tried to define that quality by developing a variety of tests to measure both specific and general abilities. Second, their research was stimulated by the practical need of the schools to explain individual differences in student performance and to identify poor performers. Third, the ferment of reform in the Progressive Era led psychologists to promote their new measures of intelligence as a means of improving the schools. The turn of the century was the time when muckrakers exposed problems ranging from governmental corruption to economic waste, and the universities were enlisted to help restructure society. Psychologists saw in intelligence tests a way to improve schools and to enhance the reputation of their science.

This chapter discusses several aspects of the emergence of the testing movement. A review of the early efforts in mental measurement in Europe and America sketches the antecedents of the intelligence testing movement. A study of Terman's development of the tests and his prescriptions for their use illustrates his leadership in the movement, as well as the nature of progressive reform. A final section places testing in the broader context of the measurement movement, and describes the first links in a network of psychologists in universities and psychological clinics who began the initial application of tests to school problems. The theme of the chapter is that before the First World War a small group of psychologists, supported by a network of institutions, and in tune with the progressive spirit, produced the first intelligence tests and experimented with their use in schools. These psychologists had created "solutions" and sought to apply them to the "problems" of their age.

The Discovery of "Intelligence" in Europe and America

In 1924 psychologist Kimball Young wrote a brief history of mental testing noting: "While American psychologists have played an important role in the development of mental testing, the cultural borrowing in this instance is so obvious that we may not escape its significance."[2] According to Young, there were at least three European contributions to the development of mental measurement: the rise of experimental psychology in Germany, the evaluation of individual differences in England, and the creation of a scale for measuring intelligence in France.

Initial attempts to study mental differences began in Germany where Wilhelm Wundt founded the first formal laboratory of experimental psychology at the University of Leipzig in 1879. Wundt's investigation of human consciousness and his rigorous experimental approach attracted several Americans who were later to figure importantly in the development of testing in the United States, among them J. McKeen Cattell, G. Stanley Hall, Edward Scripture, Frank Angell, Edward Titchener, and Charles Judd.[3]

Meanwhile, in England, Francis Galton was investigating individual mental differences. Following the publication of *On the Origin of Species* in 1859 by his cousin, Charles Darwin, Galton became interested in the inheritance of mental differences, publishing his conclusions a decade later in *Hereditary Genius*. Galton's pioneering work in statistics, as well as the opening of his own psychological laboratory in London in 1884, stimulated interest in the tests. One of Galton's students, Karl Pearson, made significant advances in developing statistical methods for the study of intelligence. After 1900 Charles Spearman and Cyril Burt argued that correlations of intelligence test scores showed the existence of a common intelligence factor, g, that was strongly influenced by heredity.

But it was the work of Alfred Binet in France that had the most direct influence on the development of intelligence tests in America.[4] In 1890 Binet joined the new laboratory of physiological psychology at the Sorbonne, where he began a systematic study of individual differences among schoolchildren in Paris. Five years later he outlined his hopes for the new profession:

The studies of individual psychology are one of psychology's most important practical applications since their aim is knowledge of the individual, and they must be envisioned and directed toward the goal we would attain . . . the study of races, the study of children, the study of patients, and the study of criminals.[5]

Through the nineties Binet experimented with a series of mental tests to detect differences among children in such things as recall, moral judgment, and mental addition.

Then a breakthrough came in the use of tests in education. In the fall of 1904 the minister of public instruction appointed Binet to study ways of identifying children in the Paris schools who were "subnormal," those who were not making adequate progress, so that they could be "segregated" into separate classes. By the next year Binet had created the first scale for measuring intelligence, a series of thirty mental tests of increasing difficulty. Using the scale, Binet could determine a child's "mental age," his relative intellectual development, and through "age norms" he could compare the child's ability with that of others the same age. In 1908 Binet brought out a revised scale that could be used to test not merely "subnormal" children, but the "normal" and "gifted." Early criticism of his test—that it contained too few tasks for each age and that its predictive powers were limited— led him to issue a second revision in 1911.

That same year both Binet and Galton died; with their passing the momentum of test development passed to the United States. One of the first Americans to study with Wundt was J. McKeen Cattell. After receiving his Ph.D. from Leipzig in 1886, he returned to head the psychology department at the University of Pennsylvania, where he established a psychological laboratory to continue his research on individual differences. In an article written in 1890 Cattell coined the term "mental test" and set the tone for America's practical application of the new measures:

Psychology cannot attain the certainty and exactness of the physical sciences, unless it rests on a foundation of experiment and measurement. A step in this direction could be made by applying a series of mental tests and measurements to a large number of individuals. The results would be of considerable scientific value in discovering the constancy of mental processes, their interdependence, and their variation under different circumstances. . . . The scientific and practical value of such tests would be much increased should a uniform system be adopted, so that determinations made at different times and places could be compared and combined.[6]

The next year he moved to Columbia University, which became the center of American test development in the 1890s.

Cattell approached his task with enthusiasm, establishing another psychological laboratory and founding several journals of importance for the young profession, *Science* and the *Psychological Review*. At his urging the American Psychological Association appointed a committee in 1895 to "consider the feasibility of cooperation among the various psychological laboratories in the collection of mental and physical statistics."[7] During the nineties he also began to forge a graduate program that would produce several leaders in the testing field after the turn of the century.[8]

Probably the most influential graduate was Edward L. Thorndike. He became interested in psychology as an undergraduate at Wesleyan University, began a doctorate at Harvard, but switched to Columbia, receiving his degree in 1898. Publishing studies of educational psychology (1903), the theory of mental and social measurements (1904), and animal intelligence (1911), he quickly rose to prominence as a leader in the field of testing research. As Thorndike remarked some years later, his early interest "concentrated on research methods of measuring mental abilities," but by 1909 he and his students focused increasingly on "scales for use in measuring school achievement in reading, writing, drawing, composition, knowledge of history and the like."[9]

Another major center of interest in intelligence testing was Clark University in Worcester, Massachusetts. G. Stanley Hall, the president of Clark, had also studied with Wundt in Leipzig. When he taught at Johns Hopkins, he founded one of the first psychological laboratories in this country in 1883. Also like Cattell, he was a pioneer in the fledgling profession of psychology, founding the *American Journal of Psychology* in 1887 and organizing the American Psychological Association in 1891. Although mostly known for his investigations in genetic and child psychology, Hall helped the emerging testing movement by sponsoring the graduate studies of several men who were to become key figures in the field. Between 1898 and 1905, five men studied at Clark who later played central roles in developing intelligence tests: Henry H. Goddard, E. B. Huey, F. Kuhlmann, J. E. Wallace Wallin, and Lewis M. Terman.

Thus by the first decade of the twentieth century several important steps had been taken toward developing tests of intelligence. From Europe had come an experimental method, a new interest in individual differences, and a scale for measuring intelligence. From America came an interest in intelligence tests that was decidedly practical. As psychologist Edwin Boring later observed, "American psychology was to deal with mind in use."[10]

Lewis Terman: Progressive Reformer

In 1914 Lewis Terman wrote: "The children of to-day must be viewed as the raw material of a new State; the schools as the nursery of the nation."[11] The 1916 publication of the Stanford-Binet intelligence test, which had launched Terman to prominence in the field of psychology, also gave him a valuable instrument for social and educational reform.

He began his professional career in the heyday of progressivism; like many reformers, he was anxious to use his science to improve society.

Terman's development of intelligence tests and his prescription for their use provide a glimpse into the workings of progressive reform. Although historians have found the precise nature of "progressivism" elusive,[12] Terman's beliefs and actions were characteristic of many members of the movement. He valued science, efficiency, conservation, and social order; he held that experts should play a greater role in shaping society; his ideas on intelligence had much in common with Social Darwinism; and his attitude towards immigrants was consonant with the nativism of the time. Terman's experience in the years before World War I provides insight into the tensions inherent in progressive reform. His views on the nature of intelligence and the school's role in its cultivation represented positions that would spark professional controversy in the twenties and widespread public debate over half a century later. A review of his professional development shows how he came to view the intelligence tests as an instrument of reform.

Born the eleventh of fourteen children on an Indiana farm in 1877, Lewis Terman quickly became an avid reader, excelled in school, and at age fifteen began to prepare for a career in teaching at the local normal school in Danville. By 1900 he had served as teacher and as principal in a township high school and over several years had completed degrees in science, pedagogy, and the arts. At the normal school Terman found an interest in psychology, reading Darwin's *On the Origin of Species*, William James's *Principles of Psychology*, and several volumes of Herbert Spencer.[13] In 1901 he entered Indiana University to begin in earnest his investigation of individual psychology. His teacher, E. H. Lindley, had just returned from a year's study in Germany and introduced Terman to the work of the early leaders in mental measurement—Wundt, Binet, Galton, Hall, and Cattell.[14] After Terman completed his B.A. in the first year and his M.A. in the second, Lindley persuaded him to pursue a Ph.D. at Clark University, where he himself had received his degree under Hall.

As Terman later recalled, the years at Clark stimulated his fast-emerging interest in mental testing: "In my efforts to find a solid footing for research with gifted and defective children, I was becoming more and more interested in the methods of tests and was reading almost everything that had been written on the subject." Although

Lewis M. Terman, 1905. Upon receiving his Ph.D. from Clark University, Terman began his career as one of the twentieth century's central figures in applied psychology and the use of intelligence tests in schools. (Reprinted by permission of the Department of Special Collections and University Archives, Stanford University Libraries.)

Hall, the president of Clark and a leader in the child study movement, was skeptical about the "quasi-exactness of quantitative methods," Terman was undaunted. He developed a variety of tests, including

measures of mathematical, linguistic, and motor ability, to assess the
intellectual processes of seven "bright" and seven "stupid" boys for his
dissertation on "Genius and Stupidity." He concluded that the nature
of intelligence could best be explained through the use of mental tests
by which an individual's performance could be quantified and compared to the "normal" performance of the population at large. In his
thesis he stated his conviction that "there are deep and fundamental
lines of cleavage among individual mentalities the existence of which is
as yet hardly suspected." He also predicted that "there is destined to
grow up eventually a large body of psychological experts who will
play a role in the future as important as that of the medical man at
present." [15]

Terman's early work contained the kernel of ideas that would shape
his later study of intelligence. In his dissertation and in two other
studies on leadership and "prematurity," he explored the relation of
intelligence to leadership, deviance, and juvenile criminality. He examined race differences in ability and the existence of a "general factor"
in intelligence. He also developed a belief in what he called "normal"
intelligence, "the natural rate of development for any particular individual." Some years later he assessed the importance of Clark for his
development: "Everything I have done since 1905 was foreshadowed
in my interests at that time—in the psychology of genius, the measurement of intelligence, the phenomena of individual differences, in
general, and the problems of hygiene." [16]

Terman's interest in the latter stemmed in part from his earlier bout
with tuberculosis shortly before Clark. After taking his Ph.D. in 1905,
ill health forced him to accept a position as principal of San Bernardino
High School in Southern California, where he could count on a good
climate to ameliorate his condition. The next year he became professor
of child study at Los Angeles State Normal School (later the University of California at Los Angeles), remaining for four "fallow" years.
Then he was called to Stanford, where Ellwood P. Cubberley was
building a new Department of Education. [17]

Arriving at Stanford in 1910, Terman returned to a study of intelligence tests. Following the advice of his Clark colleague Edmund Huey,
he began a revision of Binet's intelligence scale for use in America. In
December 1911 Terman reported on his experimental study using the
Binet tests of 400 schoolchildren near Stanford. Like Binet, Terman

first used the test to identify abnormal or feebleminded children in the schools. He reviewed the results of his investigation in six areas: the relation of intelligence to physical defects, age, school progress, "incorrigibility" or delinquency, heredity, and social conditions. He stressed his hope that a scale could be developed to measure mental development in all children as well as his view of how "fundamentally important it is to have some means available for measuring the intelligence of school children."[18]

Based on his initial research, Terman made some further observations in his report about the possible use of intelligence tests. He saw immediate application for the tests in the diagnosis of individual problems, for they offered a "more reliable and more enlightening estimate of the child's intelligence than most teachers can offer after a year of daily contact in the schoolroom." He then referred to recent studies of school "retardation"—the discovery by Leonard Ayres and others that a high percentage of students were overage for their grade level, either because they were making slow progress or because they had started late. "Before many years," he predicted, "it will probably become a matter of course to apply serial mental tests in the public schools to all pupils who are retarded or about to become retarded, or who give indication of unusual ability." He suggested that the tests could be used for "the scientific management of special classes for atypical children in the public schools," responding to the quest for efficiency that had surged earlier that year with the popularization of the ideas of Frederick W. Taylor by muckraker Ray Stannard Baker. Terman concluded: "Now that the individual treatment of pupils in the schools has begun, there is no stopping short of this idea. Tests must be developed which will enable us to differentiate all degrees of intellectual ability and all kinds of intellectual unevenness."[19]

The next year Terman put his ideas into action in a survey of the "mentally defective children" in the schools of San Luis Obispo, a coastal town of 5,000 in southern California. The newly elected superintendent, Charles R. Small—a former minister who Terman described as a "Harvard graduate and wide-awake schoolman," not an "average 'routine' superintendent"—retained Terman's services to study the "large number of overage pupils" in the elementary grades. Terman gave tests to twenty-two children and reported the results in a table that related the students' chronological and mental age (table 1.1):

TABLE 1.1

A Survey of Mentally Defective Children, 1914

Mental Age	Chronological Age in Years										
	17	16	15	14	13	12	11	10	9	8	7
17	■										
16		■									
15			■								
14				■							
13					■						
12			1			■					
11		1					■				
10		1	1					■			
9	1		3	1	1	1		1	■		
8						1		1	2	■	
7								1	2		■
6							1	1			
5											1

Source: Lewis M. Terman, "Survey of Mentally Defective Children in the Schools of San Luis Obispo," *Psychological Clinic* 6 (1912): 132.

The tests showed that all twenty-two were failing to make "normal" educational progress.[20]

Terman did not have kind words for these misfits: "They clog the educational machinery," he said. "They consume a disproportionately large part of the regular teacher's energy. They pull down the standard of achievement for other children. Finding themselves chronic failures they either become disheartened and dejected, or else they grow case-hardened and apathetic." As to why these students were so backward, Terman provided case studies and Binet tests which he said "give an extremely accurate estimate of the innate intellectual ability in general." Terman's clinical report buttressed his conclusion that these pupils were mentally deficient: "mental processes slow . . . memory poor in all school work . . . ideas vague and confused." Based on this study Terman advised Small to provide a "special class" for a majority of pupils tested to ensure that they receive individual attention. He went on to tell Small that he "could use some of the results of this survey as a good argument for the introduction of manual training, domestic science, etc., into your schools."[21]

Between 1913 and 1915 Terman presented these preliminary ideas on the use of tests in schools in several articles and in a report on his work to the Fourth International Conference on School Hygiene at Buffalo. Terman foresaw many uses for the tests: curricular reform to provide special classes for "abnormal" students, a differentiated curriculum for students of all abilities, and educational and vocational guidance. Terman argued that tests would help schools "identify the feeble-minded" and "choose the methods and matter of education which will guarantee for such children the best possible returns for their efforts," thereby improving school efficiency. He thought they would help teachers and administrators "emphasize the individual differences present among normal children" and consequently do much to "loosen up the current systems of school classification." They would enable students to be promoted "largely on the basis of intellectual ability" and bring about a more scientific education. They would lead to the "segregation of the feeble-minded" and aid in the "elimination of degeneracy" and the removal of a "demoralizing and retrograding influence from the lives of many normal children." Finally, he thought they would assist in the development of vocational guidance through which "it would then be possible to lay before each child at the end of this school course an array of occupations in which (as far as intelligence is concerned) he might reasonably be expected to succeed." Terman's rigidly deterministic views on the power of IQ tests to predict life success sowed the seeds of later controversies about the use and abuse of tests.[22]

In 1915 Terman's revision of Binet's intelligence test was complete and in 1916 he published a handbook for its administration, *The Measurement of Intelligence*. Terman's intelligence test, which he named the Stanford-Binet, was to become the most widely used individual test over the next two decades. Its appearance was significant for several reasons. Terman agreed with Binet that tests could provide a valid measure of intelligence and adopted his definition of the term: "The tendency to take and maintain a definite direction; the capacity to make adaptations for the purpose of attaining a desired end; and the power of auto-criticism." Terman translated Binet's tests into English and extended the scale at its lower and upper levels (approximately five and sixteen) by expanding the number of tests given at each age. He incorporated the concept of the intelligence quotient, or IQ, an idea originated several years earlier in Germany by Wilhelm Stern. Terman's work popularized the IQ, a ratio of mental age to chronological age, where mental age is defined by the number and kinds of intellectual tasks that can be performed by a child at any given age. The IQ allowed psychologists to express the rate of individual mental development. The Stanford-Binet was significant as well because it was standardized; that is to say, the materials of the test, as well as the administration and scoring procedures, were made uniform so that the test could be given under the same conditions anywhere. The test also included "norms," or tables that showed typical performance on the test and allowed comparisons of individuals with the rest of the population.[23]

In preparing the intelligence tests, Terman took stands that elicited controversy within the psychological community. Regarding the nature of intelligence, he argued that his test constituted a valid measure of intelligence, that the IQ was constant, and that it was greatly influenced by heredity. Early in his research he thought it would be possible to find tests "which will not be too greatly influenced by such differences in training and experience as ordinarily exist among the children of civilized people living under fairly uniform conditions of home life and educational advantages. . . . The environment of two children living in the same country under anything but exceptional conditions probably resembles a great deal more than it differs." In *The Measurement of Intelligence* he argued that he had selected "tests which are really tests of intelligence, tests which are not too much influenced by age, home environment or school instruction apart from native endowment."[24]

Terman's development of norms for the Stanford-Binet also aroused comment. The test was standardized on approximately 1,000 individuals living near Stanford. Terman believed that the schools selected for standardizing the tests "were such as almost any one would classify as middle-class. Few children attending them were either from very wealthy or very poor homes. . . . Care was taken to avoid racial differences due to lack of familiarity with the language. None of the children was foreign-born and only a few were of other than western European descent."[25]

Early work on the Stanford-Binet by Terman and others was criticized on several grounds. Some questioned the validity of this test, its reliability, and the degree to which it was influenced by heredity. They argued, too, that the sample for the Stanford-Binet norms produced standards that were biased against the lower classes, immigrants, and blacks. Others objected to the great expectations for the use of the tests, suggesting that the tests were fallible and should not be used to determine the fate of individuals.

One of the first to criticize the Binet tests was Leonard Ayres, who had conducted studies of school retardation. He argued in 1911 that intelligence tests emphasized verbal ability, measured primarily scholastic performance, and could not assess native ability. He therefore questioned their exclusive use in schools to measure performance.[26]

Ayres was followed the next year by J. E. Wallace Wallin, Terman's colleague at Clark, who had since established several psychological clinics. Wallin said of the Binet test:

This scale has recently been victimized by the indiscriminate exploiter. It has been hailed by popular writers in the daily and periodical press, and even by scientific workers, as a wonderful mental x-ray machine, which will enable us to dissect the mental and moral mechanisms of any normal or abnormal individual. But these tests are no "open sesame" to the human mind, no talisman that will transform an ordinary observer into a psychic wizard. Because the scale is coming into wide use in the public schools, the psychopathic and criminological institutes, and institutions for mental and moral defectives, and because it is being appropriated by ordinary classroom teachers and persons having no technical training in clinical psychology or knowing little about scientific method in general, it is worthwhile to point out its legitimate uses as well as its limitations and present imperfections.

Arguing that the tests "need to be safeguarded from uncritical exploitation and mystification, and rescued from the educational fakers and medical quacks," he called for a "prolonged and critical study of the scale."[27]

Although Wallin's broadside was not directed at him in particular,

Terman was extremely sensitive to this kind of criticism of testing and responded on several occasions. He deplored disputes with a "personal tinge," especially in a field as young as psychology where "methods are still tentative and insecure." He objected that the criticisms of the intelligence tests have "lacked something in spirit of fairness," have been "misleading to the lay reader," and have created an "unwarranted attitude of suspicion toward clinical psychology generally." The response of Terman to the critics exposed a number of issues that would spark controversy in the future, and revealed his tendency to overreact to criticism. These were disagreements largely among the psychologists, however, and did not seriously deflect the course of the emerging testing movement.[28]

At Stanford Terman began to establish a center from which the testing movement on the West Coast would emanate. Before the war Terman was joined in the Department of Education by two men who would contribute much to the testing movement: Jesse B. Sears, who helped develop the school survey, and William M. Proctor, who pioneered in the use of intelligence tests in educational and vocational guidance. Terman's own work on intelligence was augmented by his graduate students. They assisted Terman in preparing the Stanford-Binet, and explored in their own research the relation between intelligence and delinquency, the use of mental testing in school administration, and the correlation of intelligence with crime and unemployment. The department developed a full program to prepare teachers and administrators in intelligence testing, offering courses on retardation, the education of "defectives," the social aspects of mental deficiency, and the psychology of "exceptional" children. Terman's work in testing began to attract independent financial support; a grant from the Buckel Foundation combined with university support provided $1,000 a year for the "psychological and pedagogical study of backward and mentally defective children." Terman and Cubberley planned to offer Stanford's consulting services to "cooperate with the school systems of the state in the formation of special classes for backward or otherwise exceptional children."[29]

In the years before the war, Terman campaigned to spread the applications of his work on testing to a wider audience, in conjunction with the movements for social efficiency and eugenics. Perhaps because of his own recurring bouts with tuberculosis, Terman devoted considerable energy to the issues of school health and hygiene. In 1914 he published two major works on the subject: *The Hygiene of the School Child*, a text for teachers, and *Health Work in the Schools*, an outline for administering health programs written with Ernest B. Hoag, a Minnesota physician. Terman's ideas on the conservation of health had much in common with the ideology of the progressive movement itself:

The rapid development of health work in the schools during the last two decades is not to be regarded merely as an educational reform, but rather as the corollary of a widespread realization of the importance of preventive measures in the conservation of natural and human resources. The prevention of waste has become, in fact, the dominant issue of our entire political, industrial, and educational situation.

Health reform, Terman said, could help save lives and made good fiscal sense; it would save money by preventing "premature deaths" which entail "an economic loss upon society."[30]

At this same time Terman's services were enlisted by one of the nation's leading progressives, Hiram Johnson, governor of California and vice-presidential candidate with Theodore Roosevelt on the "Bull Moose" ticket in 1912. Johnson consulted Terman on how to increase efficiency in the state's welfare institutions: prisons, orphanages, reform schools for delinquents, and training schools for the feeble-minded. Terman responded with a series of mental surveys, including a study of the Whittier State School for Boys, San Quentin Prison, an orphanage, and the study of all schools in Merced County.[31]

Terman also lent his support to the fast-growing eugenics movement which hoped to improve society by controlling the reproduction of various "defective" individuals and by restricting immigration, primarily from southern and eastern Europe. From his work with intelligence tests, Terman had reached several conclusions consistent with the eugenics program. Increasingly, he believed that intelligence was in good part inherited. As a result, he said, "we are rapidly becoming conscious of hitherto unsuspected power to shape human destinies, and are no longer willing to remain the passive plaything of uncontrolled social and material forces." He noted that "the evolution concept is doing its work." It was, for Terman, a logical next step to think about ways to shape society's collective intelligence.[32]

Terman came to believe that social deviance was often the result of low intelligence and that the very foundations of the civilization were being threatened by what he called the "menace of the feeble-minded." He concluded that intelligence tests could help cure poverty, crime, and delinquency by identifying "feebleminded" individuals. In his survey of San Luis Obispo schools, for example, he noted that feeble-minded persons constituted "probably one-fourth of our habitual criminals and a still larger proportion of our paupers and 'white slaves.'" "The children of subnormal mental endowments undoubtedly constitute one of our greatest social problems," he continued. In a report with Ellwood P. Cubberley to Stanford alumni in 1914, Terman outlined his ideas for a genetic solution to these problems:[33]

It is clear that society has few tasks more important than that of identifying the feeble-minded and providing for their institutional care. There is a growing conviction that society, in self-defense, will be driven to provide institutional care for every feeble-minded individual throughout the reproductive period.

Terman's strong language and startling views, similar to those of other progressive reformers, served early on to polarize emerging dialogue about intelligence testing. In their quest for an ordered society, reformers often infringed upon the rights of those who were without power and were not part of the dominant culture.

Throughout the years before the war, Terman played a key role in shaping the early testing movement. The tests themselves reflected many of the prevailing currents of the period—the quest for scientific efficiency, the role of the expert, the persuasion of Social Darwinism, and the resurgence of nativism. Terman's innovation also meshed well with a heightened interest in measurement throughout the educational community.

The Measurement Movement in Education

By the First World War, Terman and other psychologists had generated substantial interest in intelligence tests and their use in schools. The rise of intelligence tests, however, coincided with the broader interest in the scientific measurement of educational products and the creation of standardized achievement tests, measures of student learning as opposed to student ability. Beginning in the nineteenth century, the measurement movement gained momentum after the turn of the century with the rise of achievement testing, the advent of the school survey, and the institutionalization of educational testing in school and municipal research bureaus. The establishment of a network of institutions concerned with educational measurement before the First World War eventually paved the way for the widespread adoption of intelligence tests.

One of the earliest attempts to develop objective tests to evaluate student performance occurred in Boston in 1845. Horace Mann, recently appointed secretary of the State Board of Education, urged the Boston Schools Committee to investigate the quality and efficiency of teaching in the city schools. The board implemented a plan, in addition to the usual mode of oral examinations, to give 5 percent of the students a test with 130 printed questions on all subjects studied in school. Although the board found the resulting poor student performance cause for "sad reflection and melancholy consideration," Mann rejoiced. The tests were "impartial," he said, and "determine, beyond appeal or gainsaying, whether the pupils have been faithfully and competently taught." So impressed was Mann with standardized, objective exams that he confidently predicted: "No committee will ever venture to relapse into the former inadequate and uncertain practice."[34]

It is doubtful that Mann's prediction came true. As city school systems became increasingly bureaucratized in the second half of the nineteenth century, however, uniform examinations—sometimes written, sometimes objective—were used not for evaluating teachers but for promoting students. After the Civil War, the idea of standardized, objective exams received broader consideration when the Pendelton Act established a permanent Civil Service Commission in 1883 to administer competitive examinations and select government appointees on the basis of merit.[35]

In education, though, it was the popularization of a series of articles by Joseph Mayer Rice that accounted most directly for the quickened interest in standardized, objective testing of student achievement. In 1892 Rice surveyed schools in thirty-six cities to determine "the causes of the marked variation in the general degree of excellence of the schools of various localities," concluding that the "obstacles to educational reform" lay in the lack of any objective standards by which effective teaching and productive learning could be measured. He soon set out to develop objective tests in four areas—spelling, penmanship, English composition, and arithmetic. Between 1894 and 1896 Rice examined some 100,000 schoolchildren in districts across the country, reporting his findings in *The Forum*. After the turn of the century, he called for a twofold educational reform based on specific standards to measure student learning and the time needed to accomplish assigned tasks. Rice's articles reached a wide audience and his studies sparked universities to develop standardized tests of achievement.[36]

Thorndike and his students at Teachers College, Columbia University, put Rice's ideas to work. The Stone Arithmetic Test, published in 1908, was one of the first standardized achievement tests. The next year Thorndike presented the first scale to measure achievement in handwriting to the annual meeting of the American Association for the Advancement of Science. To those interested in scientific measurement, Thorndike produced not only the instruments but a sense of purpose and conviction as well. His motto, "Whatever exists at all exists in some amount," served as the credo of those trying to measure educational products.[37]

The next ten years brought an extraordinary outpouring of educational achievement tests. In 1917 Walter S. Monroe reported to the annual meeting of the National Society for the Study of Education (NSSE) that there were 218 tests available for use—168 in elementary schools and fifty in high schools. This roster was only a sample of the instruments he catalogued in *Educational Tests and Measurement* that same year. Another NSSE member, Edna Bryner of the Russell Sage Foundation in New York, presented a bibliography of over 600 articles on testing appearing in thirty-three journals between 1907 and 1917. Her study showed that by the war, standard tests existed for sixteen subjects ranging from algebra, English composition, and geography to history, physics, and spelling. The educational measurement movement had come of age rapidly.[38]

The focus of measurement, however, was not exclusively student achievement. In the decade before the war, the leaders of the school survey movement examined and quantified virtually every aspect of education from teaching and salaries to the quality of school buildings. University professors frequently conducted the investigations; some of the most active surveyors included Cubberley and Sears at Stanford, Charles Judd and Franklin Bobbitt at the University of Chicago, and George Strayer at Teachers College. Between 1910 and 1925 nearly 200 cities commissioned surveys of their school systems, some sixty-seven in the period from 1910 to 1919. The surveys were of critical importance for the emerging measurement movement because they frequently employed standardized achievement tests to determine the educational quality of the school population.[39]

The survey movement stimulated some school systems to take on the task of measuring student achievement themselves; they created educational research bureaus to handle the task. As Eugene Nifenecker, assistant director of the New York City Bureau of Research and Reference said in 1918, "The city bureau of educational research is the direct and logical outcome of the combination of the survey movement and the movement for the use of measurement." By the outbreak of the war, at least twenty-three research bureaus had been founded across the country in cities ranging in size from New York, Chicago, and Philadelphia to St. Paul, Topeka, and Des Moines.[40]

Early research bureaus focused their energy on administering and interpreting standardized tests. When Frank Ballow described his experience in organizing measurement in the Boston schools for the NSSE membership, however, he revealed that the introduction of testing did not come without a struggle. In his view the research director's main task was not to administer the tests but to convince "searching and frequently unjust critics" of the tests' value. The key to the whole testing program was the classroom teacher: "The teacher must be made to realize that the results from the tests are for her information. Unless she is shown how to make use of them, and is willing to do so, standard testing *is not worth while.*"[41]

The years before the war also saw a rapid rise in psychological measurement of schoolchildren using individual intelligence tests, a program that was often carried out in psychological clinics. Between 1909 and 1914 J. E. Wallace Wallin conducted a series of surveys that documented the swift increase in mental and psychological testing. In a pool of 103 cities, he discovered that eighty-three (81 percent of those responding) were using psychological tests to identify feebleminded and backward children, and seventy-one cities were using the Binet tests specifically. Table 1.2 shows the reported use of tests by city size:[42]

TABLE 1.2
Early Use of Psychological Tests, 1914

City Size	No. of Cities 1910 Census	No. of Cities Reporting Use of Psychological Tests
Over 500,000	8	8
250,000–500,000	11	11
100,000–250,000	31	15
25,000–100,000	178	26
Less than 25,000	2,034	23
	2,262	83

Source: Adapted from J. E. Wallace Wallin, *The Mental Health of the School Child* (New Haven: Yale University Press, 1914), 406–19. Reprinted by permission.

It is hard to generalize from Wallin's data, since his eighty-three responses represented less than 5 percent of the cities in the country and the questionnaire did not evaluate the extent of use in each city. Indeed, as Wallin observed,

while this is an extremely creditable showing, particularly in view of what it portends for the future, it is necessary to emphasize that the psychological testing in most of the cities is exceedingly meager and crude, being conducted by teachers, principals, educators, psychologists and physicians who are not specialists on the physiology, psychology and pedagogy of feebleminded, backward or other types of mentally abnormal children.

Nonetheless, the number of cities reporting test use is remarkable considering that Binet had developed his intelligence scale only a few years earlier.[43]

Wallin's surveys show that the beginning of systematic mental testing was closely associated with the development of the psychological clinic, the purpose of which was to establish "the process of first-hand observation, testing and experiment." According to Wallin there were at least four functions of psychological clinics: expert diagnosis of

"mental deviation," service as a "clearing house for mentally exceptional cases," research into the nature of "mental deviation" and test
development, and the dissemination of information about the nature
and distribution of intelligence.[44]

By 1914 according to Wallin seventy clinics had been established in
a variety of institutions, as table 1.3 shows:

TABLE 1.3
Psychological Clinics, 1914

Type of Institution	Number of Clinics
Public schools	19
Universities, medical schools, and normal schools	27
Hospitals for the insane	5
Institutions for the feeble-minded and epileptic	7
Juvenile courts and other courts	5
Penal and correctional institutions	6
Immigrant stations (Ellis Island)	1
	70

Source: J. E. Wallace Wallin, *The Mental Health of the School Child* (New
Haven: Yale University Press, 1914), 399. Reprinted by permission.

Wallin's data show that the clinics set up in the public schools, colleges, and universities were the most numerous. At the time of the
survey, clinics were operating in nineteen school systems including
Chicago, New York, Oakland, Seattle, Philadelphia, Los Angeles, and
Detroit. Schoolchildren were probably given intelligence tests in the
clinics operating in juvenile courts and institutions for the feeble-
minded as well. The number of clinics in medical schools, hospitals,
and institutions for the insane suggests that intelligence testing in
America initially focused on "abnormal" and pathological individuals.
Only later did testing spread to include all students in schools.[45]

At the threshold of World War I, three important developments thus set the stage for the intelligence testing movement. Psychologists in Europe and America had begun a systematic and scientific study of individual differences and had discovered early ways to measure intelligence tests. At Stanford, Lewis Terman had developed the technology of intelligence tests and had fashioned a blueprint for their use in progressive reform. The educational measurement movement had produced a vast array of standardized, objective tests. Together these factors helped to create a network of psychologists ready to use intelligence tests on a larger scale. The solutions that applied psychologists created were eagerly awaited by schools, who faced during this same period their own set of problems.

CHAPTER 2

Problems in Search of Solutions: New Conceptions of Schooling and the Early Use of Intelligence Tests, 1890–1917

During the years between 1890 and 1917, school administrators and teachers faced complicated problems. Urban school enrollments skyrocketed because of tremendous immigration, a shift in population from the farm to the city, and newly enforced compulsory education laws. To meet the needs of increasingly diverse communities, schools developed new goals; the college preparatory curriculum of the nineteenth century gradually was replaced by one directed toward social efficiency—preparation for citizenship and the world of work, and the effective use of leisure time. Soaring costs and a campaign for efficiency put pressure on school administrators to reform the schools. In response to these problems—increasing size, diversity, rising costs, and changing objectives—the school curriculum became much more differentiated. School administrators needed a new, more efficient means of classifying students in order to assign them to different curricular tracks.

As we have seen, Lewis Terman and other applied psychologists developed intelligence tests for measuring differences in student ability during these same years. Two communities—university professors of

psychology and education, research bureau directors, and heads of
psychological clinics on the one hand; superintendents, principals, and
teachers on the other—needed each other's assistance. That was increasingly clear after the turn of the century. Applied psychologists
wanted to demonstrate the usefulness of their discipline for school
reform. School people felt that applied psychology—especially the
newly developed intelligence tests—could aid their efforts. The mutual interest of these two groups thus contributed to the beginnings of
the intelligence testing movement before the war.

A common interpretation of the testing movement among revisionist
historians is that the development of intelligence tests precipitated the
creation of a tracking system where previously there had been a more
uniform and presumably more egalitarian curriculum.[1] This chapter
tells a different story, for the process was more complicated than that.
The first section gives a brief review of the problems schools faced.
These problems are described both in terms of broad, national patterns, as well as a case study of New York, the city most dramatically
affected by mass immigration. Then the chapter examines the origins
of a differentiated curriculum in the nineteenth century. Early provisions for individuals were systematized after the turn of the century,
and school administrators used a variety of means—teachers' judgments, students' marks, and the newly developed achievement tests—
to assign students to different curricular paths. The advent of intelligence tests gave schools a new, more "scientific" means of placing
students; the tests accelerated the creation of a differentiated curriculum based on student ability, the homogeneous group. Finally, the
way intelligence tests were adopted in schools before the war is illustrated by the experience of Oakland, which became with Terman's
assistance one of the first cities in the country to use intelligence tests
for classifying students.

The Problems Facing the Schools

In the quarter-century before World War I, schools encountered a
complex and seemingly endless array of problems. How did the world
look to school administrators at the turn of the century? This section
sketches the problems they faced by describing the extraordinary growth

and increasing diversity of the American population. What these broad, demographic trends meant for the schools is illustrated by the changes that took place in school enrollment, attendance, size, and cost. In 1909 when these pressures were intense, a study by Leonard Ayres of school "retardation," *Laggards in Our Schools*, showed that many students were failing to make adequate progress and sparked a campaign for school efficiency. It was to solve these various problems that schools developed new means of classifying students.

In the years between 1890 and 1917, the character of the United States was transformed by one of the most extensive migrations in history. During that time the country's population nearly doubled, growing from 63 million to over 100 million. Much of the population growth came from immigration. The decade just after the turn of the century was a time of especially heavy immigration, with almost 9 million persons entering the country; in 1907 alone over a million reached America. Importantly, the major source of immigrants shifted during this period from northern and western Europe—primarily the British Isles, Germany, Scandinavia, Switzerland, and Holland—to southern and eastern Europe. Between 1890 and 1914 a "new" immigration brought 15 million people predominantly from Austria-Hungary, Italy, Russia, Greece, Romania, and Turkey.[2]

Mass immigration and population growth had an immediate impact on the schools as is shown in table 2.1.[3] This quarter-century was clearly a time of the "transformation of the school." School enrollment increased by over 50 percent. Students went to schools with longer terms, and attended more school days. These were the years when the public high school became part of the educational system, a development reflected in enrollments that increased over 500 percent and in correspondingly large gains in the number of high school graduates and the percentage of graduates among seventeen-year-olds.[4] The rapid expansion of schooling meant a substantial increase in school costs, over 300 percent.

Immigration explains much of the extraordinary change that took place in schools. Another reason for the surge in school enrollments, however, was the enforcement of compulsory school attendance laws. Beginning in the 1850s states had enacted laws that required at least minimal school attendance for children up to age fourteen. After 1900

TABLE 2.1

*A Comparison of School Enrollment, Attendance,
and Expenditure Figures, 1890 and 1915*

	1890	1915	Percentage Change
Total Public Day School Enrollment	12,723,000	19,704,000	55%
Total Public Elementary School Enrollment	12,520,000	18,375,000	47%
Total Public High School Enrollment	203,000	1,329,000	554%
Total High School Graduates	44,000	240,000	445%
Percentage of Population 17 Years Old Graduating from High School	3.5%	12.8%	—
Average Daily Attendance in Public Elementary and Secondary Day Schools	8,154,000	14,986,000	84%
Average Length of School Term in Days	134.7	159.4	18%
Average Number of Days Attended	86.3	121.2	40%
Total School Expenditures	$141,000,000	$605,000,000	329%
Per Capita School Expenditures in Current Dollars	$2.24	$6.03	169%

Source: U.S. Bureau of the Census, *The Statistical History of the United States* (New York: Basic Books, 1976), 368, 369, 374, 375, 379.

a coalition of organized labor, philanthropists, and reformers pushed for laws to reduce child labor and compel longer and more regular school attendance.[5] Commenting on the impact of these laws, Ellwood P. Cubberley observed:

One of the results of all this legislation has been to throw, during the past quarter of a century, an entirely new burden on the schools. These laws have brought into the schools not only the truant and the incorrigible, who under former conditions either left early or were expelled, but also many children of the foreign-born who have no aptitude for book learning, and many children of inferior mental qualities who do not profit by ordinary classroom procedure. . . . Consequently, within the past twenty-five years the whole attitude toward such children has undergone a change, and an attempt has been made to salvage them and turn back to society as many of them as possible, trained for some form of social and personal usefulness.[6]

Just what kind of "burden" the schools carried can be seen in New York, the city most affected by the new arrivals. Between 1890 and 1910 the total population of the city more than doubled, from 2.3 million to 4.8 million. In the years of heavy immigration, over 75 percent of the city's inhabitants were first- or second-generation immigrants. Approximately 40 percent of the population were foreign-born; another 40 percent had at least one parent born overseas. Only a fifth were native whites of native parents; less than 2 percent of the prewar population was black. In 1890, roughly 80 percent of the total immigrant population had come from northern and western Europe. By 1910 immigration patterns had shifted so that 60 percent of the total had come from southern and eastern Europe.[7]

While the population surged, school enrollments in New York City grew at an even faster pace. Between 1900 and 1910 the city's population grew 39 percent, while school enrollment shot up 57 percent. School attendance was up markedly around this time, rising from 136 persons in 1,000 in 1904 to 152 persons in 1916. According to one observer, Eugene A. Nifenecker, assistant director of the Bureau of Research and Reference, this was the result of immigration, an amendment to the Compulsory Education Law in 1903, and "the real attempt thereafter to enforce its requirements." To keep pace with the vast increase in students, the city embarked on a building program, adding during the decade from 1904 to 1914 some 60 elementary schools and 5 high schools to the existing totals of 414 and 19. Construction could not keep pace with demand, however, and consequently the average elementary school grew from 1,193 students to 1,407, while the average high school jumped from 1,063 students to 2,375. In 1914 there were 3 elementary schools and 2 high schools with over 4,000 students each.[8]

The pressures on school administrators intensified when superintendents, university professors, and researchers discovered that many children were failing to make it through the system in a uniform and systematic fashion. One of the first men to call attention to the problem was William H. Maxwell, superintendent of New York City Public Schools. In 1904 he published reports showing that a high percentage of students were "retarded"; that is to say they were overage for their grade level. Three years later the Russell Sage Foundation commissioned Leonard P. Ayres, former superintendent of schools for Puerto Rico, to conduct a systematic, nationwide investigation of the problem and its causes.

Ayres set out to discover why children failed. To find the answers Ayres investigated the records of 20,000 schoolchildren in fifteen schools in Manhattan and scoured the school reports from cities across the nations. Although other educators—in particular Edward L. Thorndike, George Strayer, and the graduate students at Teachers College—studied retardation, it was the publication in 1909 of *Laggards in Our Schools* by Ayres that focused national attention on the problem.

Ayres concluded that retardation was large and significant. About a third of all schoolchildren were retarded. "The general tendency of American cities," he said, "is to carry all of their children through fifth grade, to take one-half of them to the eighth grade and one in ten through the high school." Analyzing the results he found wide variations among the cities; in Medford, Massachusetts, the retardation rate was only 7 percent, while in Memphis, Tennessee, it climbed to 75 percent. He discovered, too, that girls were far more likely than boys to complete elementary school. While Ayres concluded that "there is little relation between the percentage of foreigners in the different cities and the amount of retardation found in their schools," the study did reveal sharp differences for various immigrant groups; only 16 percent of the Germans were retarded, but some 36 percent of the Italians were behind one or more years in school. Searching for the causes of retardation, Ayres came up with several, among them late entrance, irregular attendance, illness and physical defects, geographic mobility, ethnicity, and sex differences. Analyzing pupil withdrawal in six cities, he discovered that in elementary schools a change in family residence accounted for over half the departures, while most high school students left for work.[9]

For Ayres the implications of his work were clear: the public schools were shockingly inefficient. "Retardation means—not that we are spending too much—but that we are spending it wastefully," he said. The children not making normal progress are "thoroughly trained in failure." How then could the schools remedy these problems? [10]

Ayres presented a twofold plan of attack. First, more extensive and more effective compulsory attendance laws would remove the temptation of students to leave school for work. Second, the schools must be reformed to provide special classes (especially for foreigners), more flexible grading, and a curriculum "which will more nearly fit the abilities of the average pupil." He concluded: "If our conception of the mission of the common school is true then the schools must be in some measure reformed, not only on the administrative side, but also through changes in the course of study and in the methods of study." [11]

Studies done by Strayer and his students bolstered Ayres's work. Agreeing with Ayres's proposals, Strayer advocated "special classes for the bright, the slow, the backward, and the deficient." A study by one of Strayer's students, Charles Keyes, on progress in city schools reached a similar conclusion. He noted that previous efforts at reform had failed because they "accept as a fixed condition of the problem one feature of current organization that forbids the best achievement, *viz.*, the unvarying uniform curriculum." Using unusual language to describe the retarded, he proposed a "differentiated curriculum involving adjustments to arrest, to normal, and to accelerate." [12]

Schools across the country clearly faced great problems of size, diversity, and efficiency. How did they respond to these issues and to calls for reform?

Solutions: Classifying Students to Provide for Individual Differences

Ayres's call for a different means of classifying students to provide for individual differences was not new. Although provision was made in separate institutions for the physically disabled in the early 1800s, at mid-century the typical model in public education was the common school, one that offered a uniform curriculum to students of all ages, often in a one-room school. After mid-century, though, schools began to classify students according to age. Some schools, especially those in urban areas, gradually began to incorporate into the curriculum special classes for the physically and mentally disabled, for students who were either dependent or delinquent, and for immigrants who spoke no English. Throughout the nineteenth century the structure and function of the schools evolved in response to rapid industrialization, large-scale immigration, and extensive urbanization. A new classification system to treat individual differences was part of that evolution. These early attempts to provide for individual differences help explain the rise of ability grouping in the early twentieth century and the widespread adoption of intelligence tests after the war.[13]

By World War I there had been substantial changes in the structure of the schools and their purpose. The common school had become a highly differentiated elementary school offering a variety of curricula and special classes. The high school had emerged in four distinct types —college preparatory, comprehensive, commercial, and vocational. These structural modifications reflected changes in the purpose of education. In the early nineteenth century, schools attempted to provide most students with a minimum education while cultivating an elite for high school and college. By World War I educators sought to make schooling universal. A commission of leading educators in 1917 defined the purpose of high school as "life adjustment."

The movement to treat individual differences in special classes and special schools began early in the nineteenth century. Starting with the founding of the American School for the Deaf in Hartford in 1817, private and public institutions provided special education in the nineteenth and early twentieth century for the blind and cripples, orphans and juvenile delinquents, the feebleminded and epileptic. Gradually city school systems added special classes for these students and for non–English-speaking immigrants, children with physical and speech difficulties, and exceptionally gifted children.

A monograph published just before the war at Teachers College by Robert A. F. McDonald on the adjustment of school organization to various population groups outlined the history of special education. Both the history and the national pattern of special education in 1914 can be seen in table 2.2, adapted from his study. The figures indicate the total number of institutions providing for individual differences in

TABLE 2.2
Provisions for Individual Differences in Private Institutions,
Public Institutions, and Public Schools, 1914

DEAF	47	Private Institutions (1817)
	58	Public Institutions (1823)
	73	Cities having day classes (1869)
JUVENILE DELINQUENT	53	Private Institutions (1825)
	81	Public Institutions (1826)
	158	Cities having day classes (1876)
BLIND	13	Private Institutions (1832)
	48	State Institutions (1837)
	20	Cities having day classes (1900)
DEPENDENT AND NEGLECTED CHILDREN	66	Private Schools (1729)
	20	State Schools (1861)
FEEBLEMINDED, RETARDED, AND EPILEPTIC	39	Private Institutions (1848)
	39	State Institutions (1851)
	284	Cities with day classes (1896)
CRIPPLES	30	Private Institutions (1861)
	6	Private Day Schools (1890)
	6	Public Institutions (1888)
	7	Cities having day classes (1899)
NON–ENGLISH-SPEAKING IMMIGRANTS	237	Cities having evening classes (1870)
	95	Cities with day classes (1898)
OPEN-AIR SCHOOLS	137	Cities (1908)
SPEECH DEFECTIVES	17	Cities with day classes (1908)
EXCEPTIONALLY GIFTED	22	Cities (1900)

Source: Robert A. F. McDonald, *Adjustment of School Organization to Various Population Groups,* Contributions to Education, no. 75 (New York: Teachers College, Columbia University, 1915), 108.

1914. The figures in parentheses show the date when instruction first began in a particular type of institution, school, or class.[14]

As McDonald noted, special provisions for individual differences began first with students who were "subnormal," especially those with "marked pathological defects." His study did not consider school provisions for differences in age, sex, or race. Typically, these provisions were initiated by private or philanthropic agencies. State institutions then took over custody of the child and later city school systems established special day classes. His study outlined three stages in the "finer adjustments of the public school" to student differences: designation of special teachers, development of new teaching methods, and adaptation of the school curriculum. "In the education of defectives," he observed, "there is a general tendency to introduce vocational guidance, training, and placement studies in the same school." "The mind of the public school profession," he said, "has gradually come to recognize the problem of the varying groups and to perceive the need of special means for school methods."[15]

About the same time a survey was conducted for the U.S. Bureau of Education by Leonard Ayres, James Van Sickle, superintendent of schools in Baltimore, and Lightner Witmer, professor of psychology and director of the Psychological Clinic at the University of Pennsylvania. The study confirmed that provision for individual differences in the schools had become widespread. For the survey some 1,200 questionnaires were sent to the superintendents of all municipal school systems; approximately 70 percent responded. The survey showed that provision for "exceptional" children was greatest in the Northeast and Midwest, areas of highest population concentration. According to the study, 10 percent of the schools provided special classes for the "physically exceptional" (blind, deaf, dumb, and crippled, and children with physical and speech defects), and 17 percent provided classes for the "morally exceptional" (delinquents). The widest use of special classes was for the "environmentally exceptional" (non–English-speaking immigrants and late-entering students), 39 percent, and the "mentally exceptional" (defectives, the backward, and gifted), 42 percent. Evidence that schools were making extensive provision for "defective," "backward," and "gifted" children would have important consequences for the growth of the testing movement. It was precisely these kinds of "abnormal" students that the early intelligence tests were designed to identify, and it was for these special classes that the tests were first used. Meanwhile, however, the schools were experimenting with systems for classifying not only "exceptional" individuals but all students, a development that would pave the way for even wider application of intelligence tests.[16]

A parallel effort to provide for individual differences was the development of the age-graded school. In 1856 Henry Barnard, superintendent of schools in Connecticut, pointed out the enormous obstacles preventing effective teaching in the common schools. "There is a large amount of physical suffering and discomfort, as well as great hindrances in the proper arrangement of scholars and classes, caused by crowding the older and younger pupils into the same school-room," for "there cannot be a regular course of discipline and instruction, adapted to the age and proficiency of pupils," he said. Such a situation taxed the resources of even the best teacher: "With studies ranging from the alphabet and the simplest rudiments of knowledge, to the higher branches of an English education, a variety of methods of instruction and illustration are called for, which are seldom found together, or in an equal degree, in the same teacher." As a solution, Barnard proposed a system of classification by age and attainment. "By arranging scholars of the same general division in different classes, no pupil need be detained by companions who have made, or can make less progress, or be hurried over lessons and subjects in a superficial manner, to accommodate the more rapid advancement of others."[17] Barnard's comments evidently reflected the concerns of school administrators and teachers in many villages and large cities, for by the 1870s the system of age-grading had become extensive among larger, urban schools.

When William T. Harris, superintendent of schools in St. Louis in the 1870s, pondered the effects of age-grading on his students, its flaws quickly became apparent. In his annual reports Harris discussed the varied characteristics of his pupils: irregular attendance, different starting ages, and most importantly differences in "temperament and character—the slow and the swift, the weak and the strong, the careless and the earnest, the mature and the immature, the industrious and the indolent." A rigid age-grading system was inadequate to deal with such differences, he said. Such a system made the school a "lifeless machine, a Procrustean bed," recalling the mythical Greek giant who stretched or shortened his captives to fit an iron bed. It held back the bright and injured the less able. "The pupil who tries his best and then fails is deeply injured, and is apt to endeavor to preserve his self-respect by some sort of subterfuge," he said. "The root of all bitterness is loss of self-respect; the man or child who goes about thinking himself shut out from participation in the highest by his own natural incapacity is like one enclosed in a tomb while yet living." To solve these problems, Harris devised a simple solution—flexible grading. By promoting students frequently at intervals of approximately six weeks, the St. Louis schools allowed students to progress at varying rates.[18]

In the next two decades, the St. Louis system of flexible grading became fairly widespread. A survey reported by the U.S. commissioner of education in 1891 showed that 44 percent of elementary school systems in cities over 4,000 made individual promotions more frequently than once a year. The general practice was to use flexible promotions in the early grades. Over half the schools reported flexible promotion in first grade, while some 17 percent used it in the senior year of high school.[19]

In the last quarter of the nineteenth century, school administrators and teachers invented a panoply of "plans" to provide for individual differences. Some, like the St. Louis system, assumed uniform content but varied the pace of instruction and the amount of individual attention. In the Batavia Plan, as described by Cubberley, teaching assistants aided slow students, while the "left-overs" and "dull or retarded pupils" were lumped in "ungraded classes." Other programs with flexible grading included: the Pueblo Plan (individual and small group instruction with the pupil advancing at any time), the Chicago Plan (entire classes promoted when the group had achieved a certain level of performance), group teaching (instruction by teams of teachers), and departmental teaching (instruction in seventh and eighth grade in the fashion common to high schools). Probably the most widely used flexible grading system, the Elizabeth Plan, employed small group and individual instruction with promotions at any time.[20]

Of a more radical bent were programs which varied the courses of study for students of different abilities. The most widely known of this type of classification system was called the Cambridge Plan, an early form of ability grouping. The plan originated with Charles W. Eliot, president of Harvard. Addressing the annual meeting of the National Education Association in 1892 at Saratoga, New York, Eliot deplored the "undesirable uniformity" produced by rigid age-grading. This system, he said, "must suppress individual differences instead of developing them, and must leave individual capacities undiscovered and untrained, thus robbing the individual of happiness and service-ableness, and society of the fruits it might have enjoyed from the special endowments of thousands of its members."[21]

Francis Cogswell, superintendent of the Cambridge schools, quickly developed a parallel course of study, or two-track plan, to remedy the malady which Eliot had diagnosed. After the third grade, students were divided into two groups, "average" and "gifted." Those in the first group completed the subsequent course of study in six years, while the "gifted" group was given an enriched program which it completed in four years. At yearly intervals it was possible for students in one group to switch into the other.[22]

A variant of the Cambridge Plan, developed by Superintendent James Van Sickle for the North Denver schools, provided a similar method to meet the needs of the "average" and "gifted" students. Moving to Baltimore, Van Sickle introduced an important modification to the parallel course of study. In the first six grades students followed three different paths, one directed toward the "minimum essentials," a second toward the "average" group, and a third toward the "superior" group. A new type of institution, the intermediate school, then provided a differentiated course of instruction, with students in the third group preparing for advanced academic work and other taking courses oriented toward business, "household arts," and vocational courses. In rough form Van Sickle had created an early version of a three-track plan with a differentiated course of study.[23]

How widespread were these three methods of classifying students? A 1910 survey of 2,000 superintendents, principals, and teachers conducted by the Joint Committee on School Organization of the New York City Teachers' Associations provided evidence of their use in elementary schools. Table 2.3 shows the percentage of the educators surveyed who indicated they had tried a particular plan. Although the research methods used in this survey were not sophisticated, the results do allow some general observations.[24] It appears that programs involving the least amount of structural reform, such as group teaching and ungraded classes, achieved the widest use. Plans such as that used in Cambridge, involving a complex tracking scheme, appear to have been used only infrequently in these early years of the century.[25]

TABLE 2.3
The Grading and Promotion of Pupils, 1910

Classification Method	Percent Who Had Tried
Group Teaching	55%
Departmental Teaching	49%
Ungraded Classes	28%
Elizabeth Plan	28%
Pueblo Plan	21%
North Denver Plan	17%
Chicago Plan	16%
Batavia Plan	14%
Cambridge Plan	8%

Source: C. S. Hartwell, "The Grading and Promotion of Pupils," *Addresses and Proceedings of the National Education Association* 48 (1910): 296.

Around the time of the First World War, Cubberley described the structural evolution of public education in the United States. As is shown in table 2.4, the elementary school had made special provisions for individual students and had begun to adopt several plans for differentiated instruction.[26]

A similar evolution in the structure of high schools had led to the creation of four distinct institutions as already mentioned: college preparatory, comprehensive, commercial, and vocational. Cubberley also provided a more detailed description of the internal structure of most urban school systems around the time of the war, as well as his prognosis for further development (table 2.5).[27]

As the structure of American public schools changed significantly between 1840 and 1917, so too did their function as perceived by school administrators and university professors. The transformation of the high school around the turn of the century revealed the most profound shift in the function of education. In 1890 only 6.7 percent of those aged fourteen to seventeen were enrolled in public and private high schools. Already, however, the high school curriculum was changing to meet the needs of a more diversified clientele. In 1892 the National Education Association appointed Harvard president Charles W. Eliot and a group of educators to evaluate high school programs and their relation to college admissions requirements. The Committee

TABLE 2.4
Evolution of the Structure of Elementary Education

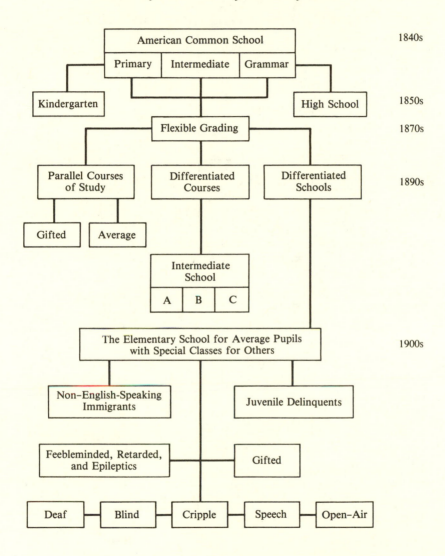

Source: Adapted from Ellwood P. Cubberley, *Public Education in the United States* (Boston: Houghton Mifflin, 1919), 401. Copyright © 1919, renewed 1946 by Helen Cubberley. Adapted with permission of Houghton Mifflin Company.

TABLE 2.5

The Reorganization of American Education, 1919

1900	Years of Age	School Grade		1925 (?)
Graduate School — Graduate Work	25 / 24	19th	**Graduate Instruction**	**Professional Schools**
	23	18th		
Professional Schools		17th		
	22			
College — Liberal Arts and Technical Courses and Departments	21	16th	**Senior College**	
		15th		
	20			
	19	14th	**Junior College**	Civic, Scientific and Liberal Arts Studies
	18	13th		
High School — Ancient Classical / Modern Classical / Scientific / English History	17	12th	**High** — Cultural / Technical / Agricultural / Manual Arts / Commercial / Home Arts / Vocational	
	16	11th		
	15	10th		
	14	9th	**Intermediate**	Some Differentiations in Courses
Elementary School	13	8th		
	12	7th		
Eight	11	6th	**Elementary School**	Six
		5th		Grades
Grade	10	4th		—
	9	3rd		Mastery of
School	8	2nd		Fundamental
	7	1st		
	6			
Kindergarten	5	Kn.		Kindergarten
Common Plan still in general use				Plan beginning to be used
The 8–4 plan				The 6–3–3 (or 5) plan

Source: Ellwood P. Cubberley, *Public Education in the United States* (Boston: Houghton Mifflin, 1919), 460. Copyright © 1919, renewed 1946 by Helen Cubberley. Adapted with permission of Houghton Mifflin Company.

of Ten, as it came to be known, recommended four different courses of study—Classical, Latin-Scientific, Modern Languages, and English. Importantly, they concluded that subjects should not be "treated differently for pupils who are going to college, for those who are going to a scientific school, and for those who, presumably, are going to neither." Although the work of the committee did signal a new direction for the high school, the reforms they proposed did not address the circumstances of the great majority of youth who went directly to work.[28]

How different was the position taken twenty-five years later by the Commission on the Reorganization of Secondary Education in 1917. By then high schools enrolled nearly one-third of the population between fourteen and seventeen. Noting that "within the past few decades changes have taken place in American life profoundly affecting the activities of the individual," the commission identified seven "cardinal principles" of education: health, command of fundamental processes, worthy home-membership, vocation, citizenship, worthy use of leisure, and ethical character. In the commission's view, an exclusive secondary school could no longer fill the needs of an educational system that was quickly becoming universal. The reports of these two commissions, though obviously not a measure of actual practice, symbolized the fact that by World War I, the educational system was on its way to becoming highly differentiated in function as well as structure.[29]

It was in good part because of a rapid expansion of education and its differentiation that intelligence tests made their first appearance as a means of classifying students. Before the war there were but few instances of their use. One of the most important, however, involved Lewis Terman and his student, Virgil Dickson, in a reorganization of the schools in Oakland, California. The Oakland experiment, one of the first examples of the use of intelligence tests for classification, was a prophetic one indeed.

Solutions: The Early Use of Intelligence Tests in Oakland

In the summer of 1917, Virgil Dickson, one of Terman's students at Stanford, became the new director of research in the Oakland Public

Schools. During the next year he organized the testing of approximately 6,500 schoolchildren with the recently developed Stanford-Binet test as well as a new intelligence test prepared by Arthur Otis, another Terman student. Based on his first year's work, Dickson observed that "standard tests, both psychological and pedagogical—group and individual—should be of great assistance in the classification of pupils according to ability and capacity to do work."[30]

Dickson's experiment in Oakland was significant, for it was one of the first systematic attempts to use intelligence tests for classifying students. An examination of Oakland as a case study in the early use of tests shows that this city, like many others across the country, faced a multitude of problems around the turn of the century. Initial attempts to cope with these strains led to special classes and flexible promotion plans. Intelligence tests were used at first to diagnose students for special classes; later their adoption led to the creation of a systemwide tracking plan based on ability. The case study of Oakland shows how a network of professionals both in the schools and at Stanford advocated the use of intelligence tests. The study reveals, as well, the ambiguity that characterized the values of those who promoted testing as a progressive reform. On the one hand, school people hoped that testing would aid in rational, efficient educational reform. On the other hand, they were occasionally overconfident about the new instruments, and their interpretation of intelligence test differences seemed to justify social prejudice by apparent scientific objectivity. The experiment with testing in Oakland in 1917 and 1918 would provide a blueprint for the intelligence testing movement after the war.

In the first several decades of the twentieth century, Oakland grappled with a variety of problems—mushrooming size, increasing diversity, and soaring costs—which faced school systems across the country. The scope of change in Oakland is depicted in table 2.6.[31] The changes in Oakland's school population came with the flood of immigrants to America around the turn of the century, with the stream of refugees who fled the San Francisco earthquake and fire in 1906, and as a result of a new compulsory school law passed by the state in 1903.[32] As Oakland's population bulged after the turn of the century, so too it became increasingly diverse; by 1918, 60 percent of Oakland's residents were first- or second-generation immigrants. The rapid growth

TABLE 2.6

*Population Growth, School Enrollment, and Attendance,
Oakland, California, 1890–1918*

Year	Population by U.S. Census	Percent Increase	Total School Enrollment	Percent Increase	Average Daily Attendance	Percent Increase
1890	48,682		9,565		6,372	
1900	66,960	38%	11,976	25%	8,512	34%
1910	150,174	124%	17,621	47%	12,919	52%
1917	206,402	37%	40,946	132%	25,797	100%
1918	246,519	19%	48,214	18%	27,304	6%

Source: *Report of the Superintendent of Schools, Oakland, California, 1917–18* (Oakland: Tribune, 1919), 234–35. Note that the population figures for Oakland in 1910 include an annexation the previous year.

in size and diversity helps to explain why school expenditures nearly doubled from $1.2 million in 1910–1911 to $2.1 million in 1916–1917.[33]

To cope with these changes, the Oakland schools introduced a series of reforms beginning around the turn of the century. In 1901 superintendent John W. McClymonds developed a system of flexible promotions and ungraded classes. Under this system, each teacher in the elementary grades, with the assistance of the principal, divided the class "according to the ability of the pupils, as nearly as possible into two equal divisions," and promotions were then made "whenever any section or division . . . completed the work of the grade." By 1915 the structure of Oakland's public school system had become highly differentiated to meet the needs of its new constituents. The system consisted of kindergartens, intermediate schools, and several high schools including a vocational school, a technical school, two comprehensive schools, and a "university" school exclusively for college preparatory work.[34]

In 1911 McClymonds hired Vinnie Hicks to establish a psychological clinic and to begin examining the "abnormal" children with intelligence tests. Working in the clinic and in the schools, Hicks identified some 365 such children, ranging from the "unruly" and the "high school subnormal" to the "feebleminded" and "idiots." In Hicks's view, isolating the "subnormal" children—"the absent, the tardy, the sickly, the unruly, the liars, thieves and cowards"—would free the teachers to work with the normal children. Furthermore, she thought the clinic could help by identifying criminals, paupers, and "defectives," proposing for the latter a eugenic program of "incarceration" and "surgical interference." Hicks offered strong medicine to cure the problems in Oakland; perhaps her zeal explains why the work of the clinic expanded slowly in the next few years.[35]

Like many urban school systems at this time, Oakland soon came under the scrutiny of reformers who hoped to centralize the power structure and streamline the schools for efficiency. In October 1914 a voluntary organization of Oakland principals called the "1915 Club" asked Jesse B. Sears of Stanford to conduct an exhaustive study of spelling efficiency in Oakland. Using standardized spelling tests developed by Ayres, his study disclosed wide variations in achievement among the schools. The Board of Education then decided to employ "a disinterested expert to investigate the reasons for the increased expense and to determine if it were possible to conduct the schools more economically without losses of efficiency." They hired Ellwood P. Cubberley, head of Stanford's Department of Education. After an extensive twelve-day investigation, Cubberley enumerated fourteen reasons for increased cost. His solutions reflected the best educational wisdom of the time: reform the school administration along corporate lines, provide the superintendent with more powerful central authority, and expand the work of the research department to provide a more scientific assessment of student abilities and accomplishments.[36]

Oakland took Cubberley's recommendations seriously and soon hired a new, aggressive superintendent, Fred Hunter. Early in his administration, Hunter identified some of the "problems" facing the city's schools:

Only One Third of the boys and girls who enter Oakland High Schools complete the high school course to graduation. . . . Almost *Eight Hundred* Oakland boys and girls leave school each year between *Grades Six and Eight*. . . . Thirteen Thousand Oakland school children (fifty-one percent of the total number in day high and elementary schools) are overage. . . . *School Methods and Organization Have Been Inflexible and Inadaptable. . . . It Costs Money to Adapt School Instruction and Organization to Child and Community Needs. . . . Sixty Per*

Cent of Oakland's population is *Foreign Born* or children of the first generation of foreign parentage. . . . *Sixteen* schools in Oakland have a percentage of foreign children ranging from *Fifty to Seventy Per Cent.* (Emphasis in the original)

With this list of particulars as ammunition, Hunter launched a campaign to reform the schools to provide for individual differences, a campaign which soon brought to Oakland's newly founded Bureau of Research a man familiar with the latest developments in intelligence testing.[37]

In the summer of 1917 Virgil Dickson came to Oakland with a master's degree from Stanford and extensive training in psychological testing with Terman. In his graduate study he had explored "the relation of mental testing to school administration" by using intelligence tests to place nearly 150 first-grade children entering schools in four towns near Stanford. With his Stanford connection and interest in the practical use of intelligence tests, Dickson seemed an obvious candidate for the Oakland position. "Fortunately," he said later, "during the summer of 1917 it was possible for Dr. Cubberley and Dr. Terman of the University to make arrangements with superintendent Hunter of the City Schools of Oakland, which would permit an educational experiment to be carried on using the Oakland Public Schools as a laboratory." Drawing from his Stanford experience, he came to Oakland with a three-pronged plan for testing the work of the schools: retardation studies, achievement testing, and psychological examinations.[38]

In September he began a systematic study of school progress and retardation in all forty-five elementary schools. The results showed less than half the students were making normal progress; in other words, a substantial percentage of Oakland students had failed one or more terms. Furthermore, the study revealed that the highest rates of failure were concentrated in the immigrant schools, as table 2.7 shows.[39] Over half the students in schools with the highest percentage of foreign parents had failed one or more grades, while under a third of the students in the schools with the smallest percentage of foreign parents had failed. Significantly, almost a quarter of the students in the latter schools had skipped one or more terms; virtually none of the students (2 percent) had skipped in the immigrant schools. For Dickson the

Ellwood P. Cubberley, Head of the Stanford University Department of Education. Cubberley's interest in school reform led to strong support for Terman's plan to use intelligence tests in schools at the time of the First World
War. (Reprinted by permission of the Department of Special Collections and
University Archives, Stanford University Libraries.)

indictment against the schools was clear: "These figures furnish evidence to convict the schools to two things: (1) the ability to discover
weakness in the child and hold him back. (2) the inability to discover
strength in the child and move him ahead."[40]

Dickson then began to analyze the abysmal record of the schools
with the help of intelligence tests. In December 1917 he administered
to about 2,000 students the group tests Terman was preparing for use

Jesse B. Sears, Professor of Education, Stanford University. An expert in the use of surveys in public school administration, Sears joined with Cubberley and Terman in 1917–1918 in one of the first systematic attempts to use group intelligence tests for classifying students. (Reprinted by permission of the Department of Special Collections and University Archives, Stanford University Libraries.)

TABLE 2.7
School Progress in Oakland Elementary Schools, 1917

	Average Rate of Progress		
Type of Schools	Rapid	Normal	Slow
Five Schools with Greatest Percentage of Foreign Parentage (60–100%)	2%	41%	53%
Five Schools with Smallest Percentage of Foreign Parentage (20–30%)	26%	42%	30%

Source: E. Morris Cox, "Survey of Nationalities," in *Report of the Superintendent of Schools, Oakland, California, 1917–18* (Oakland: Tribune, 1919), 34–38. Note that the percentages in the tables reported by Cox did not add to one hundred.

in the army. In May 1918 he secured permission from his fellow graduate student, Arthur Otis, to use his recently refined group test with some 1,600 students in the eighth and ninth grades. Throughout the year he tested over 3,000 pupils with the Stanford-Binet, concentrating on first graders. The year was a busy one indeed. Dickson addressed thirty-two gatherings of teachers and principals on "standards in classroom work" and "psychological tests," and offered two ten-hour training courses in psychological testing to one group of twenty-five first-grade teachers and another group of forty-five principals and administrators.[41]

The intelligence testing confirmed Dickson's belief that many students were failing because they "had inherent mental tendencies that make the ordinary course of study either impossible or impractical of attainment." He recommended reforming the curriculum to accommodate differences in mental ability. His plan called for "segregation" of the "mentally superior" for accelerated work, and of the "mentally deficient" for special class work. For those with ability who have "fallen behind" and for those who "work very slowly," he recommended "opportunity classes." For those "not yet mentally old enough" for first grade, he called for "special receiving classes."[42]

Dickson also foresaw an obvious place for intelligence tests in developing a more "scientific" vocational guidance. Like Terman, Dickson also saw important social consequences of the reform of school curricula through intelligence testing. When students were faced with expectations that exceeded their abilities, he noted, the "natural result" was "loss of interest, a loss of self-respect or a resort to subterfuge." Referring to the activities of the International Workers of the World, a radical labor organization, he observed: "Social unrest, sham, and the I.W.W. spirit may easily have their beginnings in these early social problems.[43]

Dickson's program for testing and classification met with hearty approval among administrators and teachers in the Oakland schools. A district administrator called the experiment "the most important factor in effective educational administration that has been introduced in years," while another called for tests to be given to all primary children so that they might be classified according to ability. The principal of the Oakland High School, C. E. Keyes, reported that intelligence tests had been used to create ability groups and to make recommendations for college as well. To Dickson, Keyes expressed the hope that "before very long the classification of the school will be based almost entirely on the results obtained from the testing." W. M. Greenwell and G. E. Mortensen, principals of the two largest Oakland elementary schools and which also had the highest concentration of immigrants, both strongly supported the testing program. They reported that ability groups based on tests reduced discipline problems and dropouts and that teachers and pupils alike seemed "happier." Teachers reported a "deeper and more sympathetic understanding of the child" and a new respect for individual differences. One said the "tests have thrown floods of light on problems that have heretofore baffled me," while another reported that they had given her "greater confidence in my judgment" and the "courage of my convictions to take action." Although these testimonies were solicited by Dickson for his Stanford doctoral dissertation, they do provide fragmentary evidence that school administrators and teachers both found intelligence tests of immense practical value.[44]

The introduction of testing in Oakland did not proceed without difficulty. Dickson for one was aware of the dangers associated with mental testing, and during the Oakland experiment warned about the "danger of over-confidence in the results of the mental test." "Altogether too many prinicipals and teachers," he said, "are perfectly

willing to shift the responsibility for using their own intelligence to
entirely too great an extent by accepting mental tests results as more
or less final." Administration and interpretation of tests by untrained
teachers and administrators led, he noted, to "extremely unfortunate"
labeling and stigmatizing of slower students. "Public criticism," he
observed, "is likely to arise unless great tact is used." Nevertheless, he
was confident that these problems could be surmounted.[45]

Although a few other school systems had also begun to use intelligence tests for classification, Oakland's experiment was one of the most
comprehensive uses of mental tests in schools before the First World
War.[46] While Dickson was busy establishing a testing program in
Oakland, his mentor, Lewis Terman, was in Washington creating the
guidelines for the massive use of tests in the army. The army experience, more than any other single factor, would demonstrate the usefulness of intelligence tests for classification. After the First World War,
school districts around the country would be following Oakland's lead.

CHAPTER 3

The Use of Intelligence Tests in World War I: Applied Psychology Comes of Age

In May 1917, a month after America declared war on Germany, Lewis Terman received word from Robert M. Yerkes, president of the American Psychological Association, that his services were urgently needed to develop group intelligence tests for use in the army. Traveling east, Terman embarked on a venture that would occupy nearly all of his time over the next two years. America's involvement in World War I would make three important contributions to the development of a national intelligence testing movement. Within a year the war experience would provide a dramatic example of the potential usefulness of intelligence tests in classifying large numbers of individuals. The war would also shape the network of professional psychologists and intelligence testers by providing a forum for university professors to share ideas they had been developing, and by giving a new group of men skill in using mental tests. Demobilization from the war would lead directly to the creation of group intelligence tests for use in the public schools.

Psychological Testing in the Army

When Congress declared war against Germany in April 6, Yerkes was meeting at Harvard with a group of psychologists known as the "experimentalists." The group agreed that the psychological profession could make a contribution to the war effort. Several days later Yerkes wrote to the members of the American Psychological Association: "In the present perilous situation, it is obviously desirable that the psychologists of the country act unitedly in the interests of defense. Our knowledge and our methods are of importance to the military service of our country, and it is our duty to cooperate to the fullest extent and immediately toward the increased efficiency of our Army and Navy."[1]

A fortnight later, Yerkes created twelve committees to explore the ways psychology might contribute, appointing himself to head the Committee on the Psychological Examination of Recruits. Yerkes also chaired the Psychology Committee of the National Research council, established by the National Academy of Science in 1916. By early May Yerkes sent a plan for psychological testing to William C. Gorgas, surgeon general and a member of the NRC. "The Council of the American Psychological Association is convinced," Yerkes's proposal said, "that in the present emergency American psychology can substantially serve the government . . . by examining recruits with respect especially to intellectual deficiency, psychopathic tendencies, nervous instability, and inadequate self-control." The plan focused in part on identifying those unfit for army service, perhaps because Yerkes had been experimenting with tests for individual psychological diagnosis at the Boston Psychopathic Hospital.[2]

Yerkes now saw a wider application for the tests. To adapt psychological tests for use in the army, Yerkes assembled a group of six psychologists, several of whom were close professional acquaintances. Walter V. Bingham, director of the Division of Applied Psychology at the Carnegie Institute of Technology, received his Ph.D. from Harvard in 1908 when Yerkes had just been promoted to assistant professor, and the two had served together as officers in the American Psychological Association in 1911 and 1912. Thomas H. Haines received his doctorate a year before Yerkes at Harvard in 1901 and later joined him on the staff at the Boston Psychopathic Hospital. Frederick L. Wells, who received his masters at Harvard before taking his Ph.D. from Chicago, held a position comparable to Yerkes's at McLean Hospital in nearby Waverley, Massachusetts. To this group Yerkes added Guy M. Whipple of the University of Illinois, an early pioneer in test development. Henry H. Goddard, president of the Vineland Training Institute, offered the use of his school's facilities to the committee.

In this group Terman was an outsider. He knew Goddard of course from their days at Clark. But as he later recalled, he did not feel part of the national psychological profession:

I was quite aware of the fact that many of the old-line psychologists regarded the whole test movement with scorn. I was probably more sensitive on this point than the facts warranted, with the result that I made at this time fewer contacts with psychologists in other fields than I should have done. Between 1910 and 1916 I made no trips East and did not even apply for membership in the American Psychological Association. . . . I had the feeling that I hardly counted as a psychologist unless possibly among a few kindred souls like Gesell, Goddard, Kuhlmann, Thorndike, Whipple, Yerkes, and a few others who had become "tarred by the same brush."

He had carried on a correspondence with Yerkes early in 1917, however, about the possibility of a joint effort to develop a new intelligence scale, a dialogue that is discussed later. This association led Yerkes to think of Terman for the committee.[3]

On the afternoon of May 28, the group met at Vineland to fashion a new series of tests. Yerkes reviewed the background of the problem for his fellow psychologists and urged that tests be created to identify "intellectually incompetent recruits," "the psychotic," "incorrigibles," and "men for special tasks." After intense discussion, however, the committee decided to expand the original proposal to identify the unfit and "unanimously agreed that an effort should be made to test all recruits." Their focus shifted from identifying "misfits" to classifying the entire army. Terman remarked that when Germany mobilized, the army was well trained: "The parts of the machine needed only to be assembled in order to begin work." America faced a crisis. Without efficient sorting of recruits, the army would remain nothing more than "an assembled horde."[4]

Terman saw the parallel between the problems the schools were facing and the situation soon to engulf the army, and he pushed hard for his plan to modify the Stanford-Binet in developing an intelligence test for the military. Fortunately, Terman brought with him Arthur Otis's new group intelligence test, a battery that Terman said "lent itself throughout to purely objective methods of scoring" and "exerted a profound influence upon the psychological testing in the army." Within two weeks they had developed the examination, "including five tests practically in the form in which Otis had used them in his own scale." After a break to test the instrument with children in public schools, university students, and people in institutions for the feeble-minded, the group reassembled and finished the revised version by early July. The committee was ready to test the army's intelligence.[5]

For Terman the potential value of the intelligence testing program was clear:

If the army is to be efficient it is evident that the work which requires most brains must be given to men with brains. We can easily imagine what would become of an army if all the men in it who were fit to command were set to digging the trenches, and if those fit only to dig trenches were made its officers. Plainly if the army machine is to work smoothly and efficiently it is as important to fit the job to the man as to fit the ammunition to the gun.

Like his prescription for using tests in schools, Terman believed his plan for testing the army would contribute to social efficiency.[6]

In August the newly formed Committee on Classification of Personnel of the War Department began a preliminary testing program. Initially, testing was conducted with Examination Alpha, consisting of eight subtests measuring ability in such areas as arithmetic, practical judgment, language, and following directions. When testers discovered a high percentage of illiterates and foreign-born among the recruits, they developed a performance test, Examination Beta, that employed subtests such as mazes, pictorial completion, and geometric construction which did not require as much familiarity with English. After testing, recruits and officers were assigned an "intelligence grade" ranging from A, very superior, to E, for men who were recommended for discharge or "special service." By May 1918 twenty-four camps had been established to test every army man; the rate of testing jumped to over 200,000 a month. At its termination in January 1919, the testing program had assessed the mental ability of 1,726,966 enlisted men and officers. Based on occupational experience, IQ scores, and personnel ratings, men were then assigned to duty.[7]

The experience of psychological testing in the army was a stormy one, however, as Daniel Kevles has observed. At several junctures, objections raised by the military threatened the entire program. Some of the earliest opposition came from career officers who resented outsiders' advice about who would make good soldiers. As one officer put it:

> The value of these examinations is almost always overrated or underrated. Generally speaking, the officer of long Regular Army experience rejects them as being valueless and his opinion is very apt to be at once adopted by any young officer who learns it. The new officer, if left to himself, accepts the results of this examination as final and conclusive and gives to the matter an unjustified value that often leads to his disappointment; and the net result in either case is a feeling of prejudice against psychological examinations, and this, I believe, is the general attitude of the service with reference to this matter.

Part of the negative reaction, Yerkes thought, was due to the "misunderstanding of psychology and prejudices against anything done in its name."[8]

Also damaging to the testing program was the skepticism of the psychologists in the army Medical Department. By nature interested in the diagnosis and treatment of individual medical problems, medical psychologists were wary of pencil and paper tests which purported to tell in fifty minutes whether a man was fit or unfit for the army. The intelligence testers also labored under the stigma of being attached to the Sanitary Corps, and in general their rank was inferior to that of their counterparts in the Medical Corps. Attempts by Yerkes to gain promotions for his men in 1918 failed several times. The ill will that the Medical Corps felt toward the testers was heightened when the results of initial examinations revealed that "medical officers as a group . . . ranked relatively low in intelligence."[9]

Opposition was not confined to those working directly with the psychological testers. Complaints—that the testers were undermining traditional army practice and that the testers were using the army for their own academic purposes—reached the secretary of war and the General Staff and prompted several investigations in 1918. Secretary of War Newton D. Baker voiced the fears of many when he said that the very word "psychology" created a "certain revulsion in the ordinary man's mind." Despite a favorable report, the General Staff only grudgingly approved the program's continuation and further showed its distaste for intelligence testing by refusing promotion requests, by blocking congressional funds earmarked for the construction of special examining stations, and by failing to issue a general order supporting the program.[10]

Facing this kind of resistance, Yerkes, Terman, and members of the psychology staff of the Surgeon General's Office tried to counter the criticism. They prepared a "Guide for Psychological Examining in the Army," containing a section entitled "Conferences with Officers" that counseled: "In order that the results of examinations may be used effectively, it is necessary that psychological examiners take pains to acquaint all officers in their stations with the nature and uses of intelligence ratings." The manual then gave advice on how to counter three common criticisms—that the scores were "greatly influenced by such accidental factors as fatigue, homesickness, illness, time of day, etc.," that the tests "do not measure real ability, but instead merely reflect the man's educational and social advantages," and that the scores may be "greatly influenced by coaching." A 1918 survey showed, they said, that three-quarters of the company officers who had become familiar with the tests during their initial, experimental use testified to their value. A typical letter from the commanding officer at Camp Sheridan stated that the psychological test was of "great value" when "properly applied." Yerkes argued as well that "the steady stream of requests from commercial concerns, educational institutions, and individuals for the use of army methods of psychological examining or for the adaptation of such methods to special needs" proved the program's importance.[11]

Through 1918 the Psychology Staff managed to parry the most overt attacks on the testing program. With the armistice in November, the need for aid in classification was greatly diminished. Proposals to continue testing in peacetime were rejected, and in January 1919 the psychological service was terminated.

Before the operation was dismantled, Yerkes made provision for an extensive analysis of the data produced in the examinations and for a history to be written by himself, Terman, and Edwin G. Boring. The army data lent support to the psychologists' contention that there were individual differences in mental ability. Moreover, the statistics on nearly two million soldiers showed that there were significant social differences in intelligence test performance, differences that would provoke a sharp debate about what exactly intelligence tests measured.

The examiners studied the relationship among Alpha and Beta scores and six variables describing the recruits: their residence, nativity, race, level of education, occupation, and the camp where they were tested. The testers soon noticed significant differences in soldier performance at the various camps. In a descriptive analysis of sixteen camps, Boring showed that in some (Lewis, Washington; Funston, Kansas; Grant, Illinois; Dodge, Iowa; and Devens, Massachusetts) the soldiers did better than average, while in others (Gordon, Georgia; Travis, Texas; Dix, New Jersey; Meade, Maryland; Lee, Virginia) the soldiers did worse. Based on this initial study, Boring was unable to make a definite statement about the causes of regional differences, but the trend to him seemed clear—recruits from the North were considerably more "intelligent" than those from the South. Examining nativity, he discovered that of the 18 percent of the army who were immigrants, those from England, Holland, Denmark, Scotland, and Germany did quite well on the tests compared with those from Turkey, Greece, Russia, Italy, and Poland. The analysis showed that an unusually high percentage of blacks received very low scores, particularly those who came from the Deep South. When looking at the effect of schooling on intelligence scores, Boring discovered a positive relationship. Evaluating occupation and intelligence test scores, he found that distribution in scores very closely reflected the status hierarchy of occupations at the time. Laborers, miners, teamsters, and barbers on average earned an army intelligence rating of C−, for example, while engineers, medical officers, accountants, mechanical draftsmen, and dental officers earned A's and B's.[12]

Boring did not attempt to explain the differences in intelligence test scores; that would await the scrutiny of psychologists in the 1920s. The men responsible for developing the tests were confident, however, that the tests measured "native intelligence" and not something else. Discussing the army experience, Terman likened the process of measuring human intelligence to assaying the quality of "a gold bearing vein of quartz": "It is only necessary to take a few random samples of the ore to an assayer, who makes a simple test and returns the verdict of so many ounces of gold per ton of rock." So too, he thought, "conceivably it might be possible to sink shafts, as it were, at certain critical points, and by examining a few samples of the mind's intellectual product to estimate its intrinsic quality by a method analogous to that of the assayer." [13]

At the close of the war, discussions about intelligence test differences were secondary to those about how the tests might be used in society. Although the army experience had not been without difficulty, many psychologists were delighted with the potential it revealed for applied psychology. The war thus served to give psychologists a new sense of confidence in their profession.

A Wider Professional Network

For the psychologists who answered Yerkes's call in 1917, the war was a turning point in creating a network of applied psychologists and developing a new sense of professional responsibility. Professional psychology had its beginnings in the late nineteenth century, a time when countless other groups, ranging from doctors and lawyers to historians and engineers, established themselves. As Burton Bledstein has observed, this emergent "culture of professionalism" was based on belief in the authority of the expert and the power of science, and the professional's "ethic of service which taught that dedication to a client's interest took precedence over personal profit." [14]

The war catalyzed the emerging profession of applied psychology. Looking back on the war years, Terman recalled:

Their most important aspect, so far as my personal development is concerned, was in the opportunity they gave me to become acquainted with nearly all the leading psychologists of America. . . . Through them and others my information was extended and my interests broadened in many fields of psychology. My intimate contact with Yerkes in particular, both in our daily work and during the long periods when I lived in his home, meant more to me than could easily be expressed. . . . One result of the war experiences was to confirm and strengthen my earlier beliefs regarding the importance of mental tests as an integral part of scientific psychology. . . . I no longer felt isolated.

The army experiment affirmed their belief, and the public's view as well, that applied psychology could make an important contribution to society. Equally important, the war experience helped convince psychologists that they did in fact constitute a national community.[15]

One of the most important professional groups in the war was the Committee on Classification of Personnel of the War Department, created in August 1917 to direct the military testing program. The membership, drawn in good part from the American Psychological Association and the National Research Council, included some of the most significant names in applied psychology before the war: James R. Angell, Walter V. Bingham, Raymond Dodge, Walter Scott, John F. Shepard, Edward K. Strong, Lewis M. Terman, Edward L. Thorndike, John B. Watson, and Robert M. Yerkes. They were an impressive group, having taken Ph.D.'s at universities that pioneered in testing around the turn of the century: Chicago, Clark, Columbia, Harvard, Liepzig, and Michigan. When the war broke out, Scott, the director of the committee, was professor of psychology at Northwestern, where he had established a psychological laboratory and where he was investigating applications of psychology in business for personnel selection. Thorndike, the chairman, was of course at Teachers College. Bingham, the secretary, had taught psychology at Chicago, Columbia, and Dartmouth before becoming director of the Division of Applied Psychology at Carnegie Institute of Technology in 1915. Terman's membership in the group undoubtedly reflected his work with the Stanford-Binet and his successful work with the Committee on Psychological Examination earlier that June.[16]

Two weeks after the Committee on Classification was created, Yerkes was appointed major and named to head the testing program under the auspices of the Surgeon General's Office. Yerkes directed the overall effort, while Terman was commissioned to develop and administer the examinations. Together they assembled a staff to implement the program. The initial group included several men who were to figure importantly in the testing movement both before and after the war: Arthur S. Otis, Charles S. Berry, Clarence S. Yoakum, Melvin E. Haggerty, and Harold C. Bingham. Eventually, over forty psychologists would serve on the staff, as military officers or civilians. In addition, an advisory panel of three prominent psychologists was appointed: Thorndike; Truman L. Kelley, a highly regarded statistician from Columbia; and Guy M. Whipple, who had pioneered in mental test development at the University of Illinois.[17]

From this core of psychologists, the Division of Psychology grew to include 384 persons, 127 officers commissioned in the Sanitary Corps, 248 enlisted men in the Section of Psychology of the Medical Corps, and a support staff. Late in December a school for military psychology was established at Fort Oglethorpe, Georgia, to train the officers in intelligence testing. After an intensive, two-month course the officers fanned out to thirty-five army camps, where they organized the work of the enlisted men in setting up the testing program.

In many respects the staff and officers of the army's Psychological Division represented the cream of talent in the young psychological profession. A study of the backgrounds of the officers shows that they were young (average age thirty) and bright. Educational information was obtained for a group of forty-seven officers, all of whom either had or would soon receive Ph.D.'s. Of the twenty-six who had Ph.D.'s, seventeen had received their degree between 1912 and 1917. Of the remaining twenty-one without a degree, all would take their Ph.D. by 1926. This educational elite came from a handful of universities. Harvard and Columbia contributed the greatest number of Ph.D.'s to the war effort (four and five, respectively), while Cornell, Chicago, Clark, Yale, Johns Hopkins, Illinois, and several others were also represented. After the war the officers pursuing advanced degrees in psychology would also attend Stanford, Ohio State, Iowa, and Princeton.[18]

Schools and universities around the country lent their men to help with the army testing program. Many were teaching in psychology departments in the East (Colgate, Cornell, Harvard, Rochester, Smith, and Wellesley), the Midwest (Indiana State, Kansas State, Miami of Ohio, Northwestern, and Texas), and the West (Oregon, Stanford, and Washington State). Some had just completed their degrees, like John E. Anderson, who received his Ph.D. from Harvard in June 1917, or like Ben D. Wood, who finished his undergraduate education at Texas that same month. Others were hard at work in the public schools. Edwin M. Chamberlain, who had finished his doctorate at Harvard in 1917, left his job as a school superintendent for the army experiment, for example, and Wilford S. Miller stepped down as principal of the University of Minnesota High School.

Other psychologists were directly involved with testing programs at the time the war broke out. Warren W. Coxe was assistant director of the Vocation Bureau in Cincinnati, while Charles A. Coburn was a vocational counselor in the Boston public schools. Garry C. Myers was a psychologist with the Brooklyn Training School, as was Edgar A. Doll with the Vineland Training School.

The profile of the 248 enlisted men is more difficult to ascertain, yet the background of a few individuals suggests that as a group they were not unlike the officers. Some came to the Psychology Division from universities where they were pursuing graduate studies and teaching. Walter Veazie taught philosophy at Columbia for three years prior to the war, while Karl Holzinger was in the math department at the University of Minnesota in 1917. Some joined through their associations with staff officers; Karl Cowdery, for example, met Terman during the survey of the Whittier State Normal School before the war. Others held positions in public education: Ernest Jackson, Robert Oberholser, and Ralph Westcott were public school principals and superintendents before the war. Still others, like Joseph Wood Krutch, came to the war from teaching in the humanities.

The experience of these men in the army helped to reinforce the sense of community among psychologists. When the war brought together these practicing applied psychologists, the leaders in the field soon saw a need to establish some kind of standards for membership in the profession. Shortly after joining the American Psychological Association in 1917, Terman was appointed to the newly created Committee on Qualifications for Psychological Examiners and other Psychological Experts. The committee, chaired by Terman's army associate, Melvin E. Haggerty, also included Mabel R. Fernald, Thomas H. Haines, Leta S. Hollingworth, Arthur H. Sutherland, Guy M. Whipple, and Helen T. Woolley. Meeting over several years, the group developed a classification for psychological examiners ranging from Class A, "persons who are thoroughly trained and experienced and able to act with freedom in making diagnoses," to Class C, "technicians with limited training." They also specified in detail the training required of examiners and proposed that the APA establish a standing committee to serve as a national certification board. After the war the association would adopt the recommendations and thus help legitimize the fast-growing profession.[19]

In a related development, Terman and fifty other individuals formed a new organization, the American Association of Clinical Psychologists (AACP), in December 1917. Meeting in Pittsburgh the association proposed:

1. To promote a mutual understanding and an esprit de corps among those working in the field of clinical psychology and a cooperative relationship with those engaged in allied fields;
2. To define, advance, and establish professional standard in this field;
3. To develop the theory and methods of mental analysis and diagnosis;
4. To encourage research and the suitable publication of scientific results in the field of clinical psychology.

Memberships standards for the group were rigorous; minimum requirements included a Ph.D. in psychology, preparation for a special field in clinical psychology, an established record of publications, and evidence of regular work in the discipline.[20]

Since many at the charter meeting were also members of the American Psychological Association, they decided to explore the possibility of merging with the APA a year later. The committee, headed by J.E.Wallace Wallin, chairman of the AACP and director of the Psycho-Educational Clinic in the St. Louis public schools, included Yerkes and Arnold Gesell of Yale. Within a year the negotiations were completed and the two groups merged. By the end of the war members of the testing community could therefore look to a single national organization for definition and direction.

When the war ended in November 1918, many of those in the Psychological Division hoped to apply their expertise in the public schools and universities around the country. U.S. Commissioner of Education, Philander P. Claxton, could well understand their need for help in getting suitable employment and saw in these psychologists a great opportunity for the public schools. In January 1919 he wrote to school superintendents around the country:

The fact that two or three hundred young men who have for several months been working in the psychology division of the Army are now about to be discharged offers an unusual opportunity for city schools to obtain the services of competent men as directors of departments of psychology and efficiency, for such purposes as measuring the results of teaching, and establishing standards to be attained in the several school studies, applying mental tests and discovering mental aptitudes of pupils, discovering defective children and children of superior intelligence, and investigating various other vital questions necessary to establish an intelligent basis for promotion, class organization and special schools.

Psychologists as well moved to promote their profession. As J. Carleton Bell, editor of the *Journal of Educational Psychology*, observed that same month: "It is now incumbent upon all those who believe in the value of scientific studies in education to engage in a vigorous and aggressive campaign to arouse public opinion to demand such studies in the schools as a matter of enlightened and progressive educational policy."[21]

Many of the psychologists in the army would return to the universities where they had been teaching before the war. Others, sparked by their experience, would pursue advanced degrees in psychology. Still others would apply their experience directly by helping set up testing programs in the schools. With the end of the war, five of the men most responsible for the army program helped the testing movement by making plans for a national effort to apply intelligence tests to school problems.

Mental Examinations for School Use:
The National Intelligence Tests

On January 23, 1919, the day the army dismantled the testing program of the Psychological Division, Yerkes and Terman wrote to the General Education Board of the Rockefeller Foundation. They requested a $25,000 grant to fund their proposal that "a group of five competent experts in mental measurement who are experienced also in school work be charged with the responsibility of developing and standardizing an intelligence scale for the group examination of school children —a scale for the measurement of native ability." To support their case, they pointed to "the amazing practical success of group psychological examining in the Army," which "has suddenly prepared the way for the introduction of similar methods in education and industry." Further, they said, "in school systems clinical psychologists are rapidly being appointed . . . who will be expected to classify children mentally as a partial basis for grading, promotion, individual treatment and vocational guidance." The need for such an examination was urgent, they believed, because intelligence tests of questionable quality were proliferating in universities and school systems around the country, and "it is far easier to supply a suitable method while none is available than to replace a number of methods which are more or less unsatisfactory."[22]

The plan was not entirely new, as Yerkes had reminded Abraham Flexner, secretary of the board, in a personal letter a few days earlier, for both Terman and Yerkes had approached the Rockefeller Foundation before the war. "The war has completely changed the setting of our plan," Yerkes noted. "Our army experience has provided us with methods and results which have a direct and important relation to the task of grading school children. What would have been impossible, or at best extremely difficult two years ago, is now obviously feasible." With the war's close, he told Flexner, "we are bombarded by requests from public school men for our army mental tests in order than they may be used in school systems." A month later the board funded the proposal in full, and a committee was assembled consisting of Yerkes, Terman, Thorndike, Haggerty, and Whipple.[23]

It was ironic that Terman and Yerkes were partners in the venture. Before the war they had engaged in a vigorous competition to win funds from the Rockefeller Foundation. That contest underscores the importance of the war in forging cooperation among psychological testers.

Fresh from publishing *The Measurement of Intelligence*, Terman had sought funds to continue his research in intelligence testing. In January 1917 he wrote to Flexner "trying to find means of financing some work in mental measurement which I have begun but am unable to complete for lack of money." Flexner, not personally acquainted with Terman, seemed interested and requested additional information which Terman quickly furnished.[24]

A few weeks later Terman received a letter from Yerkes renewing an offer to cooperate in developing a new intelligence scale. For some time Yerkes had been working on his own test, an adolescent-adult point scale. Although Yerkes observed that "our experience and points of view differ somewhat," he said he was "just now bent on securing financial aid for a job which will place the point scale on an extremely satisfactory basis." This time Terman decided to join Yerkes and wrote him with enthusiastic congratulations on his election as president of the American Psychological Association.[25]

For some reason Yerkes delayed a full month before responding to Terman. When he did write in March, he appeared to qualify his earlier proposal that they cooperate on producing a new intelligence scale. Through his position at Harvard, Yerkes had come to know many of the leading educational figures in the East and had begun an acquaintance with Flexner years earlier. In carefully chosen words, Yerkes told Terman, "I am in pretty close contact with a number of the leading men in the east who are interesting in financing such work, and I know that my plan has excellent prospect of favorable action." Describing his plan in great detail, Yerkes seemed to offer Terman a subordinate position in the venture. He concluded by reminding Terman that the West was very isolated from the centers of powers:

As you doubtless appreciate from what I have not said, I am in a much more favorable position here in the east to appreciate the chances of backing as well as to discuss matters directly with the men who will decide concerning our projects than are you in the west. I may add that I have excellent reason to suppose that financial aid will be granted for my plan. I cannot say that it would not be granted also to yours, but I believe I am speaking as much in the interest of your work as in that of general measurement when I say that we ought to get together. You must not feel, however, that I am trying to get you to help me out.[26]

Apparently that is what Terman thought. He immediately wrote to Flexner that "if the General Education Board sees fit to aid me in this task I shall be happy beyond expression." A week later he wrote Yerkes to say he would still be "more than willing to combine forces with you in a satisfactory basis of cooperation." At the same time, however, he launched a campaign to rally support to his own cause. Quickly he wrote eighteen psychologists around the country, and requested that they send affidavits to Flexner. Relying heavily on his Clark acquaintances (Gesell, Kuhlmann, Sanford, Lindley, Burnham, Goddard, and Hall), he also sent messages to Judd and Freeman at Chicago, Whipple at Illinois, and Strayer at Columbia. Flexner soon wrote that he had been "receiving a considerable number of commuications from persons interested in your plan" and was impressed.[27]

Early in April the war had broken out, however, and the General Education Board postponed any consideration of grant proposals. Yerkes named Terman to the Psychological Association's Committee on Tests, and within a month they would be working together to develop the army tests. They would jointly learn that the plan to develop intelligence tests for wider public use would have to be shelved until after the war. With the success of the army experiment, the General Education Board decided to fund the project in early 1919.

On March 28 Yerkes called to order the first of three meetings of the Elementary School Intelligence Examination Board. Beginning with "a little historical statement," he sketched his and Terman's relations with the Rockefeller Foundation and noted that "recently the demands for methods in the schools have become so urgent that we felt that something would have to be done to avoid extremes and irregularities in methods." They then began to lay the groundwork for the National Intelligence Tests. The committee agreed with Terman's view "that our present aim be to formulate a scale which will work for the last months of the 3rd grade through the 8th grade." In the next two days they decided to modify the army tests, which were developed primarily for adults. The new intelligence tests would be issued in multiple forms to discourage coaching, include both verbal and nonverbal questions, be objectively scored, and take no more than an hour to administer. Importantly, they also agreed with Haggerty's proposal that the "aim be to standardize a scale that can be used by intelligent normal school and college graduates with a reasonable amount of special training."[28]

The group then planned tryouts for the tests. Terman, who took the chief responsibility for the effort, noted that "every teacher in Oakland has had training in rating her children" and enlisted Virgil Dickson's support in evaluating the early form of the examination. After a second meeting in May, the committee then began a preliminary trial of the tests in public and private elementary schools as well as institutions for the feebleminded in six cities: New York, Cleveland, Richmond, Alexandria, Washington, and Palo Alto.[29]

In October the committee convened to put the tests in final form, and to discuss the development of norms. Regarding the creation of standard norms, there was considerable difference of opinion in the committee. In the first meeting Thorndike remarked that "for a distribution we will want a city-town of foreign population, rural districts, and a typical town of the middle states." Yerkes then suggested Washington, D.C., schools. Thorndike recommended that the committee's assistant, Margaret V. Cobb, "exercise her judgment in getting standards of 9 through 15 to represent the probable central tendency of the city of Washington" and that "we ask Terman to do it for ages 9 to 15 of what he would consider to represent the condition of the state of California." Haggerty, however, urged that the norm sample include rural children. He also pointed out to the committee, "You will have different age norms for colored children." Yerkes replied, "No, we don't want to use them. The political situation here will prevent us from going into colored schools." Pressured by time to select cities for norms, they finally decided on the public schools in Kansas, New York City, Pittsburgh, and Cincinnati.[30]

The point to be drawn from this discussion is that the examination board, like Terman in his work on the Stanford-Binet, made rather broad assumptions about the nature of American culture and what constituted the "normal" American experience. These standards were then used to judge the intelligence of many Americans whose cultural background was not adequately reflected in either the tests or the norms. These decisions would have important consequences, too, for in little more than a year, the National Intelligence Tests would be in wide use around the country.

At its final meeting the board made plans for publishing the tests early in 1920. They wrote to several publishers predicting that the tests "will be demanded by the million, for the method which the committee will recommend renders possible examination of children by classes instead of individually. It thus reduces the time and labor required to something like one-twentieth of the present requirement." For the committee Yerkes outlined the conditions for publication: "to make a good business arrangement with a thoroughly sound and reliable firm which is in a position to distribute effectively to the elementary schools of the country," "to have this material supplied as cheaply as possible," and "to have a royalty on sales returned to this organization for the work of improving these methods." Early in 1920 the committee made publication arrangements with World Book. That fall, 400,000 exams were printed and distributed for public school use, with provisions for publication of additional forms of the test at half-yearly intervals.[31]

The work of the Elementary School Intelligence Examination Board thus ensured that the work of psychological examination in the army would have a direct and dramatic impact on the public schools. What had seemed a dream to Terman and Yerkes only three years earlier was now a reality. The war provided powerful evidence of the usefulness of intelligence tests and helped to forge a network of psychologists to promote the application of test to school problems. When the work of the committee finished, the country stood poised for a massive adoption of intelligence tests in the public school for the purpose of classifying students. The adoption of that innovation was largely secured in the first half of the 1920s.

CHAPTER 4

"A Mental Test for Every Child": Terman Helps Shape the Testing Movement, 1920–1925

As the nation demobilized in the spring and summer of 1919, news of the army's testing experiment continued to spread. Within a year, schools across the country followed Oakland's lead and experimented with the new group intelligence tests to classify students. In the next decade intelligence tests were adopted and applauded with extraordinary fervor; at the same time, the practice of ability grouping spread with equal swiftness.

This sudden surge of interest was due in part to the fact that the problems schools faced before the war did not abate. School enrollments continued to soar. Between 1920 and 1930 total enrollments increased 22 percent, from 23.3 million to 28.3 million students; the high school population doubled, from 2.2 million to 4.4 million students. Immigration, which had fallen precipitously in 1915 with the beginning of the war in Europe, tripled between 1919 and 1920. In 1920 alone half a million immigrants entered the country, many enrolling in schools. The migration from the country to the city continued uninterrupted; in 1920, for the first time more Americans lived in urban than in rural areas.[1]

The postwar problems were not confined to the schools. In 1919 the progressive movement, so vigorous before the war in providing solutions to the country's problems, was afflicted by a national malaise. Wartime unity dissolved into political strife sparked by the Versailles Treaty debate and the Red Scare. The nation's economy was paralyzed after demobilization by massive unemployment, by rapid inflation when wartime controls were lifted, and by strikes that spread from Seattle to Boston. Prewar social tensions erupted in movements for women's suffrage and temperance, the resurgence of the Ku Klux Klan, and calls for immigration restriction.

In this atmosphere of crisis, many looked to the schools to help restore the social order. It was at this time, too, that Terman pressed his plans to use intelligence tests for school reform with renewed vigor. Terman assumed a position of leadership for the intelligence testing movement in the immediate postwar years, more so perhaps than any other psychologist.[2] He identified specific plans for the use of tests. His convictions about the nature of intelligence and the use of tests provided for some a sense of mission and for the movement an ideology. Terman was important, too, in helping to shape a network of psychologists and school administrators and teachers to promote the use of tests in schools. This chapter evaluates Terman's role in the testing movement from three perspectives: his prescriptions for reform, his further development of the technology of testing, and his leadership among applied psychologists. Terman's work in the twenties highlights the testing movement as part of a continuing search for solutions to the schools' problems.[3]

Prescriptions for the Use of Tests

" 'A mental test for every child' is no longer an unreasonable slogan," Terman declared in 1920. Over the next few years, he outlined his ideas on how to use intelligence tests in schools. He published two major works, *The Intelligence of School Children* in 1919, and *Intelligence Tests and School Reorganization* in 1922 as a report for the National Education Association. He wrote a spate of journal articles, and he addressed several national conventions of educators. Both Terman's analysis of the schools' problems and his proposals for reform built upon his earlier work.[4]

In *The Intelligence of School Children*, Terman concluded that next-to-

no progress had been made on solving the retardation problem identified a decade earlier by Ayres. "The problem remains," he wrote.
"The number of school laggards has decreased but little, and their
needs are almost as little provided for as before the campaign on their
behalf began." Investigators had misidentified the cause of retardation,
he said, by citing "physical defects, irregular attendance, late entrance,
too high a standard, and a lack of flexibility in methods of promotion."
Intelligence tests revealed that the "real cause" could be found in
individual differences in mental ability.[5]

During the war years Terman's students investigated mental differences with the newly revised Stanford-Binet. They measured the
intelligence of children in kindergarten, first, fifth, and ninth grade; of
students with superior intelligence; of juvenile delinquents; of all the
"retarded" children in a single county; and of the unemployed, pris-
oners, and persons in various occupations. The results showed that
individuals varied widely in their performance on intelligence tests.
The results also led Terman to conclude that the "one important cause"
of retardation lay not with social factors but with "inferior mental
ability."[6]

Terman carefully marshaled evidence to describe the problem. He
showed that the "mental ages" of children in the first, fifth, and ninth
grades overlapped considerably. As table 4.1 shows, the most able first
grader in one study was nearly on a par with the least able ninth
grader. His study also showed that student ability varied from classroom to classroom in a single grade. In an analysis of five first-grade
classes, he found the average IQ in "Room A" to be 87, while the
average in "Room E" was 112 (table 4.2). In a study of 263 eleven-
year-olds, he demonstrated that there was a high correlation (0.81)
between intelligence test performance and school progress. Students
who had fallen behind in grade level generally tested lower on intelligence tests (table 4.3). And he provided more evidence that performance varied with racial origin. An analysis of IQ scores of 148
students showed a median IQ of 78 — nearly feebleminded — for those
of "Spanish" ancestry, while "North-Europeans" and American" were
above average (table 4.4).[7]

In Terman's view individual differences in intelligence posed obvious problems for schools. He addressed *The Intelligence of School*

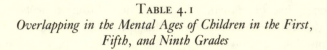

TABLE 4.1
*Overlapping in the Mental Ages of Children in the First,
Fifth, and Ninth Grades*

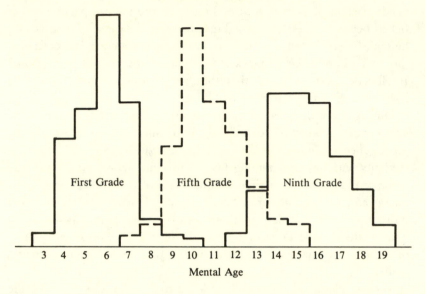

Source: Lewis M. Terman, *The Intelligence of School Children* (Boston: Houghton Mifflin, 1919), 25. Reprinted by permission.

Children to the "rank and file of teachers, school supervisors, and normal-school students to illustrate the large individual differences in original endowment which exist among school children and to show the practical bearing of these differences upon the everyday problems of classroom management and school administration." From his study Terman identified the schools' three main problems: mental ages in school grades varied widely; ability varied considerably within classes; and teachers' estimates of ability were unreliable.[8] These problems created inefficiency in schools, student frustration, and ultimately social unrest.

To solve these problems Terman proposed a systematic program of intelligence testing and classification. "A reasonable homogeneity in the mental ability of pupils who are instructed together," he said, "is a

TABLE 4.2

IQ Distribution in Five First-Grade Classes

IQs	Room A	Room B	Room C	Room D	Room E
135–up	—	—	—	1	1
120–134	—	1	—	—	1
125–129	—	—	—	1	2
120–124	—	—	—	4	—
115–119	1	—	2	3	2
110–114	1	1	—	4	1
105–109	2	—	2	5	1
100–104	5	1	2	2	3
95–99	4	—	1	2	2
90–94	3	2	6	—	1
85–89	4	3	2	2	—
80–84	6	9	4	—	—
75–79	6	4	3	2	—
70–74	3	5	4	1	—
65–69	—	6	2	1	—
60–64	1	3	—	—	—
Below 60	2	4	2	—	—
Median	87	76	85	108	112

Source: Lewis M. Terman, *The Intelligence of School Children* (Boston: Houghton Mifflin, 1919), 53. Reprinted by permission.

sine qua non of school efficiency." Thus Terman hoped to allay the frustration of students forced into a too-demanding curriculum or held back from more challenging subjects.[9]

Terman mapped out a plan that could be adopted by any school system. He proposed giving all children an individual intelligence test in the first grade. From the third grade on students would be tested at least every other year with group tests. To those who argued for more individual, selective testing, he said, "If only selected children are tested, many of the cases most in need of adjustment will be overlooked." All testing would be supervised by a school psychologist, director of research, or school administrator. To reach all students it was essential to enlist the efforts of the individual classroom teachers, since school psychologists could test individually no more than 1,000 students in a given year. "Unless the rank and file of teachers learn to

TABLE 4.3
Grade Location of 263 Eleven-Year-Olds by Stanford-Binet Mental Age

Mental Age	I	II	III	IV	Grade V	VI	VII	VIII	Total
18	—	—	—	—	—	—	1	—	1
17	—	—	—	—	—	—	3	1	4
16	—	—	—	—	—	1	2	—	3
15	—	—	—	—	2	5	6	1	14
14	—	—	—	1	6	13	2	—	22
13	—	—	—	3	12	18	1	—	34
12	—	—	1	2	22	12	—	—	37
11	—	—	2	10	42	6	—	—	60
10	—	—	6	15	20	1	—	—	42
9	—	2	3	14	6	—	—	—	25
8	1	5	6	2	—	—	—	—	14
7	1	1	3	—	—	—	—	—	5
6	1	—	—	—	—	—	—	—	1
5	1	—	—	—	—	—	—	—	1
Total	4	8	21	47	110	53	15	2	263

Source: Lewis M. Terman, *The Intelligence of School Children* (Boston: Houghton Mifflin, 1919), 117. Reprinted by permission.

TABLE 4.4
Race and IQ of 148 Schoolchildren

Race	Number	Median IQ
Spanish	37	78
Portuguese	23	84
Italian	25	84
North-European	14	105
American	49	106

Source: Lewis M. Terman, *The Intelligence of School Children* (Boston: Houghton Mifflin, 1919), 56. Reprinted by permission.

use tests," he argued, "the universal grading of children according to mental ability will remain largely a Utopian dream." Terman suggested that even in the absence of school-sponsored programs "the teacher should not hesitate to undertake the work herself."[10]

Terman further developed his ideas on the use of tests in *Intelligence Tests and School Reorganization* in 1922. "Intelligence tests have demonstrated the great extent and frequency of individual differences in the mental ability of unselected school children," he wrote, "and common sense tells us how necessary it is to take such differences into account in the framing of curricula and methods, in the classification of children for instruction, and in their educational and vocational guidance." While Terman recognized that individual differences could be treated through individual instruction, he urged that school administrators sort students into "homogeneous class groups."[11]

Hailing Dickson's experiment in Oakland—"the most thoroughgoing experiment of the kind that has yet been attempted"—Terman called for the adoption of a "multiple-track plan." While the Oakland experiment involved three tracks, Terman thought the ideal system would provide for five groups of children: "the 'gifted,' 'bright,' 'average,' 'slow,' and 'special.' " He described his plan for a typical school system of 2,000 in grades one to eight with estimates of the population of each track (table 4.5). Terman observed that the development of intelligence tests allowed for a more clearly "differentiated course of study, as regards both content and method." With appropriate revision the curricular progression for students in the different levels would be more or less continuous and could lead to different ends. The slow group, for example, would be given a course of study after eighth grade that would be primarily vocational, while the fast group would presumably prepare for college.[12]

TABLE 4.5
Multiple-Track Plan

Group	No. in Each Group	Remarks
Gifted	2½%, or 50 pupils	Two classes, four grades each
Bright	15%, or 300 pupils	One class in each grade
Average	65%, or 1,300 pupils	Four to five classes in each grade
Slow	15%, or 300 pupils	One class in each grade
Special	2½%, or 50 pupils	Three ungraded classes

Source: Lewis M. Terman, *Intelligence Tests and School Reorganization* (Yonkers-on-Hudson, N.Y.: World Book, 1922), 19. Copyright 1936 by Harcourt Brace Jovanovich, Inc. Reprinted by permission of the publisher.

Importantly, Terman recognized that any notion of a "fixed and permanent grouping" based on intelligence tests would be "repugnant to American ideals of democracy" as well as "pedagogically unjustifiable," and he argued that "the road for transfers from track to track must always be kept open." A year later in his July 1923 address to the National Education Association, he would use much stronger language to push his plan:

I predict that within a decade or two something like the three-track plan of Oakland, Berkeley and Detroit, supplemented by opportunity classes for the defectives and for the very gifted, will become standard. . . . I have no patience with those who condemn this plan as undemocratic. The abandonment of the single-track, pre-high school curriculum is the first necessary step toward educational democracy. The single-track is a straight jacket which dwarfs the mental development of the inferior as well as the gifted.[13]

Terman pressed to use intelligence tests not only for educational tracking, but also for vocational guidance. He presented studies showing that occupational status correlated with scores on intelligence tests (table 4.6). He then reasoned that an "I.Q. below 70 rarely permits

TABLE 4.6

IQ Distribution of Various Vocational Groups

Percent in Each IQ Group

Vocational Group	No. Cases	50–59	60–69	70–79	80–89	90–99	100–109	110–119	120–122	Median IQ	Lowest Fourth Below
College students	153	—	—	—	1.9	8.5	40.5	43.1	5.9	109	104 IQ
Business men	40	—	—	—	7.5	37.5	42.5	12.5	—	102	97 IQ
Express employees	47	—	4.3	4.3	23.4	19.1	19.1	17.2	12.7	95	87 IQ
Motormen and conductors	82	—	3.7	23.1	30.5	32.9	7.3	2.4	—	86	79 IQ
Firemen and policemen	30	—	6.7	26.7	36.7	20.0	6.7	3.3	—	84	78 IQ
Salesgirls	61	—	8.2	29.5	24.6	26.2	8.2	3.3	—	85	77 IQ
Hoboes and unemployed	256	5.4	14.1	21.1	26.9	16.0	9.7	5.1	1.1	89	71 IQ

Source: Lewis M. Terman, *The Intelligence of School Children* (Boston: Houghton Mifflin, 1919), 286. The "Express employees" were clerks working at a large company. Reprinted by permission.

anything better than unskilled labor," while scores above 115 "permit one to enter the professions or the larger fields of business." While cautioning that vocational and educational guidance was not an exact science, he observed that intelligence tests "can tell us whether a child's native ability corresponds approximately to the median for: (1) the professional classes; (2) those in the semi-professional pursuits; (3) ordinary skilled workers; (4) the semi-skilled workers; or (5) unskilled laborers; and this information is of great value in planning a child's education." Intelligence tests could help schools determine at an early age an individual's future vocation, thus contributing to social efficiency. Phrased another way, he said that using tests in guidance would lead to the "conservation of talent."[14]

In his analysis of school problems and in his plans for the use of tests, Terman expressed strong views on several issues relating to intelligence: the definition of "intelligence" itself, the constancy of the IQ, the influence of heredity, and the interpretation of group differences. While there certainly was no consensus on these issues among those who pushed for the use of tests, Terman's positions represented for many the ideology of the emerging testing movement.

Terman told a symposium on "intelligence and its measurement" in 1921 that "an individual is intelligent in proportion as he is able to carry on abstract thinking." He argued for the existence of a "general" factor of intelligence, "g," which could be measured by the tests. In the symposium and elsewhere, he stated his belief in the constancy of the IQ, that a person's relative intelligence would not change. he concluded, too, that heredity played a major role in determining intelligence. "The question is always raised," he wrote, "whether, in estimating a child's intelligence on the basis of the I.Q., it is not necessary to make allowance for the influence of the social environment." In his opinion the influence of several factors—language, culture, and the elements of the testing situation such as the child's attitude toward the examiner—could be controlled with standard procedures. As we have seen earlier, in his interpretation of cultural differences in test performance, Terman thought that the low scores of some ethnic groups— the Spanish, Portuguese, and Italians in the case cited in this chapter —were a sign of genetic inferiority.[15]

As to the use of tests in education, Terman consistently said that the IQ would enable schools to "predict with some degree of approxima-

tion what the child's future development will be." He dismissed those
who argued for the infinite capacity of education to improve social
opportunity:

While the law of constancy is subject to minor revisions, few things are more
certain than the essential untruth of the widespread belief that mental development knows no regularity, and that the dullard of to-day becomes the genius
of tomorrow. The fact is that, apart from minor fluctuations due to temporary
factors, and apart from occasional instances of arrest or deterioration due to
acquired nervous disease, the feeble-minded remain feeble-minded, the dull
remain dull, the average remain average, and the superior remain superior.
There is nothing in one's equipment, with the exception of character, which
rivals the IQ in importance.[16]

The ideology of the emerging test movement, as represented by
Terman's views, can be reduced to its most essential components.
Intelligence could be measured by tests and expressed in a single,
numerical ratio. This ability was largely constant and determined by
heredity. Class and racial inequality could be explained in large part
by differences in intelligence. Used in schools, intelligence tests could
be used to identify ability, prescribe curricula, and determine students'
futures.

Because of his central role in developing the tests, Terman's views
strongly influenced the attitudes of other psychologists and of school
administrators and teachers who adopted the tests. Soon Terman's
ideology would evoke a rejoinder from critics within the professional
community and from laymen. They would challenge the tests on the
grounds that they were elitist, that they neglected the role of environment in development, that they were biased in terms of social class
and cultural background, and that they were deterministic. In 1920,
however, that debate was several years away. In the meantime Terman
pressed ahead to develop the technology for the testing movement.

The Technology of the Testing Movement

While campaigning for school reform, Terman continued to develop
intelligence and achievements tests. Between 1915 and 1925 he helped
to create tests that were to become the most widely used in education:
the Stanford-Binet; the National Intelligence Tests, for grades three
through eight; the Terman Group Test, for grades seven through

twelve; and the Stanford Achievement Test, a battery of tests to measure school accomplishment in various subjects. A closer look at the development of the tests, and especially the creation of test norms, illustrates how Terman implemented his plans for school reform.

One of Terman's first tasks after leaving the army was to continue his work with the National Intelligence Tests. Once the tests were created and publication plans made with World Book in late 1919, the work of the committee turned to the difficult process of developing norms for the tests. Yerkes arranged for the cooperation of several school systems around the country to secure data and "to relieve the Committee of the heavy expense of conducting a large number of examinations." He then secured the assistance of several psychologists and school administrators to help with the project: James C. DeVoss, Kansas State Normal School; J. Freeman Guy, Pittsburgh Public Schools; J. L. Stenquist, New York Board of Education; and Helen T. Woolley, Vocation Bureau, Cincinnati Public Schools. Unfortunately the test materials did not become available until very late in the school year; consequently, usable results were received only from Guy. With the tests soon to be published, Yerkes decided to combine the Pittsburgh data with the results of testing 2,000 students in Washington to create "national" norms.[17]

Terman recognized the inadequacy of the norms Yerkes decided to print and took steps to prepare additional norms. In June 1920 he and one of his students tested all students aged eight to fifteen in the schools of Vallejo, California. The results showed large differences when compared with the Pittsburgh/Washington norms, especially at the lower and upper ends of the age scale. In material prepared for a class at Stanford and in an article early in 1921, he characterized the National Intelligence Test norms as "misleading and worthless." His Vallejo norms were superior, he said, because he had been able to reach a greater percentage of the students in the desired age range and because he believed that Vallejo was a "city of about average social and economic status." He felt that "until extensive data are available on a more nearly unselected group," the Vallejo norms should be used.[18]

Yerkes was rapidly losing interest in the project, however, and in May he wrote Terman, "I am inordinately eager to have the test job off my hands." When Terman replied in July with an "implied criticism" of the school scale work, Yerkes became even more impatient:

NATIONAL INTELLIGENCE TESTS
SCALE A — FORM 1

Prepared under the auspices of the National Research Council by M. E. Haggerty,
L. M. Terman, E. L. Thorndike, G. M. Whipple, and R. M. Yerkes

Name_____
First name　　　　　　　　Last name

Grade_____ Boy or Girl_____ Age_____
Years　　Months

Date of birth_____ Race_____
Month　Day　Year

Birthplace of parents_____
Father　　　　Mother

Teacher_____

School_____ City_____

Date_____

TEST	RIGHTS	METHOD	SCORE
1		× 2 =	
2		× 2 =	
3		=	
4		Wrongs −( ) =	
5		× $\frac{3}{10}$ =	
TOTAL	Sum of 5 scores		
MENTAL AGE IN MONTHS			

TABLE OF MENTAL AGES IN MONTHS EQUIVALENT TO SCORES IN SCALE A

Score	M.A.	Score	M.A.	Score	M.A.	Score	M.A.	Score	M.A.	Score	M.A.	Score	M.A.	Score	M.A.
41	97	61	114	81	130	101	144	121	160	141	180	161	200	181	220
42	98	62	115	82	131	102	144	122	160	142	181	162	201	182	221
43	99	63	116	83	131	103	145	123	161	143	182	163	202	183	222
44	100	64	117	84	132	104	146	124	162	144	183	164	203	184	223
45	101	65	118	85	132	105	146	125	163	145	184	165	204	185	224
46	102	66	118	86	133	106	147	126	165	146	185	166	205	186	225
47	103	67	119	87	134	107	148	127	166	147	186	167	206	187	226
48	103	68	119	88	134	108	149	128	167	148	187	168	207	188	227
49	104	69	120	89	135	109	150	129	168	149	188	169	208	189	228
50	105	70	121	90	136	110	151	130	169	150	189	170	209	190	229
51	106	71	122	91	137	111	151	131	170	151	190	171	210		
52	107	72	123	92	137	112	152	132	171	152	191	172	211		
53	107	73	124	93	138	113	153	133	172	153	192	173	212		
54	108	74	125	94	138	114	154	134	173	154	193	174	213		
55	109	75	126	95	139	115	155	135	174	155	194	175	214		
56	110	76	126	96	140	116	156	136	175	156	195	176	215		
57	111	77	127	97	141	117	156	137	176	157	196	177	216		
58	112	78	128	98	142	118	157	138	177	158	197	178	217		
59	112	79	128	99	142	119	158	139	178	159	198	179	218		
60	113	80	129	100	143	120	159	140	179	160	199	180	219		

Published by World Book Company, Yonkers-on-Hudson, New York, and Chicago, Illinois

National Intelligence Tests, 1920. Terman popularized the intelligence quotient, or IQ, a ratio of mental age to chronological age which allowed psychologists to express the rate of individual mental development. (Reprinted by permission of the Department of Special Collections and University Archives, Stanford University Libraries.)

Scale A. Form 1

Test 2

Write on each dotted line one word to make the sentence sound sensible and right.

SAMPLES $\left\{\begin{array}{l}\text{Sugar}....\textit{is}....\text{sweet.}\\...\textit{Birds}....\text{sing.}\end{array}\right.$

Begin here

1 The dog................black.

2 An airplane is able to................a great distance in a short time.

3 Mother is................doughnuts.

4 There are seven................in the rainbow.

5 Rain................snow fall from the clouds.

6 We love liberty................the United States.

7 Twenty-five cents make one................of a dollar.

8 Bananas grow in................climates.

9 He tried to................his ball among the bushes.

10 Jack came to................me mow the lawn.

11 Trees are................than bushes.

12 Winter is................in the North and short in the................

13 The man................aids his fellows will................his reward.

14 A................is made up................an engine and coaches.

15 You should never go................a crowd when................have a cold.

16 Several................have gone by since the end of the greatest................ in history.

17 Labor unions................the right to................for higher wages.

18 The visitor................the child................name.

19 Poverty cannot................down a man................is intelligent and ....hard.

20 ....should prevail in churches and libraries.

National Intelligence Tests, Test 2. Using materials developed in the First World War, Terman and other psychologists created the National Intelligence Tests and by 1920 nearly half a million exams had been published and sold to the public schools. (Reprinted by permission of the Special Collections Department and University Archives, Stanford University Libraries.)

Test 5

Scale A.   Form 1

Make under each drawing the number you find under that drawing in the key.   Do each one as you come to it.

KEY

ᑌ	ᴦ	m	⊃	ʟ	T	⊕	🗙	⅃
1	2	3	4	5	6	7	8	9

Begin here

m	ᴦ	ᑌ	m	ᑌ	ᴦ	m	⊃	ᑌ	ʟ	T	ᴦ	ᑌ	⊃	⊕	⅃	ʟ	ᴦ	m	🗙

⊃	⅃	ᴦ	🗙	T	ᑌ	⊕	ʟ	m	⊃	🗙	T	m	ᑌ	ᴦ	ʟ	⅃	⊕	⊃	ᴦ

T	m	🗙	ʟ	⅃	⊕	ᑌ	⊃	ʟ	⅃	T	ᴦ	🗙	m	⊕	ᑌ	T	ᴦ	ᑌ	⊕

⅃	🗙	ʟ	m	⊃	🗙	ᴦ	ʟ	⊕	m	⅃	T	⊃	ᑌ	m	🗙	ᴦ	T	⅃	ʟ

⊃	⊕	ᑌ	⅃	⊕	ʟ	m	ᴦ	⊃	T	🗙	ᑌ	T	⊃	🗙	⅃	⊕	ʟ	⊃	T

🗙	ᴦ	m	ᑌ	ʟ	⊕	⅃	⊃	T	🗙	ʟ	⊕	⅃	🗙	T	⊃	T	🗙	⊕	⅃

National Intelligence Tests, Test 5. Because of the large number of immi-grants in the schools, the National Intelligence Tests included performance examinations such as mazes, pictorial completion, and geometric construction which did not require familiarity with English. (Reprinted by permission of the Special Collections Department and University Archives, Stanford University Libraries.)

I do wish I had never touched the job! I had grave misgivings about the wisdom of it when I joined with you in an effort to secure funds for this work on methods. . . . If ever I fall into such an ungrateful position again as this job has placed me in I shall entirely lose respect for my intelligence! . . . How unspeakably relieved I shall be when I am through and someone else is chairman of the committee.

Shortly he got his wish. On December 30 the committee's work officially ended and responsibility for the tests was transferred to the Division of Anthropology and Psychology of the National Research Council.[19]

With the schools around the country adopting the tests, Terman continued to press for a revision of the norms. Finally, in 1923 World Book issued a supplement to the manual of directions prepared with Terman's help. The new standards improved upon the first set. Some nineteen communities and over 30,000 pupils were used to prepare age norms for the National Intelligence Test; the revised grade norms were based on nearly 40,000 students in fifty-seven communities. The limitations of the norms were still apparent though. These age norms, the manual said, "are to be understood to refer to white children." "All that can be said for the norms . . . is that they represent fairly closely the averages that will be found in school systems generally when the results for cities, towns, villages, and rural communities are combined to afford a fair sampling of the public school population of the Northern states." The manual noted as well that while national norms were theoretically possible, "scores obtained for pupils of different races, different nationalities, and different communities differ" and that special norms for special purposes might be required. Despite the difficulties in obtaining norms, the National Intelligence Tests were finding quick acceptance in the schools. The obvious problem of using these norms with black students and communities not represented by the sample would surface later.[20]

Meanwhile, Terman developed another intelligence examination, this one for high school students. By late 1919 he had prepared the Terman Group Test, a series of ten exams for use with students in grades seven through twelve.[21] He then turned his attention to marketing his test through the World Book Company.

In January 1920 Terman wrote to Casper W. Hodgson, head of

TERMAN GROUP TEST OF MENTAL ABILITY

For Grades 7 to 12

Prepared by Lewis M. Terman, Stanford University, California

EDITION I   **EXAMINATION: FORM A**

1. Name ....
   First name   Last name

2. Boy or girl...........Grade...........High or Low...........

3. Age last birthday.......Date of birthday...................
   Month   Day

4. Name of city (or county)................................

5. Name of school................................

6. Name of teacher................................

7. Date of this examination.........................19......
   Month   Day   Year

Do not turn the page until you are told to.

TEST	SCORE	REMARKS OR FURTHER DATA
1. Information		
2. Best Answer		
3. Word Meaning		
4. Logical Selection		
5. Arithmetic		
6. Sentence Meaning		
7. Analogies		
8. Mixed Sentences		
9. Classification		
10. Number Series		
Total		

World Book, informing him that the test he had proposed several months earlier was nearing completion. "It looks as though you meant business," Hodgson replied. By June the test was ready for the school market and World Book wrote that they were sending the tests to one hundred educational journals for review, "a great many to Mr. Hodgson's personal friends," and putting "a large number in the hands of persons who can use them." That fall the tests were used in cities around the country, ranging from Farmington, West Virginia, to Superior, Nebraska; from Detroit and Chicago to Colfax, Washington, and Bradford, Vermont. In November Hodgson gave Terman a preliminary report on the sales of the group test. Noting that "we are pushing hard on tests," he indicated that over 7,500 tests had been sold in a two-month period.[22]

Over the next few years, Terman's test sold well. In October 1923 he wrote Hodgson, "It seems that my group test has been given to about 550,000 children . . . during the past year." Five years later World Book reported yearly sales of over 775,000 tests. This figure represented nearly one-fifth of the total high school enrollment that year. Clearly Terman's group intelligence test for high school students received wide use.[23]

Terman's development of intelligence tests spurred his work on achievement exams. While conducting a major study of gifted children, he realized he had no reliable means of measuring school achievement. With Truman L. Kelley, who taught at Columbia and Stanford, and Giles M. Ruch, one of his students, Terman prepared in 1922 the Stanford Achievement Test, consisting of ten separate achievement tests for students in all grades.[24] At the end of the first year, Terman estimated that about 115,000 achievement tests had been sold. "Considering that probably few school men became acquainted with the Stanford Achievement Test much before the end of the school year," he wrote Hodgson in October 1923, "I think the sale of 115,000 is not bad. I shall be surprised if it does not reach a half million during the

Terman Group Test of Mental Ability, 1920. Because the National Intelligence Tests were designed for children in grades 3 to 8, Terman created a group test to measure ability of students through high school. (Reprinted by permission of the Special Collections Department and University Archives, Stanford University Libraries.)

TEST 1. INFORMATION

Draw a line under the ONE word that makes
the sentence true, as shown in the sample.

SAMPLE.   Our first President was
     Adams   Jefferson   Lincoln   <u>Washington</u>

 1 Coffee is a kind of
     bark   berry   leaf   root 1
 2 Sirloin is a cut of
     beef   mutton   pork   veal 2
 3 Gasoline comes from
     grains   petroleum   turpentine   seeds 3
 4 Most exports go from
     Boston   San Francisco   New Orleans   New York. 4
 5 The number of pounds in a ton is
     1000   2000   3000   4000 5

 6 Napoleon was defeated at
     Leipzig   Paris   Verdun   Waterloo 6
 7 Emeralds are usually
     blue   green   red   yellow 7
 8 The optic nerve is for
     seeing   hearing   tasting   feeling............... 8
 9 Larceny is a term used in
     medicine   theology   law   pedagogy 9
10 Sponges come from
     animals   farms   forests   mines................. 10

11 Confucius founded the religion of the
     Persians   Italians   Chinese   Indians............ 11
12 The larynx is in the
     abdomen   head   throat   shoulder............... 12
13 The piccolo is used in
     farming   music   photography   typewriting 13
14 The kilowatt measures
     rainfall   wind-power   electricity   water-power.... 14
15 The guillotine causes
     death   disease   fever   sickness 15

16 A character in " David Copperfield " is
     Sindbad   Uriah Heep   Rebecca   Hamlet 16
17 A windlass is used for
     boring   cutting   lifting   squeezing 17
18 A great law-giver of the Hebrews was
     Abraham   David   Moses   Saul................. 18
19 A six-sided figure is called a
     scholium   parallelogram   hexagon   trapezium.... 19
20 A meter is nearest in length to the
     inch   foot   yard   rod....................... 20

Right........

current year." Late in 1925 he reported that annual sales had climbed to 1.5 million copies.[25]

Terman's study of gifted children gave him an opportunity to introduce intelligence tests into the schools in California. Terman's interest in genius began at Clark. During his initial work with Binet's test, he had identified a handful of very bright children in the area around Stanford. In 1913 he "sifted" several high schools in San Francisco for bright students using an early version of the Stanford-Binet. In 1919 Stanford established a research fellowship for the study of the gifted which led to the discovery of 150 children with high IQs. Then in 1921 Terman received grants totaling $34,000 from Commonwealth Fund of New York to identify approximately 1,000 "gifted subjects" in California and to measure their abilities using tests of intelligence, achievement, and special traits.

A staff of six fanned out to identify gifted students in schools across the state. In each school, teachers were asked to nominate the brightest students in their classes, who were then tested for inclusion in the sample. Terman's assistants canvassed "practically the entire cities" of Los Angeles, San Francisco, Oakland, Berkeley, and Alameda and "more or less thoroughly" numerous other cities from Pasadena to Sebastopol, and from Palo Alto to Fresno.[26]

In April and September 1921, Terman appeared before the state conventions of high school principals and of superintendents to lobby for their assistance and participation. Then in December he wrote to these school administrators detailing his plan "whereby cities and counties which my field assistants cannot visit may make their own survey for the discovery of gifted children." "The plan is so simple," he explained, "that it can be carried out by any city or county which has a few teachers or principals sufficiently interested to undertake the work." He then pointed out to the school administrators the value of their work:

Terman Group Test, Information. Critics argued that intelligence tests could not measure hereditary intelligence and should not be used as a single means to group students by ability in schools. (Reprinted by permission of the Special Collections Department and University Archives, Stanford University Libraries.)

GENERAL INFORMATION — FORM I

Name ....Age.............. Grade............ High or low.............

Name of School..City ....

Date: Month and day...Year.............. Are you a boy or girl?..............

Test	Score	Age Equivalent	Grade Equivalent
1			
2			
3			
4			
Total			

TEST 1. GEOGRAPHY, HYGIENE AND ELEMENTARY SCIENCE

Draw a line under the word that makes the sentence true as shown in the two samples.
Samples: 1. The number of cents in a dollar is   **100**   **200**   **300**
           2. New York is in   **England**   **France**   **United States**

Begin here.

 1 Christmas comes in   **December**   **January**   **July** 1
 2 A food that grows under the ground is the   **cabbage**   **potato**   **tomato** 2
 3 A sweet-smelling flower is the   **daisy**   **poppy**   **rose** 3
 4 Alfalfa is a kind of   **corn**   **fruit**   **hay** 4
 5 Soap is made from   **fats**   **lemons**   **sugars** 5

 6 Bacon comes from the   **cow**   **hog**   **sheep** 6
 7 A bird that makes its nest on the ground is the   **quail**   **robin**   **swallow** 7
 8 Raisins are dried   **currants**   **gooseberries**   **grapes** 8
 9 A baboon is a kind of   **bird**   **fish**   **monkey** 9
10 Ivory is obtained from   **elephants**   **shell-fish**   **reefs** 10

11 The number of inches in a yard is   **36**   **24**   **12** 11
12 Tarts are a kind of   **drink**   **pastry**   **vegetable** 12
13 The tractor is used in   **farming**   **mining**   **racing** 13
14 Planes are used chiefly by   **barbers**   **blacksmiths**   **carpenters** 14
15 Rubber is obtained from   **animals**   **oil**   **trees** 15

16 Anchors are used on   **autos**   **ships**   **wagons** 16
17 The number of quarts in a gallon is   **2**   **4**   **6** 17
18 Muslin is a kind of   **cloth**   **color**   **drink** 18
19 The burro resembles most the   **cow**   **donkey**   **horse** 19
20 A flower that grows from a bulb is the   **lily**   **marigold**   **poppy** 20

Turn over the page to number 21

The Stanford Achievement Test, 1923. Terman prepared the Stanford Achievement Test, consisting of ten separate achievement tests for students in all grades, and by 1925 annual sales reached 1.5 million copies. (Reprinted by permission of the Special Collections Department and University Archives, Stanford University Libraries.)

We know far less about the mental, physical and character traits of the gifted then of the feeble-minded, although it is self-evident that to make the most of our resources of genius is incomparably more important to society than anything we can do for our dullards, morons and imbeciles, however important the latter problem may be.

Through this effort Terman was able to reach additional elementary schools and some ninety-five high schools enrolling roughly 70,000 students.[27]

Reporting his findings in 1925 in *Genetic Studies of Genius* and in the press,[28] Terman said the evidence dispelled some common myths that the gifted were freakish, socially awkward, and pathological: "There is no shred of evidence to support the widespread opinion that typically the intellectually precocious child is weak, undersized, or nervously unstable." The study also revealed ethnic and social class differences in the gifted group. Terman noted that there was a "marked excess of Jewish and of Northern and Western European stock represented" and that group drew "heavily from the higher occupational levels." These "facts" confirmed Terman's belief in Nordic superiority and the idea that success was largely a function of intelligence. In Terman's view the study placed "a heavy burden on the environment hypothesis." Terman also pointed out the implications of his research for the schools: "A study of superior talent inevitably raises a host of pedagogical problems . . . although new light may in time be expected from the rapidly increasing experimentation with differentiated curricula, classification by ability, and methods of individual instruction."[29]

Terman's development of the technology of testing thus stimulated the adoption of intelligence tests throughout the country and especially in California. Terman addressed part of his campaign to schools to impress upon them the importance of intelligence tests in school reform. He also tried to gain wider respect for intelligence tests among his fellow psychologists.

Leadership for the National Movement

The testing experiment in the First World War had raised Terman to national visibility and had acquainted him with the country's leading psychologists.[30] After the war Terman worked to forge a network of

leadership for the intelligence testing movement. Terman approached
the task in several ways: by bringing national recognition to Stanford's
program in education and psychology, as editor of several journals and
textbooks devoted to testing, as a member of the Psychological Corporation, and through his activities within the American Psychological
Association.

Despite the hiatus of the war, Terman continued to lay the foundations at Stanford for a program in educational psychology of national
stature. In 1922 Terman was named to head the Department of Psychology, and under his direction the program flourished. A study of
nominations for membership in the American Psychological Association conducted in the early twenties by Edwin G. Boring showed
Stanford sixth in degrees awarded, behind Columbia, Cornell, Chicago, Harvard, and Clark. Another survey by Boring in 1924 placed
the Stanford psychology department second in the country in terms of
total budget ($34,000).[31] By 1925 Terman had sponsored over thirty-
five advanced degrees in education and psychology. That same year an
analysis by the American Council on Education demonstrated that,
among sixteen universities offering the doctorate in psychology, Stanford had moved from last place in the years before the war to seventh.
In terms of overall quality, Stanford's program received the highest
rating in the country.[32]

From his position at Stanford, Terman also maintained contact with
the national network of psychologists by editing the Measurement and
Adjustment Series of nearly twenty textbooks on intelligence testing.
When World Book approached Terman about the project in the summer of 1921, Terman responded enthusiastically that the series "should
contain only books which are likely to have a very large textbook sale
or a large reading circle use."[33] That winter he solicited manuscripts
from over twenty leading figures in the testing movement, in many
cases calling upon "the club" who had served together in the war.[34]

In 1923 World Book published the first volume, Virgil Dickson's
Mental Tests and the Classroom Teacher, on the experiments in Oakland.
The occasion prompted Terman to outline his blueprint for future
works:[35]

It is the purpose of the Measurement and Adjustment Series to deal with the
entire problem of pupil testing, and of adjustments to meet the problems of
instruction and school administration arising out of individual differences.

On measurement methods the series will include texts on intelligence testing, vocational testing, the measurement of achievement in school subjects
from the first grade through the university, physical tests and measurements,
and statistical methods as applied to educational and psychological data.

On the educational adjustments necessitated by individual differences, problems to be treated in the series include the training of defectives, the education
of gifted children, the rehabilitation of delinquents, the three-track plan of
classification by ability, educational guidance, vocational guidance, etc.

Our education has been mass education. The task of this series is to focus
attention on education as adapted to individual abilities and needs.

Over the next five years came nine additional titles,[36] many written by
persons who were at the forefront of the testing movement. Five of the
authors were named in a 1929 study of "those who have contributed
most of the educational measurement movements."[37] As editor of the
World Book series, Terman thus had a great opportunity to organize
the testing network.

Although Terman devoted considerable energy to the Measurement
and Adjustment Series, he also served on the board of numerous
additional journals that served as clearing houses for reports on the use
of tests. In the early twenties he was an editor for the *Journal of Juvenile
Research*, the *Journal of Applied Psychology*, the *Journal of Educational
Research*, the *Journal of Educational Psychology*, the *Journal of Personnel
Research*, and the *Journal of Genetic Psychology*.

Shortly after the war Terman became involved with another venture
to promote the use of tests. In 1921 he joined eighteen prominent
psychologists as a founding director of the Psychological Corporation.[38] According to James McKeen Cattell, head of the corporation,
the organization's objective was "to maintain adequate standards in
applied psychology, to assure opportunities and proper payment to
those competent to do the work, and to use the profits for psychological research."[39] By the end of 1922, regional committees had been
established in Massachusetts, Pennsylvania, Ohio, Michigan, and Illinois. The next year Terman organized a branch in California.

Perhaps the most convincing evidence of Terman's rapid rise to
prominence among the nation's psychologists was his election to the
presidency of the American Psychological Association in 1922. His
address to the annual meeting of the APA in Madison, Wisconsin, the
next year gave him an opportunity to share his views on the importance of the testing movement for psychology. In a study several years

earlier, Terman had pointed out that "considerably more than half of the psychological research which is being carried on by members of the American Psychological Association . . . falls in one or another of the fields of applied psychology," especially in test development. Now in his address on "The Mental Test as a Psychological Method," he sought to demonstrate that testing had almost universal appeal in the association.[40]

"I wish to show that psychologists have too often conceived of the mental test as a mere practical device," he told his colleagues in Madison. "It has a large value as an instrument of research," he continued, and "its kinship to other psychological methods is much closer than either the average tester or the average laboratory worker appears to assume." Reviewing the history of testing, Terman said that often tests had been discontinued as research tools, because they had focused on individual differences to the exclusion of general principles, were applied to large numbers, measured the behavior not the content of the mind, made little use of laboratory apparatus, and produced results that were less exact than true experiments. He argued that "if the test had been properly constructed and validated it may at once become a tool for the investigation of important scientific problems, such as mental growth, educability, individual differences, or mental organization. It is only because tests are capable of practical application that we overlook their research possibilities and come to think of them as something to be contrasted with other methods of psychological investigation." He went on to outline some areas for study, such as individual and race differences, the interrelation of mental traits, mental growth, genius, and insanity. To the 65 percent of the association who, by his calculation, were engaged in testing research in 1923, these observations undoubtedly came as no surprise. Terman's address illustrated that applied psychology had come of age.[41]

Terman's appearance in Madison signaled a high point in his campaign to shape the testing movement. In the early twenties his prescriptions for the use of tests, his research on the technology of testing, and his conscious attempt to forge a network of applied psychologists all helped to galvanize the intelligence testing movement. Those efforts led directly to the adoption of tests in schools.

CHAPTER 5

The Use of Intelligence Tests in Schools: California Case Studies

In the years after World War I, Terman's prescription for the use of intelligence tests had a direct impact on school reform in three communities near Stanford. Oakland, which had experimented with testing before the war, launched a systemwide program of testing and ability grouping. In San Jose, where Terman had conducted research for the Stanford-Binet before the war, school administrators began a testing program in the early twenties. And Palo Alto, in Stanford's front yard, experimented with the use of tests for educational and vocational guidance. Each of these school systems had thus begun early experiments with the use of tests. Each had a direct link to Terman and Stanford. Taken together as case studies, they represent a distribution of urban communities in terms of size, ethnic diversity, and socioeconomic makeup.

The history of intelligence testing in these three cities illustrates central themes and variations in the adoption of tests for classifying students. In each instance testing was introduced in a top-down fashion by a network of psychologists and school administrators. At the center of the network was Terman, aided by his students and supported by school administrators. In each school system testing had great appeal as a means of solving problems. Oakland and San Jose in particular faced strains from the increasing size and diversity of the school population. Each school system had begun as well to differentiate the curriculum and to sort students into tracks. Palo Alto pioneered in the use of tests to solve different problems, those of educational and vocational guidance. The experience of these three cities also offers insight into the rationale of those who advocated testing and tracking plans. The tests were welcomed as a more efficient, rational, and scientific means of treating individual differences among students. In the cities with the greatest percentage of immigrants, Oakland and San Jose, nativism and a sense of Nordic superiority among school administrators and teachers also contributed to the adoption of the tests. The case studies of Oakland, San Jose, and Palo Alto that follow thus clarify why intelligence tests were adopted in the schools.

Oakland

Because of its close ties to Terman at Stanford and because of the early work of Virgil Dickson, Oakland was probably the first city in the United States to institute a systemwide program of mental testing and ability grouping.[1] After Dickson's initial experiments in 1917–1918, test use mushroomed, and there was widespread enthusiasm for the new instruments. Quickly the idea of classifying all students on the basis of tests found favor, and by 1922 a three-track plan was operating in virtually all the Oakland schools. Although there was some resistance to the use of tests, both within the system and without, evidence suggests that there was widespread support for the innovation. By the middle of the decade, the use of intelligence tests for sorting students had been institutionalized in Oakland.

As we have seen, Dickson's work began before the war when he tested 149 first-grade children with the newly revised Stanford-Binet. After his appointment as director of the Oakland Department of Research in 1917, he began, with the encouragement of the new superintendent, Fred M. Hunter, to widen the scope of the testing work through a number of experiments. In December of that year, Terman enlisted Dickson's aid in giving the army Alpha on a trial basis to 2,000 schoolchildren. Later that school year, Dickson tested the Stanford-Binet and Otis Group Intelligence examinations with 6,500 students, nearly 20 percent of the school enrollment. By the end of the war,

Dickson had established the basis for the systematic use of tests in Oakland.

With the postwar return to normalcy, Dickson proceeded with his experimental use of tests. By the end of the 1919–1920 school year, he reported that some 20,000 students had taken intelligence tests, over half of those enrolled. In several articles and an address to the National Association of Directors of Educational Research, Dickson described his success. The tests were most useful, he said, when administrators were faced with classifying large numbers of unknown students, especially in the first and ninth grades. In elementary schools the tests were used to "segregate" students by mental ability, and some early attempts were made to develop a special curriculum for the different groups. In the high schools similar experiments were conducted with ability grouping on the basis of tests. Based on these preliminary studies, Dickson said that intelligence tests could also be used to provide educational guidance for the transition between eighth and ninth grades.

One reason for Oakland's early success with testing was that Dickson did not rush the tests into the schools. A committee consisting of Dickson, Hunter, the supervisor of the primary grades, and three teachers monitored the first experiments in elementary classification based on tests. The committee recommended that the experiment be extended systemwide, a policy, Dickson noted in June 1920, that was "being gradually introduced into the schools of Oakland wherever the conditions permit." On the basis of the high school experiment, the use of tests for classification was also expanded rapidly. Yet Dickson was cautious and wished to "sound this warning": "We do not believe that the group mental test is an infallible guide. It is merely an important tool that can be used to advantage in the study and placement of groups and individuals." He pointed out that many factors could affect individual test performance: health, effort, attitude, anxiety, and time pressure. The antidote for test misuse, he said, was to employ a variety of means when estimating students' ability and when assigning them to different tracks.[2]

Despite Dickson's caution, however, the early experiments with tests contained potential for abuse, especially when they involved schools with high concentrations of immigrant children. In Oakland, the first experimental use of tests in elementary schools was conducted in neighborhoods with a high percentage of immigrants. Dickson told of two schools in the study which were "situated in a manufacturing, water-front district where the social conditions are among the least desirable of the city." Two-thirds of the children were first- or second-generation immigrants from Portugal, Italy, Austria, Assyria, Spain, Greece, England, and the Balkans. "Our problem," Dickson observed, "involved a foreign element entirely."[3]

All first-grade students in these schools were given IQ tests and were classified primarily on the basis of their scores into groups identified as "borderzone," "dull normal," and "normal." Only a few students were identified as "superior" in intelligence, and they were placed in the "normal" group. A high percentage of the students in each school was classified as below normal in intelligence. These students were then "segregated" and given a course of study "adapted to their needs."[4]

Studies of immigrant performance on intelligence tests, such as Yerkes's *Army Mental Tests* (1920), revealed wide differences in performance. Recent immigrants, especially those from southern and eastern Europe, generally tested below average. Intelligence testing in the waterfront schools in Oakland gave the impression that the immigrant students were mentally inferior.

The almost exclusive reliance on test scores for classification in this experiment reinforced ethnic and class prejudice. Dickson noted the blue-collar social status of twenty-five students in one school who received the lowest IQ scores. A survey of their fathers' occupations showed that most were laborers in the shipyards, in railroad shops, and on ferry boats. Dickson reported the experience of three teachers assigned to teach the "mentally retarded":

The first problems in the education of these children involved the teaching of cleanliness, hygiene, social adaptability, property rights, and the removal of fear of corporal punishment. Particularly do they emphasize the fact that these children get so many knocks and blows from their associates on the street and in the home, that they become victims of an attitude of fear and distrust which is very hard to overcome in the classroom. The customary thing is for the child to shrink or dodge whenever the teacher or anyone else approaches.

Immigrants, poor children, and school misfits often received low IQ scores. One result of the experimental use of tests in Oakland thus was to stigmatize some immigrants as mentally inferior.[5]

In conjunction with the first-grade experiment, Dickson explored the use of tests in the transition between junior high and high school. Using the Otis Group Intelligence Scale, he tested students at selected junior high schools in Oakland in 1919 and 1920. Results of the study showed a high correlation between test scores and school retention. In general, students who "quit school to go to work had a very much lower median test score than those who went on to high school." Those who went to business colleges and vocational schools generally scored higher than those who quit, but lower than those who went on to "regular" high school.[6]

Dickson also used the Otis scale to test all students graduating from the eighth grade in January 1920. Results of this study showed tremendous variation in test results by school, described in table 5.1. As the table indicates, median scores ranged from 48 for fifteen students in school number one to 109 for seventy students in school number twenty-nine. Dickson's study showed that test scores varied with city neighborhood, and by implication, with ethnicity and social class.[7]

The testing experiment in eighth grades led quickly to changes in Oakland school practice. Dickson noted that the tests "have contributed to a better understanding of many school problems such as retardation, elimination, and proper curriculum modifications; and they have resulted in administrative adjustments leading to greater efficiency." He listed several specific ways intelligence tests were used in "dealing with individual pupils." Low scores helped "to confirm a teacher's judgment that a child's failure in school is due to inferior capacity," while high scores for poor performers called for "special study." Test results were used for accelerated promotions, as well as educational and vocational counseling.[8]

Most important was the "differentiation of the curriculum in terms of the capacity and needs of pupils." "This problem is already a pressing one in the high schools of some of our cities," he noted, due to wider enrollments. He summed up the problem:

In short, our high schools are now attended by many pupils with a mental capacity that is only average or even below average. At the same time, many high schools have little to offer these children except a curriculum designed for the highly selected college-preparatory group that attended high school a few

TABLE 5.1
Distribution of Intelligence Test Scores Made by Graduating Classes in 29 Oakland Junior High Schools, January 1920

Score	1	2	3	4	5	6	7	8	9	10	11
150	—	—	—	—	—	—	—	—	—	—	—
145	—	—	—	—	—	—	—	—	—	—	—
140	—	—	—	—	—	—	—	—	—	—	—
135	—	—	—	—	—	—	—	—	—	—	—
130	—	—	—	—	—	—	—	—	—	—	—
125	—	—	—	—	—	—	—	—	—	—	—
120	—	—	—	—	—	1	—	—	1	—	—
115	—	—	—	1	—	1	—	—	1	—	1
110	—	1	—	1	—	—	—	—	—	2	—
105	—	—	—	—	—	—	1	—	1	—	1
100	—	—	—	—	2	2	2	—	2	1	2
95	—	—	1	2	—	3	3	—	1	3	—
90	1	—	2	—	3	4	3	1	2	1	2
85	—	1	—	—	3	6	1	—	3	—	3
80	1	1	1	2	2	1	6	1	3	—	1
75	1	1	—	1	—	3	3	2	—	1	4
70	—	2	2	—	6	2	6	1	2	1	3
65	2	2	2	—	6	7	3	1	1	—	4
60	1	2	—	2	2	2	2	1	3	1	1
55	1	5	—	2	3	5	3	—	4	—	1
50	—	2	4	—	4	4	1	1	2	2	2
45	2	4	3	2	1	3	6	1	3	2	2
40	4	1	—	2	2	1	3	—	1	1	—
35	1	—	1	—	1	1	1	—	—	1	—
30	—	1	1	—	—	2	2	—	—	—	—
25	—	1	—	—	—	—	—	—	—	—	—
20	1	—	—	—	2	1	2	—	—	—	—
15	—	—	—	—	—	—	—	—	—	—	—
10	—	—	—	—	—	—	—	—	—	—	—
Totals	15	24	17	15	37	49	48	9	30	16	27
Medians	48	53	54	64	68	69	71	72	72	75	76

Note: Read table as follows: In the eighth-grade class in school 1, one pupil made a score of 90–94, one scored 80–84, etc. There was a total of 15 graduating pupils in school 1, and they made a median score of 48. Similar data are given for the 28 other schools' graduating eighth-grade pupils.

Source: Virgil E. Dickson and J. K. Norton, "The Otis Group Intelligence Scale Applied to the Elementary School Graduating Classes of Oakland, California," *Journal of Educational Research* 3 (Feb. 1921): 110.

TABLE 5.1—*Continued*

	School										
Score	12	13	14	15	16	17	18	19	20	21	22
150	—	—	—	—	—	—	—	—	—	—	—
145	—	—	—	—	—	—	—	—	—	—	—
140	—	—	—	—	—	—	—	—	1	—	—
135	—	—	—	—	—	—	—	—	—	—	—
130	—	—	—	—	—	—	—	—	2	—	1
125	—	1	1	—	—	1	—	—	—	1	—
120	—	2	—	—	1	1	2	—	1	2	—
115	—	—	1	1	—	—	—	—	—	2	3
110	—	2	3	2	—	1	1	—	1	—	2
105	1	1	1	1	—	1	1	1	1	2	3
100	2	—	1	2	1	3	2	1	2	2	5
95	1	—	3	2	—	2	2	2	2	1	—
90	5	4	7	—	1	5	4	3	2	1	3
85	2	2	—	1	3	5	2	3	—	2	6
80	4	3	1	5	3	4	5	4	2	3	1
75	4	6	6	2	—	5	4	2	2	3	3
70	6	7	4	1	3	3	3	2	2	—	3
65	2	4	4	2	2	1	1	3	3	3	1
60	5	3	1	4	1	5	1	—	1	2	3
55	1	2	4	4	1	1	2	1	—	1	3
50	1	—	—	1	—	2	1	—	2	1	4
45	1	1	1	—	1	1	—	—	—	—	—
40	—	—	—	—	—	—	—	—	—	—	—
35	—	—	—	—	—	—	—	—	1	—	—
30	—	—	—	—	—	1	—	—	—	—	—
25	—	—	—	—	—	—	2	1	—	—	—
20	1	—	—	—	—	—	—	1	—	—	—
15	—	—	—	—	—	—	1	—	—	—	—
10	—	—	—	—	—	—	—	—	—	—	—
Totals	36	38	38	28	17	42	34	24	25	26	41
Medians	76	77	79	80	81	82	82	82	84	85	87

continued on next page

TABLE 5.1—*Continued*

| Score | School | | | | | | | Total |
	23	24	25	26	27	28	29	
150	—	1	—	—	—	—	—	1
145	—	—	—	—	—	1	1	2
140	—	—	—	—	2	—	3	6
135	1	—	—	—	—	3	4	8
130	1	1	—	1	—	3	2	11
125	1	3	—	—	1	6	6	21
120	—	1	1	2	1	6	2	27
115	1	3	2	3	3	11	7	41
110	1	4	2	—	1	11	9	44
105	—	4	3	—	2	11	7	43
100	4	3	8	2	—	9	5	63
95	4	3	2	3	3	11	3	57
90	3	6	8	2	2	13	4	97
85	6	4	6	2	—	12	3	76
80	—	4	2	2	2	10	2	76
75	3	2	4	2	3	6	1	74
70	3	3	5	2	2	7	4	85
65	1	6	4	—	1	3	1	70
60	—	7	2	—	2	5	2	61
55	1	2	1	1	—	3	1	53
50	—	2	1	—	—	1	1	39
45	1	1	—	—	—	—	—	36
40	—	—	—	—	1	—	1	17
35	1	1	—	—	—	1	—	10
30	1	3	—	—	—	—	—	11
25	—	—	—	—	—	—	—	4
20	—	—	—	—	—	—	—	8
15	—	—	—	—	—	—	—	1
10	—	—	—	—	—	—	1	1
Totals	33	67	51	22	26	138	70	1,043
Medians	88	88	90	95	95	96	109	86

decades ago. How miserably this curriculum fails, the elimination figures of most high schools clearly show. The problems of creating a new curriculum for children of average and below-average capacity is one on which intelligence tests give valuable aid.

Oakland, he was happy to report, was "using group mental tests exclusively in the upper grades as an aid in the segregation of pupils into groups of more homogeneous mental capacity."[9]

Dickson thought the use of tests to identify and classify both the gifted and the slow learners would contribute to social efficiency. Of the gifted he observed:

Conservation of power and reduction of waste is an important social ideal. A lot of the brain power in our schools is daily going to waste because it is idling far below its normal capacity. Our educational practice needs a severe earthquake that will shake us loose to the recognition of this waste.

For the less able, he thought that "courses and programs which fit their capacities and needs" would reduce "failure and discouragement." "More self-respect and better citizenship will result," he said. "Better educational guidance will naturally produce better vocational fitness for the coming worker and citizen."[10]

Dickson's experiments in 1919 and 1920 led in the next few years to a systemwide adoption of intelligence testing. In 1922 Dickson reported on the Oakland experiment in Terman's *Intelligence Tests and School Reorganization*. He announced that the total number of tests given in Oakland had reached 30,000. The reorganization of the schools had proceeded quickly after the first experimental studies. He observed that a "three-track plan" of classes for accelerated, normal, and slow classes "prevails throughout the entire city." The three-track system actually incorporated five different kinds of classes. In the "normal" sections were the vast majority of students (82 percent). Other students were placed in "accelerated" classes (10 percent), "limited" classes (6 percent), "opportunity" classes for those entering the system but needing extra help to catch up (1 percent), and "atypical" classes for students more than three years behind grade level (1 percent). The modifications in the elementary schools created a special problem for junior high schools since, as a result of the grouping in lower grades, a greater percentage of students reached seventh grade.

To accommodate more pupils of wider abilities, the junior high schools had begun to adopt a similar structure of ability grouping. This ripple effect touched the high school as well, and efforts were made to section students by ability. Commenting on Dickson's work, Terman expressed his belief that "the best hope for a satisfactory solution of the problem of individual differences lies in an extension and thorough working out of the Oakland plan."[11]

Terman's hopes received a boost when the next year he published Dickson's account of the Oakland experiment, *Mental Tests and the Classroom Teacher,* in the Measurement and Adjustment Series. Directing his book primarily to teachers but also to school principals, Dickson drew upon his Oakland experience to describe the nature of tests and their use for classification and guidance. Here and elsewhere he explained Oakland's commitment to training individual classroom teachers administering intelligence tests. By 1922 over 200 teachers—20 percent of the entire teaching force—had completed or were in the process of completing a certification course.

Dickson described the schedule of systemwide intelligence testing that had evolved over five years of experimentation. Individual intelligence tests, the Stanford-Binet, were given in certain instances:

1. For special atypical-class candidates
2. For kindergarten and primary pupils
3. For problem cases of all grades
4. For cases of disagreement between teacher's judgment and group-test results

Group tests were given in other circumstances:

1. For general classification into ability groups from third grade up, and experimental use in first and second grades
2. For cumulative record and study in grades four, six, and eight
3. For counseling and placement of pupils promoted to a higher school:
   a. Sixth grade to junior high school
   b. Eighth grade to high school
   c. Ninth grade to senior high school
4. For all pupils entering high school from out-of-town schools

He also outlined the use of tests for class organization and instruction, describing the types of classes, the method of classification (mental age, IQ, accomplishment, age, and general behavior and needs of child), the methods of adapting the curriculum to different ability groups, and the various standards for attainment and progress. Dickson's report provided solid evidence that the testing program in Oakland had matured.[12]

By the middle of the decade the reform of the Oakland public schools through the use of intelligence tests was an established fact. Superintendent Fred Hunter had, with Dickson, developed a schedule for the yearly administration of tests to the entire school system. Mental tests were given to the eighth grade in February, sixth grade in March, and fourth grade in April; achievement tests were given in grades four through twelve in May. In a special report in January 1926, Hunter reviewed the accomplishments:

To adapt instruction to individual and group needs and capacities is one of the hardest problems which the teacher and school administrator have to solve. . . . The development of mental tests upon a scientific basis, of standard tests for subject matter, and of achievement quotients has made it possible for teachers and administrators to approach the practical side of the problem upon a somewhat scientific basis. . . . Nowadays the school system that has made no beginning in the development of its curriculum along scientific lines and in the classification and promotion of its pupils in accordance with their scientifically pre-determined capacity is held to be in no sense attempting to meet the great problems before the schools.

Oakland, he was proud to announce, had begun a complete revision of the curriculum and had taken "important and far-reaching steps in the classification and guidance of pupils."[13]

Hunter's associates reported the details of the progress Oakland had made toward that end. Elise Martens, Dickson's assistant, told of a curriculum revision for the three-track system that involved over 1,000 teachers and administrators. Another assistant, Henrietta Johnson, gave an account of the expanded guidance program which included some forty-four teachers and counselors who had in the previous year administered 8,390 tests (543 individual intelligence tests, 4,002 group tests, and 3,845 subject tests). The differentiation of the school system had produced a surge in developing junior high schools as well. With only one junior high at the time of World War I, Oakland could now count sixteen. And programs in vocational education, whose genesis had come in part with the Smith-Hughes Act in 1917, now flourished under the auspices of a program of testing and classification.[14]

A decade earlier intelligence testing was in its infancy, and group tests did not exist. By 1925 Oakland had reorganized the entire system of public education based in part on the new scientific instruments. The future of testing in Oakland seemed secure.

San Jose

Like Oakland to the north, San Jose was also a pioneer in adopting intelligence tests for use in the public schools. A city of nearly 40,000 in 1920, the population of San Jose was heavily foreign as well: over half the residents were first- or second-generation immigrants. The story of measurement in San Jose illustrates how one school system used tests to solve the "immigrant problem." The history of the early years of intelligence testing in this city also brings into sharp relief the issue of ethnicity, for university researchers and schools alike interpreted differences in mental test performance as scientific proof of the "inferiority" of immigrants, especially those from southern and eastern Europe and from Latin countries. Armed with intelligence test scores, school administrators classified students by ability, one result of which appears to have been a tracking system that separated immigrants and native-born Americans.

The initial impetus for intelligence testing in San Jose came from Stanford and a group of graduate students associated with Terman. The first contact came in 1916, through an experiment Terman conducted using the Stanford-Binet to select applicants for the city's police and fire departments. In 1919 a Stanford student named Kimball Young began a study of the "mental differences in certain immigrants," under the direction of Terman and Cubberley. With the cooperation of San Jose Superintendent of Schools Alex Sheriffs, Young gathered information on all twelve-year-olds in the schools to "discover if possible some of the causes of the difficulty in the education of children of South European ancestry in our public schools" and whether their poor performance was due to "their alleged handicap" or to a "lack of mental endowments." He tested all students using the army Alpha and Beta and compiled other data including teachers' estimates of intelligence and accomplishment, grade location, and parents' occupational levels.[15]

TABLE 5.2

Retardation in Selected San Jose Schools, 1919–1920

School	Number of Pupils	Number of Retarded	Percent Retarded	Percent Latins in Schools
Total San Jose	4,939	2,098	42.4	40.0
School A	652	177	27.1	16.1
School B	629	187	29.7	17.5
School C	770	399	51.6	81.4
School D	744	464	62.1	72.4

Source: Kimball Young, *Mental Differences in Certain Immigrant Groups* (Eugene, Ore.: University of Oregon, 1922), 18. Reprinted by permission.

Among the "serious effects upon the public schools" of the recent "incursion of immigrants," Young reported in his study on discipline problems, difficulties teaching children from different cultures, and retardation. He discovered that 42 percent of the students were retarded, or behind their grade level. Examining four selected schools— "A" and "B" representing schools with predominantly northern European students, "C" and "D" representing schools with primarily Latin students—Young discovered that Latin students were the farthest behind. Retardation was nearly twice as high in Latin schools as it was in the northern European schools, according to Young's statistics (table 5.2). The study also showed that while the students in the northern European schools were fairly evenly distributed through the grades, those in the Latin schools were clustered in the first few grades. Nearly one-quarter of the students in the latter schools were in the first grade, while only 6 percent were in the eighth grade, as Young's data showed (table 5.3). Thus a disproportionate number of immigrants apparently never completed elementary school.[16]

For Young an analysis of the data provided the answer to the retardation problem. The Latin pupils "are decidedly inferior to the American pupils," he said, when measured by teachers' estimates, general intelligence (he computed the mean IQ for Latins to be 83), and economic status. Asserting that the language handicap "does not in fact exist in the case of the children of South European descent, to the great extent imagined," he concluded that "the true difficulty is

TABLE 5.3

Comparative Retardation by Grade in Schools A, B, C, and D; Also Percentage of Pupils in the Various Grades

1. For Schools A and B Together

Grades	No. Pupils	Percent Retarded	Percent in Grades
I	212	13.7	16.5
II	150	22.0	11.7
III	149	32.9	11.7
IV	137	36.5	10.7
V	161	36.6	12.6
VI	169	36.6	13.2
VII	140	24.3	10.8
VIII	163	29.4	12.7
Total	1,281		

2. For Schools C and D Together

Grades	No. Pupils	Percent Retarded	Percent in Grades
I	335	42.7	22.1
II	253	56.8	16.1
III	193	61.1	12.7
IV	208	64.4	13.7
V	145	71.0	9.6
VI	168	61.9	11.1
VII	126	61.9	8.3
VIII	96	46.8	6.3
Total	1,514		

Source: Kimball Young, *Mental Differences in Certain Immigrant Groups* (Eugene, Ore.: University of Oregon, 1922), 18. Reprinted by permission.

one of mental capacity, or general intelligence, which makes the Latins unable to compete with the children of North European ancestry in the mastery of the traditional American public school curriculum."[17]

"For the school man *now*," theoretical considerations are inconsequential, he said. "What he wants to know is *how* and *what* to do today." To solve the problems in the San Jose schools, Young called for a "new educational policy." He recommended that "standardized tests should be applied throughout the elementary schools" as a preliminary step toward regrouping students on the basis of ability. Noting that "violent reclassification cannot be brought to pass over night," he observed that "the logical places to commence in San Jose . . . are in the schools so overwhelmingly Latin in population," because "it is there that the largest numbers of backward are found." He recommended that "pedagogical," or achievement, tests be used as well and suggested that the work could be facilitated by the establishment of a research bureau. After testing, the schools should be reorganized into three tracks, for "the superior, for the average, and for the backward," and the instruction for each group modified. For Young, remaking the curriculum was "the crux of the matter." The new curriculum would provide "training for occupational efficiency, technique, and habits of work," habits of "co-operation" and "efficient living," and appreciation of the arts. For the able, the curriculum would be enriched; for the less able, it would provide training in skills and vocational education. A differentiated course of study, he said, would "fit the levels of capacity of the pupils" to "their future requirements in adult society."[18]

San Jose apparently was receptive to Young's suggestions, for in a footnote to his policy recommendations he observed that "since the above was written a new superintendent has taken over the control of the San Jose schools, and so far as this community is concerned we may look for rather radical changes in school policy. The new executive is already carrying out some of the recommendations of this chapter." That executive was Walter L. Bachrodt.[19]

The new superintendent, appointed in 1921, moved quickly to attack the difficulties in the San Jose schools. In his analysis of the problem, Bachrodt agreed with Young. In his view, the great number of foreign-born—from thirty-six countries—created an additional "burden" for the schools because the "school problem is not only one of teaching fundamentals but also of assimilation [sic]." The immigrants from Italy—by far the largest single group—presented a particular problem of "colonization" for they were represented in very large numbers in three of the nine elementary schools. Examining the retardation question, he found results similar to Young's. In three schools with a large percentage of Italians, the rate of retardation was the highest in the district (43.9, 46.6, and 58.0 percent, respectively). The problem in San Jose was compounded, Bachrodt said, by the fact that relative to other cities in California, the city had a high percentage of school-age children in the population and a low tax base. In other words, San Jose faced a financial crisis.[20]

Bachrodt's prescription for San Jose's ills followed closely Young's "new educational policy." In his first annual report in 1922, he observed that "the new field of Mental Testing has shed very valuable light upon this whole question" of retardation. He introduced his constituents to Terman's work with the Stanford-Binet and reviewed the army experiment. Acknowledging the recent criticisms of intelligence tests, he said that "as we are primarily interested in why children do or do not succeed in school," it is sufficient to know that "from thousands of cases it has been definitely proven that mental tests do test the kind of mentality that it takes to go through school."[21]

By the end of Bachrodt's first year as superintendent, intelligence testing had made a beginning in San Jose. All students had been tested in two elementary schools as well as in the entire eighth grade in all nine elementary schools for an experiment in placing high school entrants in ability groups. The scores of the group testing provided a stark contrast of relative intelligence test performance among the city's elementary schools. As in the retardation study, the three "Italian schools" were at the bottom, with mean IQs of 71, 70, and 57 respectively (the highest mean score was 94). For Bachrodt the message was plain. "It is well to face the facts," he said, "since our statistics absolutely prove it, that the children in our schools that are predominably [sic] foreign do not compare with the children of other schools either in progress through school or in marks earned on tests of native ability." Bachrodt's "facts" accurately portrayed the performance of Italians on the tests. They did not take into account, of course, the influence of culture and environment on that performance.[22]

Although intelligence testing in 1921–1922 was only conducted on an experimental basis, the structure existed to expand the program rapidly. Most of the work had been organized by the research department of San Jose State Teachers College, which had strong ties to Stanford. The eighth-grade testing had been conducted by James L. Stockton, who received his Ph.D. in 1920 under Terman. He was joined at San Jose by John K. Norton, formerly of the Oakland Research Bureau, who coauthored with Dickson an article on the use of tests in eighth grades for ability grouping and who helped to write *Mental Tests and the Classroom Teacher*. When Norton left the bureau in 1921, he was replaced by James C. DeVoss, another Terman Ph.D.

The preliminary experiments in intelligence testing and the evidence of massive retardation led Bachrodt to plan a reform for San Jose schools that was similar to Young's "new educational policy." On the basis of eighth-grade testing, he concluded that the "biggest problem that a progressive school system has to face is the readjustment of pupils into classes of like ability." He proposed to extend the ability grouping experiment, establish a junior high school, introduce a more systematic program of educational and vocational guidance, and expand offerings in vocational education. Thus in 1922 San Jose initiated a major reform of public education based on testing, classification, and guidance.[23]

Palo Alto

In Palo Alto school problems were of a different order. The population in 1920 was just a little over 7,000, immigrants were few, the community was homogeneous, and the residents prosperous. Sitting in Stanford's front yard, Palo Alto was in many respects an excellent example of a "progressive" school district, one which quickly instituted educational innovations developed at the neighboring university. Palo Alto began its own kind of experiment with the use of intelligence tests at the time of the First World War.

In some respects Palo Alto faced challenges common to many school districts in the early twentieth century. Enrollments in the high school, for example, had shot up from 306 in 1915–1916 to 571 in 1920–1921. High school graduates, numbering only thirteen at the turn of the century, reached fifty-seven in 1916 and seventy-nine in 1921. A large percentage went on to college; nearly half the class in 1920 attended Stanford. Yet increasingly the high school was enrolling students who were not headed for college.[24]

Responding to these problems, Walter H. Nichols, principal of Palo Alto High School, presented a plan for a districtwide reorganization in January 1918. Commenting on the increasing number of failures in high school, he proposed that Palo Alto expand its junior high school and diversify the curriculum. "With the beginning of the seventh grade," he said, "the course of study should recognize frankly that from a third to a half of the pupils should begin their training for definite hand occupations as opposed to brain occupations." Pupils in this age group, he argued, "are capable of being sorted tentatively into occupational groups, all educational theorizing to the contrary." In the high school he proposed establishing "two years of pre-vocational training for those pupils unable financially or unfitted mentally to complete the regular four years of high school work."[25]

When he proposed this reorganization, Nichols was receiving the assistance of psychologist William V. Proctor at Stanford. Proctor had joined Terman in the Department of Education in 1916 and soon began a series of experiments using psychological tests for educational and vocational guidance. During and after the war, he demonstrated how tests could be used at Palo Alto High School. While the primary use of intelligence tests in large urban areas was for classifying great numbers of students, Palo Alto took a different tack. In Palo Alto tests were used for sorting students, but the accent was on steering students through the educational system and on directing them toward appropriate colleges and occupations.

Consulting with Terman, Proctor began his experiment with the assistance of three graduate students—John Norton, later of Oakland and San Jose; Sam Kohs; and Mary Bess Henry. He secured permission from Nichols to examine 107 students entering Palo Alto High School with Stanford-Binet tests. The purpose of the experiment, he wrote, was to "discover whether it is practicable to use intelligence tests for the educational guidance and grouping of high school pupils according to ability." Analyzing the records of twenty-seven students who had dropped out, Proctor concluded that there was a strong relation between elimination and mental capacity and wondered whether the situation could not have been avoided through more appropriate guidance and placement.[26]

Since the intervention brought Proctor into frequent contact with Nichols, the principal sought his advise on students encountering academic difficulties. As a result of this ad hoc advising arrangement, Proctor was asked to recommend appropriate placement for all students entering high school at mid-year 1918. Pleased with the results, Nichols expanded the program to include all students entering the high school in September of that year. Word of the experiment spread fast, and the principals of four other Stanford area high schools, "upon hearing of what was being done," asked to be included in the continuing experiment.[27]

In conjunction with this original project, Proctor conducted another experiment to determine whether psychological tests could predict high school success and how they could be used in educational and vocational guidance. In the fall of 1917 he gave army Alpha tests to 1,349 students in eight Bay Area high schools. Follow-up studies confirmed earlier findings: students with lower intelligence test scores were more likely to drop out of school. From his study Proctor predicted that students entering high school who tested below normal would drop out within two years and that few such students would ever graduate. For Proctor the implications were clear. With the IQ information at hand, the principal could "plan the curriculums of his pupils more intelligently. . . . There will be fewer failures; more pupils will remain to take work that is adapted to their needs and capacities; and the high school will be less open to the charge of catering only to the intellectual aristocracy among its pupils." Proctor thus concluded that intelligence tests would contribute much to educational guidance.[28]

He then explored the use of intelligence tests in vocational guidance. Discussing an analysis of the army tests in 1920, he noted "discoverable differences in the intelligence levels of workers in various occupations." The army data, he said, pointed toward "more or less clearly defined levels of intelligence in the various occupations, corresponding roughly to the amount of intelligence necessary to succeed in them." Comparing the vocational aspirations of some 900 high school students with the occupational intelligence levels revealed by the army Alpha, as well as with vocational opportunities derived from the Federal Census, he concluded that there was an urgent need for guidance. Proctor's study is shown in table 5.4.[29]

Not only did the students aspire to occupations with average intelligence levels above their own, they sought professional and managerial positions in numbers far out of proportion to the distribution of workers currently employed. Proctor's advice: "For their own best good and the best good of the nation a great many of them should be

TABLE 5.4
Comparison of Opportunities with Vocational Ambitions

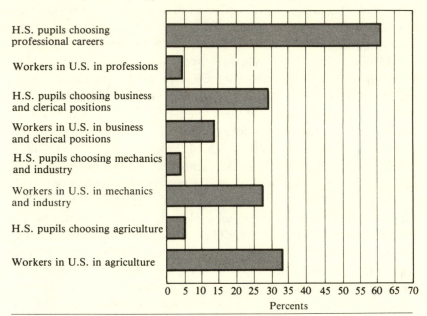

Source: William M. Proctor, "The Uses of Psychological Tests in the Vocational Guidance of High-School Pupils," *Journal of Educational Research* 2 (Sept. 1920): 540.

directed toward the agricultural, mechanical, and industrial fields." He concluded that "the mental tests, if conservatively employed, will increase the probability that the counselor will give really helpful advice," and argued that "better and more systematic educational and vocational guidance of high-school pupils" was essential to the well-run high school.[30]

Like Dickson in Oakland, Proctor decided to tell a national audience the lessons he had learned in Palo Alto. In *Educational and Vocational Guidance* (1925), he argued that the increasingly complex nature of society and the occupational structure called for a program of testing and guidance as a means of "conserving human values." The school would steer the child "along these paths of self-realization and social service to which he is best adapted by reason of his mental, moral, social, and physical endowment." In that sorting function intelligence tests would play a major role.[31]

From these case studies of San Jose, Oakland, and Palo Alto, it is possible to make some tentative generalizations about the adoption of tests. Each school system faced different problems; each reached for different solutions. Yet central themes emerge. In each instance the adoption of testing was a top-down reform, initiated by an elite: university psychologists and school administrators. Their proposals for school reform provided ready solutions for schools beset with new challenges. Reformers in each city said that testing would enhance efficiency in schools and in society. The reformers' rhetoric revealed, as well, a distinct anti-immigrant tone and suggested that the use of tests served to reinforce social prejudice. The social ideas of men like Terman and Dickson, Young and Bachrodt, Proctor and Nichols reflected the nativistic tone of the early twenties. The experiments in social reform they conducted in these three cities were probably characteristic of the adoption of testing across the country.

In Oakland, San Jose, and Palo Alto, that adoption proceeded quickly. Yet occasionally there was evidence that the adoption of testing created tensions within the school and between school and community. Dissension in these three cities was part of a national controversy over testing and ability grouping that emerged in the twenties, within both the psychological profession and the wider educational community.

CHAPTER 6

Rising Dissent: Controversies Over Intelligence Testing

At the beginning of the testing movement in 1912, J. E. Wallace Wallin warned about the inherent limitations of intelligence tests and their use by untrained persons. The tests were "no 'open sesame' to the human mind," he said, and needed to be "safeguarded from uncritical exploitation and mystification, and rescued from the educational fakers and medical quacks." Wallin's words opened a controversy that was to escalate as the development and use of tests became more extensive. After the army experiment, testing gained widespread public confidence, prompting some test developers, Terman among them, to predict that a utopia based on intelligence tests was at hand. At the same time, however, a controversy ignited about intelligence and its uses that would divide the psychological community in 1922 and 1923 and ripple through the rest of the decade.[1]

Controversies about testing were heard in three forums. Initially, applied psychologists discussed the theoretical nature of intelligence and the extent to which it could be measured by tests. As psychologists considered the influence of heredity on intelligence and the use of tests in schools, however, this internal debate became heated, leading to a special conference on the subject in 1928. The internal debate among psychologists became a public controversy when critics in the media questioned the validity of intelligence tests and the degree to which they promoted equality. At the same time, intelligence tests generated intense debate when school administrators began to use them to classify students. By the middle of the decade, some administrators, teachers, and parents spoke out against both intelligence tests and ability grouping, and in some schools the testing and tracking programs were dismantled altogether. This chapter will evaluate the debate over testing from three perspectives—the psychologists, the media, and school administrators—and the degree to which the controversy influenced public policy.

Divisions Within the Testing Community

Discussions about intelligence tests among professional psychologists focused on the nature of intelligence, its development, and the validity of the tests. In the symposium sponsored by the *Journal of Educational Psychology* in 1921, it was clear that psychologists differed on the definition of intelligence, whether it could be measured by test methods, and the degree to which it remained constant for any one individual.[2] Especially on the question of environmental influence, psychologists were sharply divided. When the early use of tests in the army and the public schools revealed distinct differences in performance for various socioeconomic, ethnic, and immigrant groups, some psychologists raised questions about the validity of the tests and the extent to which language and social factors affected individual results on the examinations.[3]

On each of these issues, Terman took strong stands, positions which elicited disagreement from his fellow psychologists. Terman defined intelligence as the ability "to carry on abstract thinking." He strongly believed that exams such as his Stanford-Binet and the National Intelligence Tests were valid and reliable measures of ability and that intelligence remained relatively constant. Convinced of the essential correctness of Galton's theories on hereditary genius and based on his own research with the gifted, he concluded that intelligence was greatly controlled by genes and was but little influenced by other factors. As we have seen, he decided early in his work that test score differences among ethnic, national, and occupational groups could be explained primarily in terms of inherited intelligence.[4]

In the symposium Terman's position brought a sharp attack from psychologist Beardsley Ruml, who argued that because psychologists' terminology was vague, "the nature of intelligence can hardly be debated at the present time." Ruml questioned the assumptions of Terman's work—the definition of intelligence, his use of statistics, and IQ constancy. Terman, joined by his Stanford colleague Truman Kelley, responded with a crisp rejoinder. Dismissing Ruml's "philosophical approach" as lacking "the essential genius which leads to discovery," they compared the work of intelligence testers to that of Newton and Einstein and argued that their own work must be viewed as scientific exploration. "The concept of the IQ will not fall," they said, "as a result of mere verbal attacks, but only when it is experimentally shown not only that it is inconstant, but how it varies." Terman and Kelley then presented a list of "interpretative concepts of the movement" that they hoped would be "refined, not discarded": "the constancy of the IQ; a practical limit to general mental development somewhere in the neighborhood of age 16; the bearing of mentality upon delinquency and insanity; the general linear (usually rectilinear) positive correlation between desirable traits; the great relative importance of individual differences in determining our success in meeting life tasks; the importance of the intelligence level in fields far removed from the scholastic, as in army assignments."[5]

The intraprofessional debate intensified in April 1922 when William C. Bagley of Teachers College delivered a paper entitled "Educational Determinism; or Democracy and the I.Q." at a convention of school superintendents in Chicago. Bagley challenged the definition of intelligence advanced by psychologists such as Terman and suggested that the tests were so unrefined as to make scientific prediction unwarranted. Disclaiming any "personal animus," he warned that the "present tendency" to increase the use of tests beyond a "very restricted field" is "fraught with educational and social dangers of so serious and far-reaching a character as to cause the gravest concern." The heart of his attack was the use of tests for classification. Such a use would promote a "fatalistic" labeling of slower students and an undemocratic emphasis on the training of the gifted. Focusing in particular on Terman's proposals for tracking in *The Intelligence of School Children*, Bagley criticized this "cool proposal to separate the sheep from the goats at the close of the sixth school year." Bagley offered his own assessment of the plan:

With his instruments of selection admittedly faulty, with his measures that measure something that no one has yet been able to define, the determinist proposed this policy and seeks to justify his proposal on the high grounds of social welfare and especially of social progress.

Bagley attacked this policy as shortsighted. The extensive use of tests, he said, would undermine democracy by promoting an increasingly stratified society.[6]

Terman felt compelled to reply. He unleashed an ad hominem attack, charging that Bagley's "vision is blurred by the moist tears of sentiment and the eloquent address closes with a rhapsodic peroration on the miracles that skillful teachers work with morons and on the ultimate illumination of the world by gleams of light struck from dull minds." Terman reasserted his belief in individual differences and defended his plan for a differentiated curriculum with students classified according to ability. He dismissed with a grim analogy Bagley's plea for increased attention to children with low IQs: "No one has ever proved the impossibility of life returning forty-eight hours after death, yet we do not hesitate to bury our dead within that time."[7]

Terman's rebuke elicited a rejoinder from Bagley later that year. The testers' "dogmatic disregard" of environmental factors (such as the influence of schooling) had caused them to misinterpret the results of the army tests for different occupational and immigrant groups, he said, and in so doing weakened "public faith in education." His complaint was not with the tests themselves but with hereditarian assumptions. He termed it the "height of folly" for "education not to avail itself of these instruments in detecting individual differences in learning capacity whether such differences be innate or acquired." On the other hand, he observed, the tests will "render a gratuitous and disastrous disservice if they encourage in the teacher the conviction that the illumination of common minds is either impossible or a relatively unimportant task."[8]

Other psychologists tried to close the breach between Terman and Bagley the next year. At Stanford, Truman Kelley, a former student of Bagley's, was grieved "that they were battling for the Lord" when they "ought to be shoulder to shoulder in the fight." He "salvaged from the storm" areas of agreement and disagreement. They appeared to agree that individual differences—both innate and acquired—existed, that the purpose of education is improvement, and that "intelligence tests are valuable instruments if properly used." They disagreed on the relative influence of nature and nurture, the best means to secure improvement, and the "proper use of" test scores. Concluding his consensus statement, Kelley noted that the ranks of the critics "need augmenting" for "the test movement has secured the popular hold of such a sort as to constitute a guarantee that it will be misused."[9]

Other members of the Stanford community, John C. Almack, James F. Bursch, and James C. DeVoss, tried to arrange an "armistice." They evaluated the use of tests in the schools by asking three questions: Does the knowledge of the limits of future development adversely influence an individual's self-image?; Does classifying an individual by intelligence change the way he is viewed by society?; and Has the use of intelligence tests created a new basis for classifying or cataloging individuals? They argued that while knowledge of limits might discourage the less able, it might also encourage the talented who held themselves in low esteem. They said, too, that other factors such as wealth, race, sex, and occupational status often exerted a profound and occasionally detrimental influence on the way an individual was viewed by society; intelligence tests could balance those other factors. Finally, they argued, "we have always striven to find some basis for classifying human beings" and the recent movement was merely a refinement of old practices, not a revolution.[10]

These cautionary statements brought a momentary lull, but Terman rekindled the debate. Writing early in 1924 on the "possibilities and limitations of training," he resumed his campaign for the differentiated curriculum. "We have established one type of school and uniform methods of instruction for all children," he said. Declaring that the "results of intelligence testing during the last decade present a challenge which is without parallel in the history of education," he dismissed the notion that education could bring infinite growth for the individual as a "beautiful faith . . . long ago destroyed." He argued that if studies could be conducted to support his contention that differences in intelligence were mainly due to heredity, a revolution would be at hand:

If this, or even half of it, should be found true, the practical consequences would be well nigh incalculable. Eugenics would deserve to become a religion. Educational effort, while it would deserve to continue, would largely have to be redirected. The first task of the school would be to establish the native quality of every pupil; the second, to supply the kind of instruction suited to each grade of ability. Either group instruction would be abandoned, or, if it were retained, a three-track or five-track plan would operate from the first grade on, each with methods and a curriculum peculiar to itself.

Terman concluded his article with an important announcement. He had been named to chair a committee of the National Society for the Study of Education which would investigate the nature-nurture question and report in early 1928.[11]

Terman confidently predicted that a series of carefully planned scientific investigations would "fairly well settle the question" of how much heredity influenced intelligence. Over the next four years, he chaired the NSSE committee on nature and nurture, a group whose members represented a broad cross section of opinion on the matter: Bagley, Baldwin, Brigham, Freeman, Pintner, and Whipple. Backed by funding from various foundations, private, and university sources, the committee sponsored some twenty-two separate studies of the influence of nature and nurture on intelligence and sixteen studies of its influence on achievement. In February 1928 the society gathered in Boston to hear the results.[12]

Following an opening paper by Truman Kelley and Barbara Stoddard Burks, a Terman protégé, on "statistical hazards" in nature-nurture studies, researchers presented the results of their findings on factors influencing intelligence test scores: family, social environment, race, schooling, health, IQ, constancy, and coaching. They then turned their attention to factors influencing achievement test scores: intelligence, school attendance, teaching ability, school expenditures, and effort.[13]

The evidence on the nature-nurture issue was mixed and seemed to preclude a final answer. There were so many investigations on different subjects with different methodologies and different conclusions that one could assemble support for hereditarian or environmental positions. The introduction which Terman wrote for the yearbook suggests that even he, one of the strongest defenders of the notion of a constant, hereditary intelligence measured by tests, had been forced to modify his claims slightly. "For certainly it must be admitted," he wrote,

that no final answer to the nature-nurture question has been attained or even approximated. The most that can be justly claimed is that the bounds of our knowledge have been in some measure extended. . . . It is conceivable that the elusive nature of the problem is such as to preclude for a long time to come, if not forever, a complete and final solution.

Assessing the evidence after the conference, however, Terman defended his earlier prediction. "My interpretation of the evidence . . . ," he said, "is that it places the IQ and other indices of intelligence on a solider foundation than ever before. Everything goes to show that the IQ does count, that it is not easily influenced by environmental factors, and that it is therefore relatively constant."[14]

For Terman, the conference had an importance that transcended the nature-nurture question. Studies of school achievement seemed to show that it was relatively little influenced by such factors as the quality and methods of teaching, school expenditures, attendance, the improvement of physical defects, or the size of the class. The findings prompted him to issue one of his last published statements on the use of tests in an editorial entitled, "The Ultimate Influence of Standard Tests." "A hundred years from now," he predicted, "the educational historian will probably characterize the present era as the one which saw the birth and development of the testing movement." Not surprisingly, he predicted that the use of standardized tests of intelligence and achievement in schools would be viewed as "of capital importance." The results of the NSSE conference, however, had forced him to modify his prescriptions for reform and his plans for improving the efficiency of the school machine. He continued to advocate the use of tests for educational and vocational guidance. He concluded, though, that an "exaggerated" concern with subject-matter achievement should be replaced with an emphasis on "the ethical and social ends of education" and care "about making the school a wholesome place in which to live."[15]

During the decade of the twenties, psychologists debated the value of intelligence tests and their use in restructuring schools. While psychologists discussed the issues among themselves, certain individuals in the media began to listen. Eventually they themselves joined the controversy.

Controversy in the Public Forum

Although many in the nation had become aware of the development of intelligence tests through the army experiment, little of the initial intraprofessional argument reached the public. In 1922 as concern mounted over immigration and Congress considered proposals for restrictions even more severe than those of the 1921 quota, several writers issued interpretations of the army test results for mass consumption. Lathrop Stoddard, in *The Revolt Against Civilization*, and Charles Gould, in *America, A Family Matter*, both claimed that the hierarchical order in intelligence scores of immigrant Americans provided convincing, scientific proof for the superiority of Nordic peoples and the inferiority of southern and eastern European peoples. Others like Albert Wiggam argued in "The New Decalogue of Science" that efforts to improve intelligence through changes in the environment were foolish. Often it was alleged on the basis of the army data that the average mental age of Americans was near thirteen. Through such sensationalized reports of the army intelligence test results, the public learned of the controversy brewing in the testing community.[16]

In the waning months of this supercharged year, the *New Republic* carried a series of six critical essays about intelligence testing by Walter Lippmann and a rejoinder to the attacks by Terman. It was in this exchange that the controversy broke open in full view of the public, or at least the readers of the Lippmann column.

Lippmann wrote in an indignant tone. He aimed to provoke in true muckraking fashion. His articles contained four basic arguments. First, he said, intelligence tests did not measure "intelligence," for the testers had no adequate definition of the term. Further, the tests could not be said to measure hereditary intelligence, for it was impossible to sort out the myriad of environmental factors affecting individual performance. Importantly, he agreed with Terman that the tests might be of "some practical benefit" for more homogeneous classification of schoolchildren if the tests were "administered in skepticism and sympathy." Yet he argued that such a benefit was "in great danger of being offset by dangerous abuse" due to the exaggerated claims of the intelligence testers.[17]

Lippmann developed these arguments over several months. He spent considerable time discussing the definition of intelligence and method of test construction. Because intelligence "is not an abstraction" and because "the intelligence tester starts with no clear idea of what intelligence means," Lippmann concluded that the tests could not purport to measure it. Likening the process of creating a mental test to that of making a set of graded puzzles, Lippmann questioned the more-or-less arbitrary categories used to classify individual performance in the tests as well as the process of standardizing the tests on very small groups of people. Analyzing the army tests, he concluded that time pressure and individual anxieties could make the tests unreliable. Finally, he questioned the usefulness of the tests in predicting life success when they were validated only by school performance.[18]

In later articles Lippmann examined the claim that the tests could measure hereditary intelligence. Focusing on data from early use of the Stanford-Binet, he challenged Terman's interpretation of results which were said to prove strong hereditary influences in intelligence. Terman had misread the data, Lippmann said, and was "obeying the will to believe, not the methods of science." In Lippmann's view the evidence showed that environmental factors played a significant role in developing intelligence.[19]

Setting aside discussions of test theory, Lippmann gave strong support to the use of tests in schools for classifying children:

A fair reading of the evidence will, I think, convince anyone that as a *system of grading* the intelligence tests may prove superior in the end to the system now prevailing in the public schools. The intelligence test, as we noted in an earlier article, is an instrument of classification. When it comes into competition with the method of classifying that prevails in school it exhibits many signs of superiority. If you have to classify children for the convenience of school administration, you are likely to get a more coherent classification with the tests than without them.

What concerned Lippmann, then, was not the use of tests but their potential for misuse.[20]

In his first article Lippmann had warned that because of unreasonable claims and faulty assumptions the tests were "in danger of gross perversion by muddleheaded and prejudiced men." In his final essay, "A Future for the Tests," he explored the possible key role in schools for tests should the view become common that they measured heredi- tary intelligence. The tests and their makers would "occupy a position of power which no intellectual has held since the collapse of theo- cracy." The testers would become gatekeepers at the door to opportu- nity:

If he were really measuring intelligence, and if intelligence were a fixed hereditary quantity, it would be for him to say not only where to place each child in school, but also which children should go to high school, which to college, which into the professions, which into the manual trades and common labor.

By his choice of words, one can measure the intensity of Lippmann's campaign to forestall this development. Leveling his main charges against Terman, he described the work of the intelligence testers with the following language: "dogmatize," "a purely statistical illusion," "revival of predestination," "a will to power," "self-deception," "van- ity," and "pretention." Arguing that testers should turn their efforts toward developing specific tests for special abilities, Lippmann con- cluded that by abandoning the notion of hereditary general intelligence "psychologists will save themselves from the reproach of having opened up a new chance for quackery in a field where quacks breed like rabbits."[21]

After reading this final broadside, Terman decided to respond in kind. Within a week he dashed off "The Great Conspiracy" and dispatched it to the *New Republic* for publication later in December. Terman's rebuttal employed heavy sarcasm in which he likened Lippmann's essays to William Jennings Bryan's antievolutionist rant- ings. He scrutinized seven of Lippmann's assertions, showing that Lippmann had misunderstood portions of the army data himself and that his grasp of statistical principles was weak. He dismissed Lippmann's fear of the potential abuse of tests in schools as an example of "what horrible possibilities an excited brain can conjure up" and asserted that abuse was not "one of the recognized rules of the game." Responding to Lippmann's statement that testers had mistakenly discounted the environmental effects of the first four years of life, Terman said that perhaps it was "high time that we were investigating the IQ effects of different kinds of baby-talk, different versions of Mother Goose, and different makes of pacifiers and safety pins."[22]

That Terman saw himself on a crusade against the critics of the tests seems clear from his correspondence with World Book regarding the whole exchange. After the first four Lippmann pieces had appeared in print, Terman wrote World Book asking that the company distribute reprints of his reply to Bagley the previous June. The head of World Book, Caspar Hodgson, replied that "we have been following here the criticisms of the tests" and "are inclined to think that these attacks on tests may help the business rather than damage it, but agree with you that we ought to be on our toes all along the line." Within a month World Book sent out over 7,000 reprints, to all superintendents in cities over 25,000, to teachers in charge of summer school classes on tests and measurements, and to individuals who requested them. Early in December Terman wrote again to World Book telling Hodgson that he hoped the *New Republic* rejoinder "succeeds in setting people laughing at" Lippmann and asking that the company consider reprinting his Lippmann rebuttal for distribution in a similar fashion.[23]

When Lippmann replied to Terman's piece, implying that he was "loose-minded," Arthur Otis contacted Terman about the advisability of continuing the controversy. He wrote to suggest:

that we go slow on passing out reprints of your reply. . . . Now that Lippmann has replied in the way he did, I feel all the more certain that it would be unwise to call attention to this controversy. You will realize of course that all the readers of the New Republic who have seen Lippmann's series of articles will see your article anyway, and I believe that those who know nothing of the controversy will be just as well off to remain in ignorance of it. . . . In view of the turn that the controversy has taken, I believe we should withdraw with as few words as possible.

Supportive letters he had received from "school people" led Terman to believe that Otis and Hodgson were "entirely mistaken," but he deferred to their judgment. A few days later he confided in Cattell at the Psychological Corporation of his misgivings. "I hope I shall never be led to take part in such a controversy again," he said, observing of the nature-nurture question, "I wonder if there is any other scientific problem in the world fraught with more significance for mankind than that one."[24]

The Lippmann-Terman tête-à-tête quickly disappeared from the

page of the *New Republic* and the details of their disagreement undoubtedly faded rapidly from the public memory. Writing later that spring
in the *New Republic*, Lippmann offered his final assessment of the
controversy and the testing movement: "Mental testing has now clearly
passed the peak of its pretensions." But the debate about the nature of
intelligence and the use of tests lingered in the public domain, surfac-
ing occasionally with the publication of tracts such as Carl Brigham's
Study of American Intelligence. As the fires of the Lippmann-Terman
debate cooled down, though, new criticisms of intelligence testing
were heard from another quarter: the schools themselves.[25]

The Use and Misuse of Tests in Schools

"The avidity with which the educational public has seized upon group
intelligence examinations is both encouraging and alarming," M. E.
Haggerty told the National Association of Directors of Educational
Research at Atlantic City in March 1921. "It confirms our faith that
such tests meet a real need in school work," he said, "but it also raises
a doubt as to the existence of a wholesome critical attitude of mind
toward the proper selecting of tests and the proper use of test results."
Haggerty's admonition sounded an early warning from the group most
closely connected with the development and use of intelligence tests in
schools, and it would be followed by increasingly critical comments
from other members of the psychological community. After the first
rush of enthusiasm for reorganizing schools with intelligence tests,
reaction to their use also built up among school administrators. Across
the country people in communities served by the public schools also
questioned the use of intelligence tests, although the nature and extent
of their opposition is hard to document. With an innovation that
promised so much, reaction and disappointment seemed inevitable.[26]

After Haggerty's comments in Atlantic City came attempts from
other applied psychologists to moderate an overenthusiastic promotion
of tests. In February 1922 at the joint meeting in Chicago of the
National Society for the Study of Education and the Department of
Superintendence, called to consider the NSSE report on "Intelligence
Tests and Their Use," Marion R. Trabue discussed the "pitfalls" in
the administrative use of tests. Trabue likened the use of tests to a
"walk through the open country at night, on account of the deserted

mine-shafts and unprotected pits that await the feet of one who travels without a light." He pointed out the dangers that would stem from confusion about the nature of the tests, exaggerated confidence in their accuracy, deterministic applications of test results, and inappropriate use in the schools. A leitmotif heard throughout the address was the danger of test use without guidance from experts. He warned that such a use could "involve scores of innocent boys and girls in an educational and vocational snare, which would affect their lives profoundly and in many cases permanently." School administrators should "acknowledge frankly" that intelligence tests were measures of a "relatively specific ability to do abstract thinking," should correct the "tendency" to use tests "as the basis for the promotion and classification of pupils, more or less regardless of the judgments of teachers," and recognize that school reorganization "with the aid of intelligence tests is not in itself a desirable educational objective." He closed with a plea that "for the present, and until the science of mental measurements is much older, more highly developed, and better understood, the psychologists and the school administrators must cooperate at every step."[27]

Trabue's appeal was echoed in similar statements from those connected with test development around the country. From Harlan C. Hines at the University of Washington came the plea "we need to 'calm down.' " He noted that the tests have "fallen sometimes into the hands of persons who have, willfully or no, perverted the purpose for which they were intended." Arthur Otis of World Book spoke on the value and limitations of group intelligence tests to school administrators gathered at the University of Pennsylvania in April 1922. Addressing the same group, Frank Graves, president of the State University of New York and New York State commissioner of education, observed that "there has arisen a perceptible fear lest we ruin the prospects of great service from psychological tests and the measure of intelligence by overdoing them." At an early stage in the movement, university professors and test developers thus moved to restrain the excesses in the use of intelligence tests.[28]

The controversy had expanded to include not merely the use of intelligence and achievement tests but the whole notion of grouping students by ability. In a 1924 revision of his widely used textbook on *Educational Tests and Measurements*, Walter S. Monroe discussed the classification of students, giving special consideration to Terman's five-track plan. Noting that Terman was "one of the most ardent advocates of the multiple-track plan of classifying pupils," Monroe questioned whether such a plan was desirable. The answer, he said, was likely to have "a very significant influence upon our future life as a state and as a nation" and a wrong answer "serious consequences." Monroe reviewed the arguments for and against grouping, the scientific evidence on the use of tests for classification, and the effects of segregation on school and society. He urged moderation and counseled that the superintendent "should give very thoughtful consideration to the matter before reorganizing his school system on either a three-track or a five-track plan."[29]

Later that year Frank N. Freeman of the University of Chicago wrote a consensus statement on testing, "Sorting the Students," that probably reflected the views of many university psychologists. Freeman's article, called by the editors a "timely and judicious discussion of the reasons for and against the growing practice of grouping students according to ability and achievement tests," argued that the classification of students was based on a well-established existence of differences in the "capacity" of students to do schoolwork. The issue of classification, he said, really had to be considered apart from intelligence tests which were "only a somewhat better measure" of ability than was school accomplishment. He rejected assertions that grouping "branded" students, arguing that individuals must cope with many kinds of labels. Considering the sociological criticisms that grouping was undemocratic, he said that these statements were built on the faulty reasoning that democracy meant total equality and that classification, by recognizing inequalities, was therefore undemocratic. Freeman's article suggests university psychologists accepted the value of providing for individual differences through grouping and believed that a careful use of intelligence tests could contribute to the classification of students.[30]

While university professors were debating the merits and demerits of testing and classification, school superintendents, principals, and directors of research bureaus were wrestling with the practical application of intelligence tests. In 1921 Edmund Lyon, principal of East High School in Cincinnati, reported that simple solutions to the need to provide for individual differences contained an "element of danger," especially for the "submerged tenth." For a group to be known as the "slow group" or the "dummies of the school" would involve "discrimination which may at once defeat the purpose" of any classification scheme. "It is not natural for a boy's mother or father to believe that a son or daughter is dull," he said, "and to classify students strictly along the lines of their intelligence involved odious comparison."[31]

Others agreed that classification of students by intelligence tests created a self-fulfilling prophecy. John L. Stenquist of the Bureau of Reference, Research and Statistics in New York City made a "case for the low I.Q." Many successful individuals in the past, he pointed out, had been rather illustrious school failures. The advent of intelligence tests had added a greater burden to school failure by creating "ficticious stigmas." "There is a strong and universal notion," he said, "that a low score in such tasks as have here been called intelligence tests constitutes a disgrace, that must be shunned at all costs."[32]

The issue of labeling was but one of the many "problems arising in the administration of a department of measurements" which Helen Davis faced in Jackson, Michigan, in 1922. According to Davis, it was essential to acquaint the teachers with the theory and application of testing and keep them informed of classification and testing plans through regular announcements in bulletins and frequent meetings. She noted that students were often fearful of the tests and recommended that "when calling a child from the room" for individual tests, "avoid arousing the comments of his classmates, and assure him at once that he is being called out to do you a favor and not for any misdemeanor." Since the research bureau was occasionally at odds with school administrators, she found it necessary to assemble evidence "for convincing the school officials" of the value of classification.[33]

Tensions surfaced as well between school and community. Meeting parents' objections was a delicate task best left to teachers, she said, and recommended that "to avoid misunderstandings, a brief outline of the plan of classification to be followed, and its purpose, together with arguments for meeting objections to it, should be put in the hands of every teacher who is likely to be called upon to defend the administration and its policies." The community also needed to be informed of testing programs, through parent-teacher meetings, and through talks at business organizations and women's clubs. Explanations of the testing program in the local newspaper were important, but she cautioned that "experience has shown that to avoid serious misunderstandings, any material submitted for publication should be prepared by the department (and if at all important, endorsed by the superintendent) and given to the reporter with the understanding that it appear *verbatim*." Davis's experience in Jackson suggests that adopting a program of intelligence testing was a highly sensitive venture, one which needed to be handled with good judgment and diplomacy.[34]

Often it seemed one or the other was lacking. In 1924 Charles G. Reigner, a school administrator in Baltimore, offered a perspective on the measurement movement from the "man in the street." His quarrel was not with achievement tests but tests of general intelligence. Basing his observations on several years' work in giving and scoring the tests, and on close work with teachers in several communities, he announced, "Mr. Intelligence Tester, you haven't yet proved your case to the man in the street." Difficulties with administering the tests and divisions among psychologists about the nature and value of the intelligence tests led him to say, "you must excuse us from taking the quite revolutionary steps which are urged upon us."[35]

Other administrators were not so cautious in their criticisms of the intelligence tests. R. T. Hargreaves, principal of Central High School in Minneapolis, delivered a paper on the use of intelligence tests in guidance to a session of the National Association of Secondary-School Principals in 1924. Hargreaves criticized educators who had been carried away by enthusiasm for objective measurements and who had used tests to predict the vocational future for individuals. Attacking such a plan as an "iridescent dream," he said:

Under the influence of some such ideal one group of psychologists and professional educators, seized with a desire to play Providence in the name of science to others has taken a few facts, gone up on to the mount to confer with biologists, and has come down to us with a new decalogue of science by which they are going to predict the future of individuals, and with a technique which they are going to use to find out what folks are fit for and to fit them for it. . . . They have set up a *those who* classification of children, God's elect and the godforsaken.

Another principal, E. F. Orr of Hobart, Indiana, issued an equally strong rebuke of the testing movement that same year. Having instituted a testing program two years previously, having "done no little thinking on the subject," and having read about the " 'war among the psychologists,' " he came to the conclusion that the tests had "little if any value."[36]

The testimony from men like Hargreaves and Orr represented the views of some principals; the program of Principal R. O. Billet in Paineville, Ohio, typified the experience of others. "What honest-to-goodness, practical service, if any," he asked of intelligence tests, "can they render to real, bread-and-butter school administration and class-room procedure?" Four years' use of intelligence tests, combined with other measures such as grades, teachers' judgments, and achievement tests served to convince him that "the mental test is invaluable as an aid in learning the pupil's probable ability." In some schools, then, the judicious use of intelligence tests and other measures led to approval for ability grouping.[37]

In some communities, however, resistance to testing came from groups outside the school. Controversy in the national media occasion-ally affected local reception of testing programs, as revealed by Guy M. Whipple's report in 1923 on intelligence testing's objectors, "con-scientious and otherwise." Much of the recent criticism of testing, he noted, was simply "the favorite indoor sport" of journalists, feature writers, and psychologists. What alarmed him were reports of contro-versy within the schools:

One hears almost daily of conservative school superintendents who are ap-palled by these tirades against the testing program, of school principals who raise objections to the appearance in their classrooms of competent school psychologists, of parents who are afraid to have their children tested.

Controversy lingered even after the debates vanished from the press. Superintendent William Stark reported on the battles in Stamford, Connecticut, between "the scientific mind" and "popular prejudice." His plan to introduce standardized achievement tests in the schools met opposition, from teachers "suspicious of the scheme," from "boardinghouse-keepers," and "all-wise businessmen." The local paper noted dissatisfaction with the tests and urged readers to write the schools.[38]

One of the most well-documented campaigns mounted against intel-ligence tests occurred in Chicago in 1924. When Superintendent William McAndrews introduced several innovations—the platoon school, the junior high, and intelligence tests—in the Chicago schools, the reforms were greeted by representatives of labor as an " 'unholy trinity' forced upon the people of the city by vested interests." Led by Victor A. Orlander, secretary-treasurer of the Illinois State Federation of Labor, labor fought the changes at the Board of Education and in the local press. To Orlander and other labor figures, the reforms were a thinly disguised attempt at class control, for the use of tests in educational and vocational guidance would simply perpetuate the social order. "Has a new natural law been discovered which binds each individual to a place in society and against which protest or struggle is hopeless?" a labor newsletter asked. The intelligence testers, it charged, "have brought into America the ancient doctrine of caste." [39]

From the testimony of psychologists, journalists, school administrators, and teachers, it is clear that the adoption of intelligence testing and ability grouping in the early twenties sparked controversy. Much has been made of these divisions, especially the exchange between Terman and Lippmann. [40] The debates were highly visible and symbolized deep value conflicts over the use of tests. Yet for a complete understanding of the testing movement, we must ask to what degree the controversies affected public policy.

CHAPTER 7

National Patterns in the Use of Tests

By the middle of the 1920s, thousands of people—including university professors, school administrators, teachers, publishers, and the directors of philanthropic foundations—had collaborated to bring intelligence testing into the nation's schools. This movement was diffuse. No single agency shaped policy, and leadership was decentralized. The work of Lewis Terman has illustrated how and why tests were developed and the way in which they were introduced into three school systems in California. What were the contours of the broader testing movement? To what degree was Terman's experience representative?

This chapter offers a tentative portrait of the national testing movement. The first section describes the outline of the movement—when and where standardized tests were developed—through an analysis of early bibliographies of mental tests. The use of tests for classification and guidance is documented through national surveys conducted in the twenties. Selected evidence from schools across the country illustrates some of the specific circumstances that led schools to adopt tests.

The Scope of the Movement

As we have seen earlier, the testing movement began around the turn of the century, was stimulated by World War I, and rapidly gained momentum in the first half of the 1920s. By the end of the decade the movement had matured to a point where educators thought it necessary to catalogue the array of educational tests on the market. Initial efforts by the University of Illinois Bureau of Educational Research[1] and the U.S. Bureau of Education[2] culminated in *A Bibliography of Mental Tests and Rating Scales* (1933) by Gertrude A. Hildreth, a psychologist working under the direction of Rudolph Pintner at Columbia. Hildreth surveyed the relevant psychological and educational literature, previously published test bibliographies, publishers' test lists, library catalogues, and important individuals in the field. She included all standardized, objective tests that were intended for more than local or experimental use and that were generally available to the public. An analysis of Hildreth's bibliography provides a quantitative portrait of the testing movement.[3]

After the first tentative efforts at the turn of the century, American psychologists began producing mental tests at a fast clip. Especially important was the creation of mental tests for the classification of large numbers of students, shown in table 7.1.[4]

TABLE 7.1

The Development of Mental Tests in the United States, 1900–1932

	Binet Tests & Revisions	Preschool & Kindergarten	Elementary Ages 6–14	High School Ages 14–18	Total
1900–04	—	—	2	—	2
1905–09	—	—	2	—	2
1910–14	14	—	3	—	17
1915–19	5	1	10	1	17
1920–24	6	6	19	7	38
1925–29	—	16	8	8	32
1930–32	—	8	1	2	11
No date	1	2	6	5	14
TOTAL	26	33	51	23	133

Source: Adapted from Gertrude A. Hildreth, *A Bibliography of Mental Tests and Rating Scales* (New York: Psychological Corporation, 1933), 1–202.

By 1930 over 130 such instruments were on the market. Approximately a fifth had been produced before the war; nearly half were created in the boom years after the war, from 1918 to 1925. Psychologists fashioned four principal kinds of tests for school classification: individual Binet tests, preschool and kindergarten tests, elementary tests for ages six to fourteen, and high school tests for ages fourteen to eighteen. Initial interest focused on individual tests, with Terman publishing the most widely used version, the Stanford-Binet in 1916. Attention then shifted from the individual to group tests for elementary schools, as the National Intelligence Test was fashioned right after the war. When these early group tests proved less reliable for the lower and upper age ranges of schoolchildren, psychologists created improved instruments for preschool and high school.

Although early exploration in mental testing began in Europe, the United States quickly took the lead in producing tests for school use. The comparative development of mental tests here and abroad is shown in table 7.2.[5]

Table 7.2

A Comparison of the Development of Mental Tests in the United States and Other Countries, 1900–1932

	United States	Germany	Great Britain	France/ Belgium	Other European	Other	Total Non-U.S.
1900–04	2	—	—	—	—	—	—
1905–09	2	2	1	4	—	—	7
1910–14	17	4	5	6	4	—	19
1915–19	17	4	2	—	—	—	6
1920–24	38	13	11	3	—	1	28
1925–29	32	13	5	8	7	3	36
1930–32	11	5	2	—	1	3	11
No date given	14	—	6	—	2	—	8
TOTAL	133	41	32	21	14	7	115

Source: Adapted from Gertrude A. Hildreth, *A Bibliography of Mental Tests and Rating Scales* (New York: Psychological Corporation, 1933), 1–202.

Between 1900 and 1932 the United States produced half of all mental tests, with Germany second, Great Britain third, and France fourth. The mental tests produced elsewhere were largely translations of Binet's and Terman's tests.

Mental tests for school classification were only a part of the vast production of standardized tests—over 2,500—in the early twentieth century, as is shown in table 7.3.[6]

TABLE 7.3
The Development of Mental Tests in the United States,
Classified by Type of Test, 1900–1932

Type of Test	Number	Percent
Tests of Mental Capacity for		
School Classification	218	8.5
Binet Tests & Revisions	26	
Preschool & Kindergarten	33	
Elementary (Ages 6–14)	51	
High School (Ages 14–18)	23	
College Level	27	
Adult Level	23	
Scholastic Aptitude Tests—		
College & Adult Level	15	
Tests for the Blind & Deaf	13	
Tests for Backward, Subnormal &		
Abnormal Subjects	10	
Mental Capacities—Single Tests	202	7.9
Performance Tests—Form Boards &		
Mazes	80	3.1
Psychomotor tests	44	1.7
Achievement & Educational Tests	1,298	50.7
Fine Arts Tests	64	2.5
Character & Personality Tests	329	12.9
Vocational Tests	231	9.1
Environmental & Teacher Rating		
Scales	62	2.4
Unclassified Materials & Miscellaneous	30	1.2
Total Number of Tests	2,558	100.0

Source: Adapted from Gertrude A. Hildreth, *A Bibliography of Mental Tests and Rating Scales* (New York: Psychological Corporation, 1933), 1–202.

The mental tests most used in classifying students, those included in table 7.1 and represented here at the top of table 7.3, were less than 5 percent of the total. Tests of all types of mental capacity—including college and adult levels, backward subjects, and specific mental abilities such as memory—accounted for a little over 15 percent. The other major types of tests produced were those measuring achievement, character and personality, vocational interest, and performance.

In sheer volume tests of educational achievement accounted for half the tests produced. The creation of achievement tests began before the war and increased dramatically throughout the twenties, as is indicated in table 7.4. As we have seen earlier, these tests were also used to place students in homogeneous groups. It seems reasonable to conclude from the data in tables 7.1 and 7.4 that the heydey of intelligence testing peaked in the early twenties, with achievement testing receiving greater attention later in the decade and into the thirties. Why this was so we can only speculate. Perhaps a sufficient number of reliable intelligence tests had been produced by the mid-twenties to meet demand. Or perhaps criticism of intelligence tests led schools to adopt achievement tests to help in classifying students. In any case the sales of both achievement and intelligence tests continued to boom through the twenties, securing for tests a significant role in classifying students.

Mental test development was concentrated in a few key universities, as well as in research bureaus affiliated with school systems. In the field of elementary and high school tests, development was dominated by several members of the group that created the National Intelligence Tests: Terman, Melvin E. Haggerty, Guy M. Whipple, and Arthur S. Otis. Terman, as we have seen, brought out his Group Test of Mental Ability in 1920, while his colleague Otis, who had become Director of Test Service for the World Book Company after the war, brought out four exams between 1919 and 1923. Haggerty returned to the University of Minnesota where he brought out two intelligence tests for grade school use in 1920. Whipple at Illinois created tests for gifted children and general intelligence tests for grades four to eight that same year. He later joined B. R. Buckingham and W. S. Monroe in revising the Illinois General Intelligence Scale in 1926. The other members of the original NIT group concentrated their energies elsewhere. Thorndike continued as a leader in the testing field, but worked mostly with achievement tests, while Yerkes for the most part ended his involvement with the testing movement in 1921.[7]

Publishers pushed hard to market these tests. World Book gained a prominent position in the elementary and high school market by securing the rights to publish the work of Terman and Otis. Four publishers

TABLE 7.4

The Development of Achievement Tests in the United States, 1900–1932

	Composit.—General/Unclass.	Agricultural	Education	Psychology/Psych. Meas.	Teacher	Commercial Subjects	English	Foreign Languages	Handwriting	Home economics/Industrial art	Mathematics	Physical education	Reading	Religious education	Science	Social Studies	Spelling	TOTAL
1900–04	—	—	—	—	—	—	1	—	—	—	—	—	—	—	—	—	—	1
1905–09	—	—	—	—	—	—	—	—	—	—	3	1	—	—	—	—	—	4
1910–14	—	—	—	—	—	1	3	—	6	—	4	1	1	—	—	1	3	20
1915–19	1	—	—	—	—	—	20	11	18	2	24	2	18	—	8	18	9	131
1920–24	14	5	2	2	1	8	33	23	9	11	31	10	34	7	15	35	9	249
1925–29	22	2	6	9	10	20	65	61	13	25	64	10	44	7	40	71	23	492
1930–32	18	1	3	6	4	12	39	20	4	13	31	4	16	—	39	42	3	255
No date given	6	3	1	4	7	3	20	7	8	6	25	3	18	5	10	16	4	146
TOTAL	61	11	12	21	22	44	181	122	58	57	182	31	131	19	112	183	51	1,298

Source: Adapted from Gertrude A. Hildreth, A Bibliography of Mental Tests and Rating Scales (New York: Psychological Corporation, 1933), 1–202.

—the Public School Publishing Company in Bloomington, Indiana; the C. H. Stoelting Company of Chicago; Teachers College/Columbia University Press; and World Book—produced over half the tests. The remaining tests were produced by a handful of independent publishers, as well as university presses and school research bureaus. For the Binet and preschool tests, the story was much the same, with Stoelting and Warwick and York of Baltimore leading the production. Printing mental tests for school use was thus concentrated in the hands of relatively few houses.[8]

The introduction of tests into the schools did not result merely from a push from the publishers. There was a large nationwide network which paved the way. Looking back on "ten years of educational research" in 1928, Walter S. Monroe, director of the Bureau of Educational Research of the University of Illinois, surveyed the rise of educational measurement after the First World War. Among the causes of the measurement movement in general and the intelligence movement in particular, he cited: the financial support of the foundations such as the Carnegie Corporation, the Commonwealth Fund, the General Education Board; the information collected and disseminated by the United States Bureau of Education; the influence of the school survey movement; the role of educational periodicals in spreading information about tests; the stimulus provided by national organizations like the National Society for the Study of Education, the National Education Association, and the National Research Council, as well as by national conferences such as that sponsored on a yearly basis by Indiana University; and the activities of research bureaus at the state, city, and university level.[9]

Textbooks on measurement written by key figures in the testing movement also speeded up the adoption of intelligence tests. Following Terman's *Intelligence of School Children*, several psychologists published introductions to mental testing. Like Terman, most university professors directed their works to administrators and teachers in the field. These textbooks, used in schools of education across the country, helped train a new generation of teachers and administrators in mental measurement.[10]

In the decade after the First World War, the scope of the intelligence testing movement was well defined. In the afterglow of the army's experiment with intelligence testing, applied psychologists moved quickly to exploit public enthusiasm and developed a wide variety of individual and group intelligence tests as well as a host of achievement examinations. A network of organizations and individuals then moved to introduce the tests into the schools. This movement was propelled by the creation of a rich literature on intelligence tests and how they could be used for classifying students and for educational and vocational guidance. The test movement was in no way confined to the rarified atmosphere of universities, national educational organizations, and national publishing houses, however, for school administrators and teachers rushed enthusiastically to adopt the tests after the war.

The Use of Tests for Classification and Guidance

Before the First World War, we have seen how schools developed a variety of ways to classify students to provide for individual differences. After the war psychologists created a new lexicon for sorting students, coining such phrases as "ability grouping," "homogeneous grouping," and "tracking." While the testing movement presented a new incentive for grouping, it built on previous practice too. These changes in actual school classification practices and in the use of tests are illustrated by several educational surveys conducted at the time.

In 1923 Fred C. Ayer of the University of Washington sought to describe "the present status of promotional plans in city schools." He surveyed superintendents in a sample of 200 schools stratified by region (New England, Middle Atlantic, North Central, South, and West) and the size of city (100,000+, 25,000–100,000, 5,000–25,000, 2,000–5,000). Although his sample was more representative of large cities than small, and more representative of the densely settled Northeast and North Central region than the South and West, his work nonetheless allows us to make some tentative generalizations about what he termed the "startling array" of promotional plans and classification schemes. He reported on the plans currently in use in 124 cities (table 7.5).[11]

Ayer observed that the larger cities were more likely to use special classification plans, as were the cities in the Middle Atlantic and North Central states. His findings showed that 64 percent provided classes

TABLE 7.5
The Status of Promotional Plans According to Frequency of
Appearance in 124 Cities

Rank	Plan	Cities	Percent Total
1	Departmental teaching	88	70.9
2	Semiannual promotion	85	68.5
3	Classes for subnormal	79	63.7
4	Evening schools	72	58.0
5	Vacation schools	68	54.8
6–7	Supervised study	67	54.0
6–7	Double promotion	67	54.0
8	Junior high schools	61	49.1
9	Adult instruction	57	45.9
10	Ungraded rooms	52	41.9
11	Industrial classes	50	40.3
12–14	Elizabeth Plan	45	36.2
12–14	Non–English-speaking classes	45	36.2
12–14	Auxiliary teaching	45	36.2
15	Opportunity classes	38	30.6
16	Trade schools	34	27.4
17	Open-air classes	28	22.6
18–19	Speech defects classes	27	21.7
18–19	Classes for deaf	27	21.7
20	Special arts classes	23	18.5
21	Home-training classes	22	17.7
22–23	Classes for cripples	18	14.5
22–23	Disciplinary classes	18	14.5
24	Overage classes	17	13.7
25–27	North Denver Plan	15	12.0
25–27	Platoon system	15	12.0
25–27	Classes for blind	15	12.0
28	Pueblo Plan	13	10.4
29–30	Batavia Plan	12	9.6
29–30	Parental schools	12	9.6
31	Supplementary classes	9	7.2
32	All-year schools	6	4.8
33–35	Quarterly promotion	4	3.2
33–35	Classes for epileptics	4	3.2
33–35	Santa Barbara Plan	4	3.2
36	Cambridge Plan	3	2.4

Source: Fred C. Ayer, "The Present Status of Promotional Plans in City Schools," *American School Board Journal* 66 (Apr. 1923): 37. Reprinted with permission from *The American School Board Journal* (Apr.). Copyright 1923, the National School Boards Association. All rights reserved.

for subnormal students, 42 percent "ungraded rooms" for slow learners, and 31 percent "opportunity classes" for bright pupils. The study demonstrated in "an astonishing fashion the great attention which is being given to variate children," he said, noting the high percentage of systems providing special education for children with speech defects, the deaf, blind, and crippled. A "decidedly less number" of programs for bright pupils were reported, such as the Elizabeth, North Denver, Pueblo, Santa Barbara, and Cambridge plans.[12] A comparison of Ayer's findings with previous studies of classification schemes at the turn of the century indicates that provision for "subnormals," slow and bright learners, and those with special educational problems all increased significantly in the early twentieth century, suggesting that schools were becoming more highly differentiated. Although Ayer made no special attempt to measure the use of tests in classifying students, he did observe that "the present contribution of achievement and intelligence tests and individual records has increased rather than diminished the total number of classification schemes." "These same instruments will ultimately determine the fate of the 36 promotional plans herein described," he predicted.[13]

A survey conducted in 1925 by the U.S. Bureau of Education, "Uses of Intelligence and Achievement Tests in 215 Cities," offered convincing evidence of the rapid increase in the use of tests for classifying students.[14] W. S. Deffenbaugh, chief of the bureau's City School Division, asked all superintendents in cities of over 10,000 to report on the purposes for which they used intelligence and achievement tests in the elementary and secondary public schools. He presented the replies from 215 cities (a 35 percent response rate).

Deffenbaugh reported first the use of group intelligence tests (table 7.6). The data showed elementary schools were most likely to use tests, high schools least likely, with junior highs in between. Group tests were used most often to classify pupils into homogeneous groups. Nearly two-thirds of the elementary schools, over one-half of the junior high schools, and two-fifths of the high schools employed the tests for this purpose. Supplementing teachers' estimates of student ability and diagnosing failure were the next most frequent uses in all schools. Junior high schools and especially high schools reported extensive use of tests in educational and vocational guidance. There was

Table 7.6
The Use of Group Intelligence Tests in Elementary, Junior High, and High Schools in Cities of Over 10,000, 1925

Purposes For Which Tests Are Used	Elementary Schools		Junior High Schools		High Schools	
	Percent of Cities	Rank of Purpose	Percent of Cities	Rank of Purpose	Percent of Cities	Rank of Purpose
Classification of pupils into homogeneous groups	64	1	56	1	41	1
Supplementing teachers' estimates of pupils' ability	62	2	44	2	33	2
Diagnosis of cause of failure	46	3	29	3	24	3
Establishment of classes for subnormal children	43	4	14	10	7	13
Extra promotions	40	5	21	4	8	11
Comparison with other school systems	26	6	18	7	13	7
Admission to first grade of elementary school	25	7	0	21	0	21
Placement of new pupils from other schools	23	8	19	6	10	10
Regular promotion of pupils	22	9	15	9	6	15
Determining comparative efficiency of teachers	20	10	11	13	10	9
Establishment of classes for supernormal children	20	11	6	17	2	20
Diagnosis of cause of success	19	12	16	8	12	8
Demotions	17	13	8	16	7	12

Determining changes in method of presentation of lessons	14	14	13	11	6	15
Determining changes in subject matter of courses of study	11	15	0	14	7	14
Determining class marks	10	16	7	19	4	18
Establishing special supervised study groups	8	17	6	17	3	19
Vocational guidance	0	—	13	12	17	6
Determining number of courses to be carried at one time by high school pupils	0	—	9	14	21	5
Guidance in the selection of high school course	0	—	19	5	24	4
Admission to organized school activities	0	—	3	20	5	17

Source: W. S. Deffenbaugh, "Uses of Intelligence and Achievement Tests in 215 Cities," Department of the Interior, Bureau of Education, City School Leaflet no. 20 (Washington, D.C., 1925).

a variation among the three types of schools in the other uses of group tests, which included establishing special classes and making rapid promotions.

The survey then described the use of individual intelligence tests (table 7.7). All schools used individual tests less frequently than group tests. Establishing classes for subnormal children, classifying students into homogeneous groups, supplementing teachers' judgments, and diagnosing failure ranked among the most frequent uses. Use was most widespread among elementary schools, where individual and group intelligence tests served almost identical purposes.

Finally, Deffenbaugh reported on the use of standardized educational, or achievement, tests (table 7.8). Standardized achievement tests were about as widely used as group intelligence tests in all schools. They were used for different purposes, though, especially to evaluate the performance of schools. Achievement tests were used to classify students into homogeneous groups, but all schools were more likely to use group intelligence tests to that end, especially in junior highs and high schools.

In a follow-up analysis of the Bureau of Education survey, Bertha Hebb described "The Classification of Elementary School Pupils into Homogeneous Groups." She reported that 80 percent of the cities (172 of 215) were using standardized tests to classify elementary school pupils. Analyzing the data by size of city, she found little variation. To place students, schools were most likely to use group intelligence tests, then standardized achievement tests, and finally individual intelligence tests.[15]

In 1926 the Bureau of Education released another study, "Cities Reporting the Use of Homogeneous Grouping."[16] This survey, also sent to superintendents in cities of 10,000 or more, probed similar issues regarding intelligence testing and student classification. A tabulation of the returns from 292 cities (probably a better response rate even though the number of cities had increased over the previous year) revealed the pattern shown in table 7.9 in the provision of ability groups. As the survey demonstrated, ability grouping had become very widespread by the mid-1920s, especially in cities of over 100,000.

Elementary schools were the most likely to have ability grouping (85 percent), followed by junior high schools (70 percent) and high schools (49 percent). The survey also sought to determine the methods used to group students, reporting the following instances in which IQ or mental age was employed (table 7.10). Thus by the 1920s school systems across the country had become highly differentiated and frequently used intelligence and achievement tests to classify students.

While the practice of ability grouping based on intelligence tests was common, there were many variations on this theme. Indeed, when Henry J. Otto of Northwestern surveyed 395 superintendents in cities ranging from 2,500 to 25,000 to determine the "administrative practices followed in the organization of elementary schools," he found that "the measures which are applied in classifying the pupils for instructional purposes differ so much for the various school systems that no one practice can be designated the prevailing one." Conducting his survey in 1929, he discovered 20 different plans to classify students within classrooms, and 122 different promotion schemes.[17]

The diversity of testing and classification practice that the surveys reported is perhaps best illustrated by the actual reports from schools during the twenties.

Reports on the Adoption of Tests

Throughout the 1920s educators filled the pages of professional journals with reports of their experiments using intelligence tests for classification and guidance. Those contributing to this national discussion included university professors, directors of research bureaus, school administrators, and teachers. Their reports fill in the details of the testing movement outlined by the surveys and help describe national patterns in the adoption of intelligence tests.

As a group, university professors played several roles in the adoption of tests in schools. Some, like Terman, participated in a highly visible way by developing and marketing tests. Others, however, concentrated on experimenting with and reporting on developments concerning the nature of intelligence and the use of tests. In national forums which brought together educators of all stripes to discuss the testing movement, university professors helped to define the central

TABLE 7.7

The Use of Individual Intelligence Tests in Elementary, Junior High, and High Schools in Cities of Over 10,000, 1925

Purposes For Which Tests Are Used	Elementary Schools		Junior High Schools		High Schools	
	Percent of Cities	Rank of Purpose	Percent of Cities	Rank of Purpose	Percent of Cities	Rank of Purpose
Establishment of classes for subnormal children	67	1	18	3	8	7
Classification of pupils into homogeneous groups	40	2	22	2	14	3
Supplementing teachers' estimates of pupils' ability	38	3	24	1	16	2
Diagnosis of cause of failure	37	4	23	4	25	1
Extra promotions	33	5	16	5	7	10
Demotions	25	6	9	7	4	16
Placement of new pupils from other schools	23	7	9	8	5	12
Diagnosis of cause of success	16	8	12	6	11	4
Regular promotion of pupils	13	9	7	10	2	19
Establishment of classes for supernormal children	13	10	8	9	6	15
Admission to first grade of elementary school	12	11	—	—	—	—
Determining comparative efficiency of teachers	9	12	6	13	7	8
Comparison with other school systems	8	13	5	14	7	9

Determining changes in method of presentation of lessons	8	14	5	15	5	13
Determining changes in subject matter of courses of study	7	15	4	17	5	14
Establishing special supervised study groups	5	16	4	16	1	20
Determining class marks	4	17	3	19	3	17
Vocational guidance	—	—	7	11	10	5
Guidance in selection of high school courses	—	—	7	12	10	6
Admission to organized school activities	—	—	2	20	3	18
Determining number of courses to be carried at one time by high school pupils	—	—	4	18	7	11

Source: W. S. Deffenbaugh, "Uses of Intelligence and Achievement Tests in 215 Cities," Department of the Interior, Bureau of Education, City School Leaflet no. 20 (Washington, D.C., 1925).

TABLE 7.8

The Use of Standardized Educational Tests in Elementary, Junior High, and High Schools in Cities of Over 10,000, 1925

Purposes for Which Tests Are Used	Elementary Schools		Junior High Schools		High Schools	
	Percent of Cities	Rank of Purpose	Percent of Cities	Rank of Purpose	Percent of Cities	Rank of Purpose
Supplementing teachers' estimates of pupils' ability	61	1	41	1	27	1
Comparison with other schools systems	57	2	34	3	16	3
Classification of pupils into homogeneous groups	54	3	35	2	20	2
Diagnosis of cause of failure	44	4	28	4	14	5
Extra promotions	41	5	26	5	9	8
Determining comparative efficiency of teachers	38	6	18	7	15	4
Regular promotion of pupils	32	7	21	6	7	11
Placement of new pupils from other schools	27	8	15	9	6	16
Establishment of classes for subnormal children	25	9	9	15	2	18
Determining changes in method of presentation of lessons	20	10	15	8	8	10
Determining changes in subject matter of courses of study	20	11	14	11	7	12
Demotions	19	12	8	16	3	17
Diagnosis of cause of success	18	13	15	10	6	15

Determining class marks	14	14	10	14	6	14
Establishment of classes for supernormal children	11	15	6	17	1	20
Establishing special supervised study groups	10	16	5	18	2	18
Guidance in the selection of high-school course	—	—	12	12	10	6
Vocational guidance	—	—	11	13	9	7
Admission to organized school activities	—	—	3	20	7	11
Determining number of courses to be carried at one time by high school pupils	—	—	4	19	9	7

Source: W. S. Deffenbaugh, "Uses of Intelligence and Achievement Tests in 215 Cities," Department of the Interior, Bureau of Education, City School Leaflet no. 20 (Washington, D.C., 1925).

TABLE 7.9

Homogeneous Grouping in Cities of Over 10,000, 1926

Size of City	Elementary Schools			Junior High Schools			High Schools		
	Number with Ability Groups	N	%	Number with Ability Groups	N	%	Number with Ability Groups	N	%
100,000+	36	40	90.0	28	40	70.0	26	40	65.0
30,000– 100,000	66	89	74.2	57	89	64.0	36	89	40.4
10,000– 30,000	145	163	89.0	119	163	73.0	81	163	49.7
TOTAL	247	292	84.6	204	292	69.9	143	292	49.0

Source: Adapted from "Cities Reporting the Use of Homogeneous Grouping and of the Winnetka Technique and the Dalton Plan," Department of the Interior, Bureau of Education, City School Leaflet no. 22 (Washington, D.C., 1926), 1–11.

TABLE 7.10

The Use of Intelligence Tests in Classification, 1926

Size of City	No. of Cities	Total Cities	Percent
100,000+	36	40	90.0
30,000– 100,000	67	89	75.3
10,000– 30,000	147	163	90.2
TOTAL	250	292	85.6

Source: Adapted from "Cities Reporting the Use of Homogeneous Grouping and of the Winnetka Technique and the Dalton Plan," Department of the Interior, Bureau of Education, City School Leaflet no. 22 (Washington, D.C., 1926), 1–11.

purposes of the testing movement and to sound a cautionary note against an overzealous and uncritical acceptance of tests by schools.

The 1922 annual meeting of the National Society for the Study of Education on "Intelligence Tests and Their Use" was typical of convocations called to assess the testing movement. Several key figures in the field—among them Guy M. Whipple of Michigan; Edward L.

Thorndike, Rudolph Pintner, and Marion R. Trabue of Columbia; and W. S. Miller of Minnesota—gathered in Chicago in February to discuss the nature, history, and general principles of intelligence testing as well as the administrative use of intelligence tests. The convention featured reports on the use of tests ranging from the lower primary grades to colleges and universities. Time and again the participants sounded the refrain that intelligence tests would make education more scientific, promote efficiency, and conserve talent. Some speakers urged caution in the adoption of tests. Indeed, as Whipple noted, the tests had been occasionally misunderstood and the "result too often has been either an unreasoning and blind antagonism or a superlative and uncritical acceptance of these means for discovering and directing pupils' abilities and attainments." It was at national meetings of organizations like the National Society for the Study of Education, as well as in reports in educational journals, that psychologists and educators defined the potential use of intelligence tests in the schools.[18]

A natural ally of the university professors in their promotion of intelligence tests were research bureaus and psychological clinics, especially those in the city school systems. The founding of research bureaus and psychological clinics, begun after the turn of the century, accelerated after the war. These organizations conducted individual and group testing, made recommendations for classifying students, and in some cases developed the tests themselves. Most bureaus and clinics carried on a campaign to convince teachers and the public of the worth of intelligence tests. The actual power of the bureaus and clinics to effect school reorganization, however, varied considerably.[19]

One such organization that had great success with a testing program was the psychological clinic in Detroit. One of the first of the clinics founded, it conducted individual tests before the war. After the war the clinic was directed by two men who had served together in the Psychological Division, Charles S. Berry, professor of educational psychology at the University of Michigan, and Warren K. Layton. In the winter of 1920, the superintendent of schools approved a plan for testing and classifying all pupils in Detroit's first-grade classes. Berry's staff developed its own intelligence test which it administered to 10,000 students in September 1920. By June another 48,000 children were tested and by November another 20,000: all in all, over half the students in the system. On the basis of these tests, the children were rated on an A-to-E scale, and the children were then classified into "X," "Y," and "Z" groups representing, respectively, the top 20 percent, the middle 60 percent, and the lowest 20 percent of the students in terms of ability. As Layton observed, "it was believed that to give the new plan of classification a fair trial it would be wise to classify, by means of a group test, all pupils entering school for the first time, and then to maintain intact the divisions thus formed as far as possible throughout the six years of the elementary course." It was up to the individual principles to decide what use should be made of the test results, however, and in Layton's view the voluntary nature of the program was essential in securing a "constant and substantial increase in the number of group mental tests in Detroit." Indeed, Layton specifically rejected the idea of a systemwide program mandated by the superintendent, even though he acknowledged the national "tendency toward just such a situation."[20]

Vigorous support for the widespread use of intelligence tests came from school superintendents, especially those facing the challenges common in large urban centers. Reporting on the classification of students in Newark, New Jersey, David B. Corson confidently announced in 1920, "All children are not born with the same endowment of possibilities; they cannot be made equal in gifts or development or efficiency. The ultimate barriers are set by a power inexorable." The "radical and absolutely necessary action," he said, "is to accept a classification of children according to ability and attainment, and not according to physiological age." In Muskegon, Michigan, Superintendent Paul C. Stetson echoed Corson's feelings. "The preponderance of evidence is in favor of the use of intelligence tests supplemented by the personal testimony of the pupil's former teachers." He hoped that "as intelligence tests are perfected . . . it may be possible to classify pupils entirely on the basis of intelligence tests." And the New York City district superintendent of high schools, John L. Tildsley, enthusiastically told the participants at the National Association of Secondary School Principals in 1921 about the possibilities arising from the use of intelligence tests. Reminding his audience of the adage "you can't make a silk purse out of a sow's ear," he observed:

Now that we are able to discover in the early years of the elementary school, with a reasonable degree of accuracy, through the use of these tests, which is the pure silk and which the sow's ear, is it not reasonable to demand that we as educators shall so modify, adjust, and apply the educational process to the materials in our charge whose qualities we know that the silk shall be made into a silk purse and the sow's ear into a pigskin purse which in the view of many of us is of no less value to society than is the silken purse?

Of course, not all superintendents were equally euphoric about the possibilities of testing.[21]

It appears that school principals may well have been less ready than superintendents to embrace the exclusive use of intelligence tests for grouping their students. Closer to the day-to-day operation of the schools, principals were aware of the difficulties associated with intelligence testing programs: teacher resistance, the effect of testing on the morale and self-image of the students, and parental suspicions of the instruments. Elementary principals like Cora Campbell of the Bancroft School in Kansas City, Missouri, favored a go-slow approach in developing a testing program, noting that "it was not the desire of the faculty of this school suddenly to overturn the established organization of the school." "Violent revolutions in school policy," she said, "are apt to arouse so much suspicion and opposition that only disaster can result." Others, like Leonard Power in Port Arthur, Texas, cautioned experimenters to be aware of "all the handicaps one labors under when trying scientifically to test a whole school." In the high schools as well, administrators sometimes faced an uphill battle to institute a testing program. Gustave A. Feingold, vice-principal and director of intelligence in Hartford, Connecticut, had to overcome several "chief objections to the sectioning of classes in the senior high school on the basis of intelligence," namely that classification will "break down the spirit of democracy," that students in slower tracks "will feel disheartened by finding themselves condemned to a life of inferiority," and that these students will lack the stimulus provided by association with brighter students. Over the years as principals began to assemble longitudinal studies of their students' performance on intelligence and achievement tests, they often concluded that intelligence tests alone were not adequate for classification.[22]

The best-laid plans of school administrators for schoolwide programs in testing and classifying students ultimately depended for their success on the willingness of teachers to join in the reform efforts. Although it is difficult to measure how teachers felt about intelligence tests, it seems as though their support was occasionally only luke-warm. Part of their lack of enthusiasm stemmed from the fact that administrators used intelligence test results to measure teaching effec-tiveness, by comparing student accomplishment with tested ability. Intelligence tests also served to undermine teachers' authority and professional expertise when it was revealed that mental tests were more reliable predictors of school success than were an individual teacher's marks. When intelligence tests were directed to answer the question, "how much mental ability does a teacher need?" teachers undoubtedly felt a sense of insecurity as well. Teachers' reservations were captured in the words of "Miss Winthrop," a fictitious fifth-grade teacher, who said to her principal, "Educational measurements may be the last word in school procedure, but I do not see that they have anything to offer me as a class-room teacher."[23]

University professors were among the first to see that teachers would have to be convinced of the worth of the testing movement. J. Carleton Bell, editor of the *Journal of Educational Psychology*, urged in 1919 that tests be used primarily for diagnostic, not supervisory, purposes. Should this be done, he predicted, "measurements, instead of being looked upon by the teacher as the mysterious functions of a remote bureau, will come to be regarded as the teacher's useful tools, whereby she can determine quickly and accurately the needs of her pupils and the most effective adjustment of her energies." B. R. Buckingham and Walter S. Monroe of the University of Illinois argued that the superintendent "who contemplates initiating a testing program" will "have to 'sell' the idea to his teachers."[24]

This message was not lost on school administrators. Samuel S. Brooks, superintendent of schools in Silver Lake, New Hampshire, was particularly effective in "getting teachers to feel the need for standardized tests." Brooks introduced a systematic testing program in his rural school district and, after two years, "invited" his teachers to "submit a short paper on the advantages of using standardized tests." He deftly dismissed those opinions that were unfavorable. According to Brooks, one teacher's mind was frozen in "the last stages of its plasticity," another was a "local crank," and a third the daughter of a school board member who was not interested in "anything but her salary and a good time." Most teachers, he said, affirmed the tremendous value of the tests in conserving time and effort, in promoting more efficient teaching, and in facing "an irate parent with much greater assurance when he or she demands to know why James was not promoted." "I think that standardized tests are the greatest boon that has ever been invented for the benefit of teachers," said one.[25]

Other superintendents reported similarly encouraging receptions for testing. Hobart Corning of Trinidad, Colorado, polled his teachers on the advantages and disadvantages of classification and found the instructors overwhelmingly in favor of both testing and ability grouping. Yet even the best sales campaigns often failed to ignite the interest of teachers in the testing movement. At the end of the decade, I. N. Madsen of the State Normal School in Lewiston, Idaho, observed that the testing movement had failed "to enlist the intelligent cooperation of the classroom teacher" and that testing programs often engendered among teachers "a passive or even a hostile attitude because the implication is that they are on trial."[26]

Intelligence tests met with varying receptions in different types of schools. Reports from the field suggested that test use was most extensive in the lower grades and that tests were more often used for educational and vocational guidance in upper grades. Field reports also provided tentative evidence to explain why the use of intelligence tests for classification and guidance was less frequent in smaller cities and in rural areas. Helen Davis, director of measurements and special education in Jackson, Michigan, pointed out that administrators in small schools were reluctant to adopt testing programs because there were fewer pupils in each grade and because they lacked extra classrooms and teachers. In Pennsylvania, Charles Myers of the State Education Association added to the list of handicaps facing rural schools wishing to adopt intelligence tests: poor organization, little supervision, poorly trained teachers, strained finances, and extremely heterogeneous student groups. Even New Hampshire superintendent Brooks met residual resistance to testing, prompting him to deride a "common fallacy in his district" that under proper conditions and with proper instruction "every child barring the obviously feebleminded is about equally capable of making satisfactory progress in any study." But not all testing programs in rural areas and small cities encountered such turbulence. An extensive program of classifying pupils by ability in Enid,

Oklahoma, suggested that intelligence tests were employed success-
fully in school systems outside of the large urban areas.[27]

In reports about the use of intelligence tests for guidance, school
administrators and teachers in the twenties described an increasing
role for the school as a "selective agency." As B. R. Buckingham
observed early in the decade, "within the past few years the means
have multiplied by which the school has become consciously the direc-
tive and selective agency which it has always been unconsciously."
There was great potential in this regard, he said, for "our educational
and intelligence tests permit us to ascertain the capacities of pupils far
more accurately than ever before." His comment was reinforced by
another key figure in the guidance movement, Richard D. Allen,
director of research and guidance in Providence, Rhode Island. In
1925 he remarked that even though all "the paths have not yet been
blazed," the possibilities for the use of tests in guidance "are almost
unlimited."[28]

From the testimony of school administrators and teachers, from
surveys, and from reports on test development we can thus describe
national patterns in the testing movement. By all accounts the use of
intelligence tests flourished in the 1920s. The use of tests began in
urban areas and focused initially on elementary schools. Quickly testing expanded into junior high schools and high schools and reached
into the rural parts of the country. For classifying students, the group
test was most frequently used, supplemented by achievement tests and
individual intelligence tests. Early differentiation of the school curriculum paved the way for the introduction of intelligence tests; but the
testing movement exerted a powerful influence on the rise of ability
grouping and tracking. Certainly there were dissenters from the movement and their voices would become louder in future years. But in the
1920s intelligence testing was widely perceived as an innovation that
would increase efficiency in schools and in society. As the movement
gained support, intelligence testing became common practice in American schools. Today we live with the consequences of that reform.

Lewis M. Terman, 1941. At the close of his Stanford University career, Terman looked back on his thirty-five-year effort to make intelligence tests a permanent feature of the American educational experience. (Reprinted by permission of the Department of Special Collections and University Archives, Stanford University Libraries.)

Conclusion

From 1890 to 1930 powerful forces transformed the American educational system. The purpose of education, as well as the structure, function, and control of schools, were all vastly different at the end of this period. One of the forces shaping the system at this time was the intelligence testing movement. The development and use of intelligence tests for classifying students—by Lewis Terman and others—changed the way Americans thought about ability.[1] The movement also produced a new means of sorting students in schools. As this history has shown, schools in America began to classify students by a variety of schemes early in the nineteenth century. The invention of intelligence tests, however, speeded up the rise of schools as sorters by providing school administrators and teachers with instruments which they saw as more efficient and more scientific. In the words of contemporaries, the testing movement dramatically enlarged the role of the school as a "selective agency."

In recent years both the nature of intelligence tests and their use in sorting students have become issues for intense debate. Beginning in the 1960s controversy about tests led several cities and entire states to ban the use of group intelligence tests. In Washington, D.C., in the early seventies, for example, Judge J. Skelly Wright abolished tracking based on aptitude testing in a much-heralded case, arguing that the system deprived the city's poor and black students of equal educational opportunity.[2] The debate about the influence of heredity on intelligence, sparked by the Jensen article, continued through the seventies.[3] The National Education Association joined the fray by calling for a moratorium on the use of all standardized tests. Throughout the seventies and eighties the use of tests has been challenged, in professional circles, in the media, and in the muckraking press.[4]

This study was undertaken for two reasons. One purpose was to provide a better understanding of the introduction of tests and their role in transforming schools in the early twentieth century. A second purpose was, through this history, to provide perspective on the current problems faced by policymakers in education. Two questions were posed: why were intelligence tests adopted so rapidly in the schools, and what was the historical relation between testing and tracking? Three related answers to these questions have emerged.

A group of newly emergent professionals—university professors of psychology and public school administrators—joined hands to push for the widespread use of tests to classify students. Supported by a network of institutions, they hoped to reform schools to provide for individual differences in a more rational, scientific, and efficient fashion. The reforms these men proposed were largely top-down, conceived by an elite to improve society.

Their calls were heeded because the schools at this time urgently needed a new means to classify students. Schools in America had sorted students systematically at least as early as the beginning of the nineteenth century. But a host of new and pressing problems—increasing size, diversity, changing objectives, and rising costs—called for a more efficient and effective means of classifying students. Teacher judgments and student achievement were no longer adequate to classify the great number of students clamoring into the schools after 1890.

Reforms proposed by psychologists were not value-free, and intelligence tests were adopted in schools precisely because they reinforced central themes of the progressive movement. Tests were efficient, scientific, and rational. They gave power to professionals at a time when "experts" were increasingly called upon to solve society's problems. For some the tests were appealing as well because they confirmed widespread assumptions about the superiority of Nordic Europeans, the inferiority of the masses thronging to America from southern and eastern Europe, and of blacks migrating into cities in the North and West.

These three themes—the professional network, problems the schools faced, and progressive values—combined to accelerate the rapid and widespread adoption of intelligence tests in the 1920s. The study of the adoption of tests helps also to explain the rise of tracking. For nearly a century before the invention of intelligence tests, American schools had experimented with various means to provide for individual differences. While the appearance of intelligence tests did not create tracking, the tests, and especially the early beliefs that they measured "inborn capacity," acted as a catalyst for the institutionalization of classification plans. The very words "tracking," "homogeneous grouping," and "ability grouping" became part of the educational vocabulary just when intelligence tests were developed. Clearly the rise of testing and tracking were closely intertwined.

How did the rise of intelligence testing and tracking influence the role of the school in promoting social opportunity? From this study the record appears mixed. Schools sorted students well before intelligence tests—by grades, teacher judgments, early kinds of "objective" tests, as well as by age, sex, and race. For some, especially immigrant children just arrived in the United States, school administrators around the turn of the century often had to base classification decisions on scanty, largely subjective information. As Ray Rist has shown in his study of "The Self-Fulfilling Prophecy in Ghetto Education," classification based on subjective judgments often serves to reinforce social class differences in schools. In the context of early twentieth-century school problems, intelligence tests therefore may well have enhanced opportunity for some individuals by providing a less subjective measure of ability.

In the psychologists' initial assumptions about intelligence and in the early interpretation of group differences in performance, however, we have seen a recurring theme of Nordic superiority and ethnic inferiority. By promoting tests as measures of "hereditary capacity," psychologists like Terman helped to reinforce social class differences in schools. Tracking systems and classification practices that relied heavily on intelligence tests often erected road blocks to opportunity for certain groups, notably blacks and immigrants from southern and eastern Europe. By identifying the "misuse" of intelligence tests in the twenties, critics both inside and outside the psychological profession helped to correct some of the early "abuses" of tests. Yet, the widespread criticism of testing in the sixties, seventies, and eighties suggests that the use of intelligence tests in schools in the half century after World War I continued to influence individual fates and arouse political contention and led to controls on the use of group intelligence tests.

In coming to this explanation of the testing movement, I have built upon elements contained in previous studies; in important ways, though, this study revises earlier interpretations of the testing movement. Revisionist assessments were correct in noting the link between economic change and the transformation of the school, and in many cases they accurately interpreted the reforms as a means of social control. Too often, however, the revisionists have asserted that testers were motivated by self-interest and racism; too often they have paid more attention to rhetoric than to actual school practice. Their notion that testing produced tracking is a simplification of a complex evolution of the sorting function of schools. The argument that the rise of intelligence tests was inevitable does not withstand close analysis; had there been no intelligence tests, the creation of standardized achievement tests might well have accomplished much the same purpose in schools.

If the revisionists have blurred important details of the picture, so too have "house" historians neglected important elements in the history of testing. At times the rhetoric of the testers was elitist, hereditarian, and defensive. By overselling their reform, they provoked an angry response. By claiming for themselves and their instrument an extraordinary power to predict human destiny, they met sharp resistance from those who believed in America as a place for opportunity, not self-fulfilling prophecies. These interpretations of the movement have neglected the way tests influenced social opportunity. The widespread adoption of intelligence tests in the twenties should dispel the notion that the testing movement was simply an imposition from a power elite. It is hard to conceive of a movement spreading so rapidly and so widely without a high degree of initial consensus among psychologists, administrators, and teachers.

What implications for public policy today can be drawn from this history of intelligence testing? One is that we must avoid seeing the schools as a panacea to cure all society's problems. When intelligence tests were heralded as the way to utopia, expectations were raised, only to be shattered later. Another lesson is that the process of educational reform must recognize the needs and interests of all individuals and groups, not just a select few. Reformers in the Progressive Era saw intelligence tests as a means to improve society; but not everyone shared their vision of the shape of that "improved" society. Regarding the use of tests, one implication is that educators must use a variety of measures to assess talent and provide instruction tailored to individual needs. When tests were developed they were often promoted as the only way to measure student ability. As recent accounts show, tests are still misused where they are relied upon exclusively for making judgments about students. We need to do a better job instructing educators and the public on the appropriate and inappropriate use of tests. Looking back on the history of intelligence testing and ability grouping, we can see more clearly the causes and consequences of the rise of schools as sorters.

Appendix:
Discussion of Terms

Because this study deals with the complex subject of psychometrics, or the numerical measurement of mental ability, and the adoption of tests by schools, it is necessary to provide a definition of the terms frequently used. The language of testing can be discussed in three parts: those terms describing the nature and types of tests; those terms describing test construction and interpretation; and those terms describing kinds of abilities.

The Nature and Types of Tests

As Lee J. Cronbach has observed, for psychometric purposes a test can be defined as a "systematic procedure for observing a person's behavior and describing it with the aid of a numerical scale or category-system."[1] *Intelligence tests* or *mental tests* are those that measure abilities useful in thinking. The terms *mental ability* or *mental capacity* are often used to describe tests of intelligence, though it should be pointed out that psychologists today prefer the word "ability"—a measure of present performance—to the word "capacity"—used by early psychologists to suggest a trait that is inborn and fixed.

There is no agreement on the meaning of the word *intelligence*, and there has been much debate about the degree to which tests can measure it and the degree to which such performance is influenced by heredity or environment, nature or nuture. Common descriptions of intelligence refer to the capacity for critical thinking and abstract reasoning. Terman included three qualities in the definition he adapted from Binet: "the tendency to take and maintain a definite direction; the capacity to make adaptations for the purpose of attaining a desired end; and the power of autocriticism.[2] Frequently, psychologists have simply defined intelligence as "what the tests measure."

An associated term is *intelligence quotient*, or *IQ*, a concept popularized by Terman. The IQ is a ratio of *mental age* to chronological age, where mental age is defined by the number and kind of intellectual tasks that can be performed by a child at any given age. The IQ is used to express the rate of intellectual development. Early psychologists, Terman in particular, believed that the IQ was *constant*, that a person's relative standing would not change, an idea later challenged.

There are two basic forms of intelligence tests. The *individual test* can be either written or oral and is given to single persons by a psychologist. A *group test* is a written exam that can be administered to large numbers of persons at a single sitting.

There are a variety of other kinds of ability tests. *Aptitude tests* are used to predict success in a course of training or an occupation. *Achievement tests* measure success in past study. The word *educational test* is often used to refer to any kind of test given to students. *Performance tests* usually require a nonverbal response. Tests of *special abilities* are used to assess individual performance in things ranging from manual dexterity to perception. Other tests measure aptitude in the fine arts and for certain vocations, as well as character and personality traits.

Test Construction and Interpretation

One characteristic of early intelligence tests was that they were *objective*, factually oriented evaluations which reduced subjectivity in grading. True-false and multiple-choice tests are examples of objective tests. Another characteristic was that they were *standardized;* that is to say, the procedures for test administration, the test materials, and methods of scoring were established so that the same procedures could be followed anywhere, anytime. The word also is used to describe tests with *norms*, tables showing typical performance on the test. Adequate norms represent a defined and clearly described population that forms an appropriate standard group. They include a sufficient number of cases, are based on a random sample of the defined population, and reflect a representation of the group in question.[3] Typically, *specialized norms* describe variance in performance by age, sex, race, occupation, geographic location, type of school, and the like. As the population changes, norms become obsolete.

Performance on intelligence tests, like the existence of certain biological traits such as height, conforms to a *normal distribution*, a smooth, systematic frequency curve. Regarding early test developers, Cronbach observed that they "thought it a natural law that abilities are normally distributed. It is now realized that such a statement is meaningless, since the shape of the distribution depends on the scale of measurement as well as on the subjects' experience."[4]

The *validity* of a particular test can be measured in several ways: in terms of its ability to predict future performance, in terms of a comparison of test performance with the behavior the test is supposed to measure (content), and in terms of the actual concepts used to interpret performance (construct). Test *reliability* provides information on the degree to which the test results can be replicated and on the standard measurement error. *Correlations*, statistical summaries of the relation between two variables, are used to determine validity and reliability.

Test *bias* is a complicated term generally used to suggest that particular tests are unfair to individuals or groups. Tests are unbiased to the extent to which they compare individuals from similar backgrounds and experience. It is generally recognized, however, that intelligence tests measure a certain amount of language ability, school experience, and cultural background.

The Language of Ability

With the appearance of intelligence tests came a new vocabulary to describe kinds of abilities and levels of performance. The early tests of intelligence developed by Binet and Terman involved a series of mental tasks arranged in order of difficulty. To describe individual performance, testers developed a hierarchy of terms. Average performance was termed *normal*. Those who did above average were called *superior*. Particularly high scores were termed *exceptional*, *gifted*, or *genius*. Those scoring just below average were labeled *dull;* those farther down the scale were called *borderline* or *borderzone*. The bottom group was identified as *feebleminded*, a term that in today's terms might be translated as "mentally retarded." It is important to note that at the turn of the century the term *retardation* described students who were overage for their grade level, either because they were making slow progress or because they started late, and did not necessarily indicate some kind of mental disability.

Notes

Introduction

1. Terman, "Methods of Examining," 299–546; Terman, *Intelligence*, xiv; Hildreth, *A Bibliography of Mental Tests*, 3; "Cities Reporting the Use of Homogeneous Grouping," 1–11.

2. "Homogeneous Grouping," 1926.

3. Hoffman, *The Tyranny of Testing*. A particularly useful survey can be found in Haney, "Validity, Vaudeville, and Values," 1021–34. The flavor of the sixties' critique of testing can be sampled in the following: Gilbert, "On the IQ Ban," 282–85; Goslin, "The Social Impact of Testing," 676–82; Goslin and Glass, "The Social Effects of Standardized Testing," 115–31; Gross, *The Brain Watchers*; Joseph O. Loretan, "The Decline and Fall of Group Intelligence Testing," 10–17; Rosenthal and Jacobsen, *Pygmalion in the Classroom*.

4. Nairn and Associates, *The Reign of ETS*; Owen, *None of the Above*; James Crouse, "Does the SAT Make Better Selection Decisions?" 195–219; Hanford, "Yes, the SAT Does Help Colleges," 324–31; Jensen, *Bias in Mental Testing*, 1–24. Also see Jensen, *Straight Talk About Mental Tests* for a readable account of the technology of testing.

5. Wigdor, "Ability Testing," 6–8, 26; Garner and Wigdor, eds., *Tests: Uses, Consequences, and Controversies*, vols. 1 and 2; Bernard Gifford, "Testing, Politics, and the Allocation of Opportunities," 431; and Snyderman and Rothman, "Science, Politics, and the IQ Controversy," 91.

6. Committee of Ten, *Report*; Kingsley, *Cardinal Principles of Secondary Education*.

7. See Hofstadter, *Social Darwinism in American Thought*; and John Higham, *Strangers in the Land*.

8. Wiebe, *The Search for Order*; Kennedy, ed., *Progressivism: The Critical Issues*; also consulted was Filene, "Obituary," 24–43; and Burnham, "Psychology, Psychiatry, and the Progressive Movement," 457–65. For a general history of the progressive period, see John M. Blum et al., *The National Experience: A History of the United States*, 4th ed. (New York: Harcourt, Brace, Jovanovich, 1977).

9. Echols, "The Rise of the Evaluation Movement" offers a particularly detailed account of the rise of the measurement community. The following is a list of some of the major journals consulted, identifying the editor and date of first publication: *Ameri-*

can School Board Journal (1890); *School Review* (1893), James McKeen Cattell; National Society for the Study of Education, *Yearbook* (1900); *Journal of Educational Psychology* (1910), William C. Bagley; *Schoolmen's Week* (1914), University of Pennsylvania; *School and Society* (1915), University of Chicago; *Educational Administration and Supervision* (1915), W. C. Bagley, W. W. Charters, David S. Snedden, and George Strayer; National Education Association, *Journal* (1916), Department of Secondary School Principals, *Yearbook* (1921), Department of Elementary School Principals, *Yearbook* (1922); *Elementary School Journal* (1971); University of Illinois, Bureau of Educational Research, *Bulletin* (1918); *Journal of Educational Research* (1920), B. R. Buckingham, W. S. Monroe, and G. D. Strayer; *Educational Research Bulletin* (1923), Ohio State University.

10. Seagoe, *Terman*; and Russell Marks, "Testers"; Terman, "Trails," 297–331; Boring, "Lewis Madison Terman, 1877–1956," Ernest R. Hilgard, "Lewis Madison Terman, 1877–1956," Sears, "L. M. Terman, Pioneer in Mental Measurement."

11. For a comprehensive introduction to the issues in testing, see Cronbach, *Essentials of Psychological Testing*.

12. Cremin, *The Transformation of the School*; Rudy, *Schools in an Age of Mass Culture*, 31, 48; Joncich, *Sane Positivist*; Callahan, *Cult*.

13. Baritz, *The Servants of Power*, xi; Kevles, "Testing the Army's Intelligence," 579.

14. Haller, *Eugenics*, 3, 95.

15. Karier, "Testing for Order," 344.

16. Marks, "Testers," 46; also see Marks, "Lewis M. Terman," 336–55.

17. Joel H. Spring, "Psychologists and the War," 13; also see Spring's *Education and the Rise of the Corporate Order*.

18. Bowles and Gintis, *Schooling in Capitalist America*, 199, 191, 195, 200; also see Bowles, "Unequal Education," 1–30; and Carnoy, "Educational Reform and Social Control," 115–55.

19. David K. Cohen and Marvin Lazerson, "Education and the Corporate Order," *Socialist Revolution* 2 (April 1972): 48, 53, 54, 69.

20. Kamin, *The Science and Politics of I.Q.*, 1–2; also see James M. Lawler, *IQ, Heritability and Racism* (New York: International Publishers, 1978); for Jensen's article and critical responses, see *Harvard Educational Review, Environment, Heredity, and Intelligence*, reprint series no. 2, and *Science, Heritability, and IQ*, reprint series no. 4, 1969.

21. Cronbach, "Five Decades," 1, 8.

22. Tyack, *One Best System*, 180, 216.

23. Samelson, "Putting Psychology on the Map," 152, 155.

24. Gould, *The Mismeasure of Man*, 24–25, 174–92, 21.

25. Fass, "The IQ," 446.

26. O'Donnell, *Behaviorism*, ix.

27. Resnick, "History of Educational Testing," 174.

28. Sokal, ed., *Psychological Testing and American Society*. See in particular his introduction, "Psychological Testing and Historical Scholarship—Questions, Contrasts, and Context," 1–20; and Minton, "Lewis M. Terman and Mental Testing," 95–112.

29. Sokal, "History of Psychological Testing," 425–28.

1. Solutions in Search of Problems

1. Lewis M. Terman, *Measurement*, vii.

2. Young, "The History of Mental Tests," 2.

3. For the early development of professional psychology, see O'Donnell, *Origins of Behaviorism*. Also useful is Camfield, "Professionalization," 66–75. On Cattell's development, see Sokal, *Psychological Testing*, 21–45; Scripture would lecture at Columbia and later become professor of phonetics and director of the phonetic institute, 1922–1933; Angell would head the department of psychology at Stanford for thirty years; Titchener would become professor of psychology at Cornell in 1895 where he would remain for thirty years; Judd would become professor of psychology and head of the department of education at Chicago between 1909 and 1938.

4. Boring, *A History of Experimental Psychology*.

5. Binet and Henri, "On the Psychology of Individual Differences, 1895," 431.

6. Cattell, "On Mental Tests," 424. Cattell's early contributions have been well analyzed by Sokal, "James McKeen Cattell and Mental Anthropometry," 21–41.

7. American Psychological Association, quoted in Peterson, *Early Conceptions*, 93.

8. The following is a list of some of the most prominent graduates, with the dates of their degrees: Edward L. Thorndike (1898), Robert S. Woodworth (1899), Clark Wissler (1901), Walter F. Dearborn (1905), Albert T. Poffenberger (1912), Truman L. Kelley (1914), and Arthur I. Gates. (1917).

9. Edward L. Thorndike, quoted in Joncich, *Sane Positivist*, 559.

10. Boring, *A History of Experimental Psychology*, 506; Henry H. Goddard played a significant role in early test development which is well recounted in Zunderland, "The Debate over Diagnosis," 46–74.

11. Terman and Hoag, *Health Work in the Schools*, 4.

12. See Filene, "Obituary."

13. Seagoe, *Terman*, 9.

14. Terman, "Trails," 310.

15. Ibid., 318; Terman, "Genius and Stupidity," 310, 312.

16. Terman, "Preliminary Study," 413–51; Terman, "Study in Precocity," 145–83; Terman, "Trails," 321.

17. Terman, "Trails," 321.

18. Terman, "The Binet-Simon Scale," 204.

19. Ibid., 2–5; Ayres, *Laggards*; Callahan, *Cult*; see chapter 2 for a fuller discussion of the retardation issue.

20. Terman, "Survey San Luis Obispo," 131, 132.

21. Ibid., 136, 137, 133–35, 137.

22. Terman, "Report of the Buffalo Conference," 554; Terman, "The Significance of Intelligence Tests for Mental Hygiene," 122, 124.

23. Terman, *Measurement*, 45.

24. Terman, "A Tentative Revision and Extension of the Binet-Simon Measuring Scale of Intelligence," 62; Terman, "Stanford Revision," 1917, 128. For other reports on the Stanford-Binet, see Terman, "The Stanford Revision of the Binet-Simon Scale and Some Results from its Application to 1000 Non-Selected Children," *Journal of Educational Psychology* 6 (Nov. 1915): 551–62, and "The Mental Hygiene of Exceptional Children," 529–37.

25. Terman, "Stanford Revision," 1917, 29.

26. Ayres, "The Binet-Simon Measuring Scale for Intelligence," 187–96.

27. J. E. Wallace Wallin, *Experimental Studies of Mental Defectives* (Baltimore: Warwick and York, 1912), 1–2; also see Wallin, "Practical Guide," 217–38; Wallin's role in the measurement movement is discussed in Cravens, *The Triumph of Evolution*, 245.

28. Terman, "The Binet Scale and the Diagnosis of Feeble-Mindedness," Nov. 1916, 530.

29. For a complete list of the Ph.D. and M.A. research sponsored by Terman, see Seagoe, *Terman*, 205–10; Terman, "To Help Backward School Children," Stanford *Alumnus* (Apr. 1914): 1, 3–4.

30. Lewis M. Terman and Ernest B. Hoag, *Health Work in the Schools;* Terman, *Hygiene*, 1, 4.

31. Terman et al., *Surveys.*

32. Terman, *Hygiene*, 1.

33. Terman et al., *Surveys*, 26; Terman, "Survey San Luis Obispo," 132; Terman, "Backward Children," 2.

34. Boston Schools Committee, "Report of the Visiting Committee," in Caldwell and Courtis, *Then and Now in Education*, 168, 180; Horace Mann quoted in Caldwell and Courtis, 238–43.

35. For discussions of the changing structure of urban schools in the nineteenth century, see David B. Tyack, "Bureaucracy and the Common School: The Example of Portland, Oregon, 1851–1913," *American Quarterly* 19 (Fall 1967): 475–98; Katz, "The Emergence of Bureaucracy," 56–104; and Marvin Lazerson, *Origins of the Urban School;* for a brief discussion of testing in the civil service, see DuBois, *A History of Psychological Testing*, 5–6.

36. For the early measurement movement, see Rice, *The Public School System;* "A New Basis in Education," and "Obstacles to Rational Educational Reform."

37. See Joncich, *Sane Positivist.*

38. Monroe, "Existing Tests and Standards," 71–104, Monroe, *Educational Tests and Measurements*, 1917; Bryner, "Selected Bibliography."

39. Sears, *The School Survey.*

40. Nifenecker, "Bureaus of Research," 52; for further discussions of the rise of municipal and educational research bureaus, see Ashbaugh, "Cooperative Work," 57–70; Courtis, "Training Courses in Educational Measurement," 133–38; Chapman, *Organized Research in Education*, 210–12; Deffenbaugh, "Research Bureaus"; Gill, *Municipal Research Bureaus;* Judd, "Educational Research," 165–77; Martens, "Organization of Research Bureaus"; Monroe, "Ten Years of Educational Research"; and Theisen, "Operation of Bureaus of Educational Research," 382–91.

41. Ballou, "General Organization of Measurement Work," 50.

42. Wallin, *The Mental Health of the School Child*, 406–19.

43. Ibid., 393.

44. Ibid., 23, 138, 152, 154.

45. Ibid., 23, 399.

2. *Problems in Search of Solutions*

1. For revisionist interpretations see Karier, "Testing for Order," and Marks, "Testers."

2. Jones, *American Immigration*, 179; see also Oscar Handlin, *The Uprooted* (Boston: Little, Brown, 1951).

3. U.S. Bureau of the Census, *Statistical History*, 368–69, 374–75, 379.

4. For interpretations of the rise of the high school, see Krug, *The Shaping of the High School, 1880–1920* and *The Shaping of the High School, 1920–1941;* and Sizer, *Secondary Schools.*

5. Tyack, *One Best System*, 71, 183; Ensign, *Compulsory School Attendance and Child Labor.*

6. Cubberley, *Public Education*, 381.

7. Nifenecker, *Problems of School Maladjustment in New York City*, 7, 132, 150–51.

8. Ibid., 10, 191, 79.

9. Ayres, *Laggards*, 4, 6, 5, 6.

10. Ibid., 10.

11. Ibid., 7, 218.

12. George D. Strayer, *Report of Commissioner of Education of New York State*, 1910, cited in Blau, *A Special Study on the Incidence of Retardation*, 58, 65; see also for studies of retardation: Van Denburg, *Causes of the Elimination of Students*, Volkmar and Noble, "Retardation," 75.

13. On the evolution of school structure, see Tyack, *One Best System* and Samuel P. Hays, "Politics of Reform," 157–69.

14. McDonald, *Adjustment of School Organization*, 108, 120–45. Even though McDonald's study did not define the sample, the data nonetheless seem useful in suggesting how provisions were made for special education.

15. Ibid., 104, 106, 105.

16. Van Sickle, Witmer, and Ayres, "Provisions for Exceptional Children," 5–92.

17. Barnard, "Gradation of Public Schools," 455, 456, 458.

18. Harris, "The Development of the Short-Interval System in St. Louis," 328, 312, 304.

19. Boykin, "Class Intervals," 981–1009. A questionnaire regarding grading practices in schools was addressed to superintendents in all cities and villages of 4,000 and over. Of 816 questionnaires sent, approximately 465 were returned, a response rate of 57 percent. Note that column entitled "Total Replies" does not equal 465 since for each grade, approximately 25 answers were labeled "vague or indefinite."

20. Cubberley, *Public Education*, 374.

21. Eliot, "Undesirable and Desirable Uniformity," 271–300.

22. Cogswell, "Promotions," 346–48.

23. Ellwood P. Cubberley, *Public School Administration*, 306.

24. Hartwell, "The Grading and Promotion of Pupils," 296; replies were received from half the group surveyed. Responses came from 325 superintendents; 513 principals; 20 teachers; 25 college presidents and professors; 66 normal school presidents, teachers, and supervisors of training schools; and 21 others including members of boards of education. Responses came from all 48 states and territories, Puerto Rico, Manila, and Canada. After eliminating "vague replies," 965 answers were left. Because the survey does not indicate any more precisely how the sample was selected, it is difficult to know how representative are the data.

25. For other discussions of pupil classification during this period, see: Dutton and Snedden, "Grading and Promotion,"; H. S. Jones et al., "Report on City School Systems," 276–84; Holmes, *School Organization and the Individual Child*; Richman, "A Successful Experiment," 23–29; Shearer, *The Grading of Schools*; and Van Sickle, "Plan of the North-Side Schools of Denver," 341–46.

26. Adapted from Cubberley, *Public Education*, 401.

27. Ibid., 460.

28. Grant and Lind, *Digest*, 44; Committee of Ten, *Report*, 6; for discussions of the "cardinal principles," see Krug, *The Shaping of the High School, 1880–1920*, Sizer, *Secondary Schools*, and Karier, *Man, Society, and Education*, 69–79.

29. Grant and Lind, *Digest*, 44; Kingsley, *Cardinal Principles of Secondary Education*, 7, 11.

30. Dickson, "Scientific Methods," 225.

31. Source: *Report of the Superintendent of Schools, Oakland, California, 1917–18* (Oakland: Tribune Publishing, 1919), 234–35. Note that the population figures for Oakland in 1910 include an annexation the previous year.

32. On March 24, 1903, the California legislature approved "an act to enforce the educational rights of children and providing penalties for violation of the Act." Shortly thereafter the Oakland Board of Education hired a truant officer who subsequently made some 775 visits to schools and families to investigate 200 cases of truancy in the following school year. *Annual Report of the Public Schools of the City of Oakland, 1903–04* (Oakland: Oakland Enquirer, 1904), 12, 16.

33. Ibid., 33, 239.

34. Ibid., 56; *Annual Report of the Public Schools of Oakland, California, 1911–12* (Oakland: Oakland Enquirer, 1912), 6.

35. Hicks, "Report of the Child Study Laboratory," 68, 70, 71.

36. Sears, *Spelling Efficiency*; Cubberley, *Report of the Public School System of Oakland*, 3.

37. Fred M. Hunter, "A School System for All of the Children of All the People," *Report of the Superintendent of Schools, Oakland, California, 1917–18* (Oakland: Tribune Publishing, 1919), 33.

38. Dickson, "Mental Testing," 1917; Dickson, "Mental Testing," 1919, 5.

39. Cox, "Survey of Nationalities," 34–38. Note that the percentages in the tables reported by Cox did not add to one hundred.

40. Hunter, *Report, 1917–18*, 181.

41. Ibid., 173.

42. Dickson, "Mental Testing," 1919, 99.

43. Hunter, *Report, 1917–18*, 226.

44. Dickson, "Mental Testing," 1919, 72, 74, 76, 79, 84, 86.

45. Ibid., 94, 95.

46. For other early experimental testing, see for example: Goddard, "Two Thousand Children," 870–78; Haggerty, "Specific Uses of Measurement," 25–40; Pintner, "Mental Survey," 597–600; Starch, "Standard Tests," 143–48; Whipple, "The Use of Mental Tests," 149–160; Woody, "Tests and Measures," 61–66.

3. *The Use of Intelligence Tests in World War I*

1. Yerkes, "Psychology in Relation to the War," 86; for biographical sketches of Yerkes, see: Carmichael, "Yerkes," 1–7; Elliott, "Yerkes," 487–94; and Yerkes "Autobiography," 381–89. For a recent assessment of Yerkes's role, see Reed, "Yerkes and the Mental Testing Movement," 75–94.

2. Yerkes, "Psychology in Relation to the War," 91, 89; for an excellent analysis of the war experiment, see Kevles, "Testing the Army's Intelligence," 565–81; another more recent account can be found in Von Mayrhauser, "The Manager, the Medic, and the Mediator," 128–57.

3. Terman, "Trails," 324.

4. Terman, "Methods of Examining," 299; Terman, "The Use of Intelligence Tests in the Army," 177.

5. Lewis M. Terman to O. S. Reimbold, 18 May 1920, Lewis M. Terman Papers, Stanford University Library, Stanford, California.

6. Terman, "Tests of General Intelligence," 160.

7. Yerkes and Yoakum, *Army Mental Tests*, 16; the eight subtests in the army Alpha included commands, arithmetic, practical judgment, synonym-antonym, disarranged sentences, number series completion, analogies, and general information; the army Beta subtests included maze, cube analysis, x-o series, digit-symbol, number checking, pictorial completion, and geometric construction.

8. Yerkes, "History and Organization of Psychological Examining," 111, 97.

9. Ibid., 97; Kevles, "Testing the Army's Intelligence," 574–75.

10. Newton D. Baker quoted in Bell, "Editorial," 1918, 400–401.

11. Yerkes and Yoachum, *Army Mental Tests*, 49; Yerkes, "History and Organization of Psychological Examining," 109.

12. Boring, "Measurement of Intelligence in the United States Army," 697.

13. Terman, "Tests of General Intelligence," 163.

14. Bledstein, *The Culture of Professionalism*, 87. Also see Camfield, "Professionalization," and O'Donnell, *Behaviorism*.

15. Terman, "Trails," 325–26.

16. The other members of the committee were also leaders in the psychological community. James R. Angell was head of the Department of Psychology at the University of Chicago before the war, became acting president in 1918–1919, and assumed the presidency of Yale after the war. John F. Shepard was associate professor of psychology at Michigan. Edward K. Strong was professor of psychology at George Peabody Teachers College and after the war would head the Bureau of Educational Research at Carnegie Institute of Technology before becoming professor of psychology at Johns Hopkins. Raymond Dodge would become professor of psychology at Yale after the war.

17. Harold C. Bingham would teach at Wesleyan and Yale after the war. Melvin E. Haggerty was professor of educational psychology at the University of Minnesota. Clarence S. Yoakum would author *Army Mental Tests* with Yerkes and direct a vocational survey at Carnegie Institute of Technology after the war.

18. To establish the background for those in the Psychological Division, three principal sources were consulted: Bowman and Ryan, eds., *Who's Who in Education; Who's Who and Why in After-War Education;* and Wolfle, ed., *American Psychological Association Directory, 1948.* I am indebted to Daniel P. Resnick for suggesting this line of research to me and to Michael Vandervelden for assisting in the bibliographic work.

19. "Report of the Committee on the Qualification of Psychological Examiners and Other Psychological Experts," Terman Papers.

20. "Proposed Constitution and By-Laws of the American Association of Clinical Psychologists," Terman Papers.

21. Claxton, "Army Psychologists for City Public School Work," 204; Bell, "Editorial," 1919, 55.

22. Lewis M. Terman and Robert M. Yerkes to Abraham Flexner, 23 January 1919, Terman Papers.

23. Robert M. Yerkes to Abraham Flexner, 17 January 1917, Terman Papers.

24. Lewis M. Terman to Abraham Flexner, 9 January 1917, Terman Papers.

25. Robert M. Yerkes to Lewis M. Terman, 12 February 1917, Terman Papers.

26. Ibid.

27. Lewis M. Terman to Abraham Flexner, 22 March 1917; Lewis M. Terman to

Robert M. Yerkes, 29 March 1917; Abraham Flexner to Lewis M. Terman, April 1917, Terman Papers.

28. Elementary School Intelligence Examination Board Minutes, Meeting of 28 and 29 March 1919, Terman Papers.

29. Ibid., 45.

30. Ibid.; Ibid., Minutes of Meeting of 17 and 18 October 1919, 68; Elementary School Intelligence Examination Board, "Report to the National Research Council," 17 March 1921, 29, Terman Papers.

31. "Report to the National Research Council," 24, 25, Terman Papers.

4. "A Mental Test for Every Child"

1. U.S. Bureau of the Census, *Statistical History*, Series H., no. 418, 424.

2. Odell, "Who Have Contributed Most?" 751–54; Odell's study of leadership provides quantitative evidence of Terman's relative importance in the measurement movement. He tabulated the frequency of reference to individuals on twenty issues in a selected list of publications between 1926 and 1929. Terman ranked first on the number of sources containing a reference to his work and third on frequency of citation, behind Giles Ruch of Stanford and Edward L. Thorndike. A weighted average for the two measures placed Terman and Thorndike at the top of the list.

3. Heberle and Gusfield, "Social Movements."

4. Terman, "The Use of Intelligence Tests," 20; Terman, *Intelligence;* Terman, ed., *School Reorganization*.

5. Terman, *Intelligence*, 111, 115; Terman may have overestimated the extent of the problem, for Leonard Ayres concluded about the same time that retardation had diminished by 50 percent.

6. Ibid., 116.

7. Ibid., 25, 53, 117, 56; note that the psychologists in the twenties used the term "race" to describe what today is meant by "ethnicity."

8. Ibid., xi.

9. Terman, ed., *School Reorganization*, 7.

10. Ibid., 22, 291, 24.

11. Ibid., 3, 17; this reference to "homogeneous grouping" is one of the first uses of the term, which later became widespread in education.

12. Ibid., 18, 19, 20.

13. Ibid., 21; Terman, "Conservation," 364.

14. Terman, *Intelligence*, 286; Terman, "The Use of Intelligence Tests," 31; Terman, "Conservation," 359.

15. Terman et al., "Intelligence Symposium," 128; Terman, *Intelligence*, 11.

16. Terman, *Intelligence*, 10.

17. "Report to the National Research Council," 20, Terman Papers.

18. Terman and Whitmore, "Age and Grade Norms," 128; see also Terman and Whitmore, "Tentative Age and Grade Norms for the National Intelligence Scale," Memorandum for Education 57a, Stanford University, Terman Papers.

19. Robert M. Yerkes to Lewis M. Terman, 20 May 1920 and 29 July 1920, Terman Papers.

20. Lewis M. Terman et al., *National Intelligence Tests, Manual* (Yonkers-on-Hudson, N.Y.: World Book, 1923), 3–4.

21. The subtests for the Terman Group Test included: information, best answers, word meaning, logical selection, arithmetic, sentence meaning, analogies, mixed sentences, classification, and number series.

22. Caspar W. Hodgson to Lewis M. Terman, 13 January 1920; Ernest Hesse to Lewis M. Terman, 28 June 1920; Caspar W. Hodgson to Lewis M. Terman, November 1920, Terman Papers.

23. Caspar W. Hodgson to Lewis M. Terman, 15 October 1923; O. S. Reimbold to Lewis M. Terman, 1 February 1928, Terman Papers.

24. The ten separate parts of the Stanford Achievement Test battery included: geography, hygiene and elementary science; language and literature; history and civics; music and art; advanced arithmetic—reasoning; advanced arithmetic—computation; advanced reading and language; word meaning; sentence meaning; and language usage.

25. Lewis M. Terman to Caspar W. Hodgson, 15 October 1923; A. E. Wiggam, interview with Lewis M. Terman, 1925, Terman Papers.

26. Lewis M. Terman, "Mental and Physical Traits of a Thousand Gifted Children," in Terman, ed., *Genetic Studies*, 1:8.

27. Lewis M. Terman, "Survey of Gifted Children in California," 30 December 1921, Terman Papers; *Genetic Studies*, 1:9.

28. Terman, "California's Gifted Children Tested by Science," *San Francisco Examiner*, 12 April 1925; Terman, "Bright Children Upset Notions About 'Genius,' " *New York Times*, 19 July 1925.

29. Terman, *Genetic Studies*, 1:634, 639.

30. Terman, "Trails," 325; Terman noted in his autobiography that "among the war associations which meant most to me were those with Yerkes, Thorndike, Whipple, Scott, Woodworth, Kelley, Bingham, Yoakum, Mabel Fernald, Bridges, Boring, Dodge, Goddard, Strong, Wells, and May."

31. Edwin G. Boring, "Analysis of Nominations and Elections in the American Psychological Association in 1920–22," 3, Terman Papers; Boring, "Confidential Memo," 31 January 1924, Terman Papers.

32. Seagoe, *Terman*, 111.

33. Lewis M. Terman to O. S. Reimbold, 7 November 1921, Terman Papers.

34. Terman's initial inquiry went to: Grace Fernald, University of California; E. L. Thorndike, Rudolph Pintner, W. A. McCall, Leta Hollingsworth, Arthur Gates, Columbia; Frank Freeman, Chicago; Walter F. Dearborn and Daniel Starch, Harvard; W. S. Monroe, Illinois; Bird T. Baldwin, Iowa; Guy M. Whipple, Clifford Woody, Michigan; M. E. Haggerty, Minnesota; V. A. Henmon, Wisconsin; Arnold Gesell, Yale; Virgil Dickson, Oakland Public Schools; Raymond Franzen, Department of Research, Des Moines, Iowa; Arthur S. Otis, World Book Co.; A. H. Sutherland, Los Angeles Public Schools; and F. L. Wells, Boston Psychopathic Hospital.

35. Lewis M. Terman, "Memorandum for Mr. Ferguson," World Book Co., 20 April 1923, Terman Papers.

36. The Measurement and Adjustment Series issued the following works: Ben D. Wood, *Measurement in Higher Education*, 1923; Louise Stedman, *Education of Gifted Children*, 1924; Arthur S. Otis, *Statistical Method in Educational Measurement*, 1925; Joseph Peterson, *Early Conceptions and Tests of Intelligence*, 1925; Norman Fenton, *Self-Direction and Adjustment*, 1926; Florence Goodenough, *Measurement of Intelligence by Drawings*, 1926; Truman L. Kelley, *Interpretation of Educational Measurements*, 1927; Giles M. Ruch and George D. Stoddard, *Tests and Measurements in High School Instruction*, 1927; Clark L. Hull, *Aptitude Testing*, 1928.

37. Odell, "Who Have Contributed Most"; the five were Giles M. Ruch, Arthur S. Otis, Truman L. Kelley, Ben D. Wood, and Clifford Woody.

38. For a discussion of Cattell's role, see Sokal, "The Origins of the Psychological Corporation," 54–67. The founding members of the Psychological Corporation were: James R. Angell, President of Yale; W. V. Bingham, Carnegie Institute of Technology; Cattell; Raymond Dodge, Wesleyan University; S. I. Franz, Government Hospital for the Insane; G. Stanley Hall, Clark; H. L. Hollingsworth, Barnard; Charles H. Judd, Chicago; William McDougall, Harvard; W. B. Pillsbury, Michigan; Walter Dill Scott, Northwestern; Terman; Thorndike; E. B. Titchener, Cornell; Howard Warren, Princeton; Margaret Washburn, Vassar; J. B. Watson, J. Walter Thompson Co.; R. S. Woodworth, Columbia; and Robert Yerkes.

39. James McKeen Cattell, "Charter Announcement," Psychological Corporation, 1921, Terman Papers.

40. Terman, "The Status of Applied Psychology," 3; Terman, "Mental Test," 93–117.

41. Terman, "Mental Test," 100, 96, 108.

5. The Use of Intelligence Tests in Schools

1. Dickson, Mental Tests, xiii.

2. Dickson, "First-Grade Children," 480; Dickson, "Mental Tests in Guidance," 609.

3. Dickson, "First-Grade Children," 475, 476.

4. Ibid., 475.

5. Ibid., 476, 479.

6. Dickson, "Mental Tests in Guidance," 602.

7. Dickson and Norton, "Otis Group Intelligence Scale," 110.

8. Ibid., 106, 114–15.

9. Ibid., 115; Dickson, "Mental Tests in Guidance," 608.

10. Dickson, "The Gifted Child," 300; Dickson, "Mental Tests in Guidance," 610.

11. Dickson, "Classification of School Children," 32–34; see also Dickson, "The Treatment of Gifted Children," 26–28.

12. Dickson, Mental Tests, 215, 216–17.

13. Hunter, "The Principal and the Educational Expert," 372; Hunter, Superintendent's Bulletin, 12.

14. Hunter, Superintendent's Bulletin, 18.

15. Terman, Intelligence; Terman et al., "Trial of Mental and Pedagogical Tests," 17–29; Young, Mental Differences, 3, 94.

16. Young, Mental Differences, 18.

17. Ibid., 63–64.

18. Ibid., 66, 67, 97.

19. Ibid., 66.

20. Bachrodt, Annual Report, 18.

21. Ibid., 21.

22. Ibid., 31, 22.

23. Ibid., 32, 112, 113, 120–21, 126.

24. Palo Alto High School, Board Meeting, Minutes, 4 December 1920, 2; "Palo Alto High School Graduates," Board Meeting, Minutes, 13 December 1915, Archives, Palo Alto Unified School District, Palo Alto, California.

25. Walter H. Nichols, "School Reorganization Within the Boundaries of the Palo Alto Union High School District," 6 January 1918, 6, 13–14, Archives, Palo Alto Unified School District, Palo Alto, California.

26. Proctor, "The Use of Intelligence Tests," 474, 506.

27. Ibid., 507.

28. Proctor, "Psychological Tests and Probable School Success," 270.

29. Proctor, "The Use of Psychological Tests," 538, 540.

30. Ibid., 535, 546.

31. Proctor, *Educational and Vocational Guidance*, 8, 17.

6. Rising Dissent

1. J. E. Wallace Wallin, *Experimental Studies of Mental Defectives*, Baltimore: Warwick & York, 1912, 1–2.

2. Terman et al., "Intelligence Symposium," 123–44, 198–216, 271–75. Participants included: E. L. Thorndike, L. M. Terman, F. N. Freeman, S. S. Colvin, R. Pinter, B. Ruml, S. L. Pressey, J. Peterson, L. L. Thurstone, W. F. Dearborn, M. E. Haggerty, and B. R. Buckingham.

3. The studies of racial and ethnic differences in intelligence test performance are extensive. See for example: Schwegler and Winn, "A Comparative Study," 838–47; Rudolph Pintner and Ruth Keller, "Intelligence Tests of Foreign Children," *Journal of Educational Psychology* 13 (Apr. 1922): 214–22; Sheldon, "The Intelligence of Mexican Children," 139–42; and Bere, *Children of Foreign Parentage*.

4. Terman et al., "Intelligence Symposium," 128.

5. Beardsley Ruml, quoted in Terman et al., "Intelligence Symposium," 143; Terman and Kelley, "Dr. Ruml's Criticism," 462–63.

6. William C. Bagley, "Educational Determinism; or Democracy and the I.Q.," *School and Society* 15 (Apr. 1922): 373. Earlier that year he gave the same address to the Society of College Teachers of Education in Chicago, a talk which was reprinted in his book *Determinism in Education*.

7. Terman, "The Psychological Determinist," 3, 5.

8. Bagley, "Professor Terman's Determinism," 376, 377, 384–85.

9. Kelley, "Again: Educational Determinism," 10, 11, 18.

10. Almack, Bursch, and DeVoss, "Democracy, Determinism, and the I.Q.," 292–93, 294.

11. Terman, "The Possibilities and Limitations of Training," 335, 336, 340.

12. Ibid., 340.

13. Terman, Introduction to "Nature and Nurture," 1–7.

14. Ibid., 6; Terman, "Influence of Nature and Nurture," 370.

15. Terman, "The Ultimate Influence of Standard Tests," 57, 59. The 1928 conference did not mark the end of Terman's involvement in the test controversy. In 1940, for example, he served as critic in a symposium on "Intelligence in a Changing Universe," *School and Society* 51 (Apr. 1940): 465–70. In 1932 he identified a list of "credos" in his autobiography, "Trails to Psychology," that included the observation that "the major differences between children of high and low IQ, and the major differences in the intelligence test scores of certain races, as Negroes and whites, will never be fully accounted for on the environmental hypothesis." It is significant that in his personal copy of "Trails" Terman noted in the margin in 1951, "I am less sure of this now" and later "And still less sure in 1955!" Despite these concessions late in his life, Terman

continued to be identified with a strong hereditarian position throughout his years in the profession.

16. For a discussion of nativism, see Higham, *Strangers in the Land.*

17. Lippmann, "Future," 10.

18. Lippmann, "Mental Age," 213–14; Lippman, "The Mystery of the 'A' Men," 248.

19. Lippmann, "Tests of Hereditary Intelligence," 330.

20. Lippmann, "The Reliability of Intelligence Tests," 276.

21. Lippmann, "Mental Age," 215; Lippmann, "Future," 10, 9–10.

22. Terman, "The Great Conspiracy," 10, 13.

23. Caspar W. Hodgson to Lewis M. Terman, 1 December 1922; William C. Ferguson to Lewis M. Terman, 22 December 1922; Lewis M. Terman to Caspar W. Hodgson, 7 December 1922, Terman Papers.

24. Arthur S. Otis to Lewis M. Terman, 4 January 1923; Lewis M. Terman to Arthur S. Otis, 11 January 1923; Lewis M. Terman to James McKeen Cattell, 16 January 1923, Terman Papers.

25. Lippmann, "Mr. Burt and the Intelligence Tests," 263.

26. M. E. Haggerty, "Recent Developments in Measuring Human Capacities," *Journal of Educational Research* 3 (Apr. 1921): 241.

27. M. R. Trabue, "Some Pitfalls in the Administrative Use of Intelligence Tests," *Journal of Educational Research* 9 (June 1922): 1, 2, 4, 5, 9, 11.

28. Hines, "Measuring Intelligence," 35; Otis, "Group Intelligence Tests, 55–67; Graves, "The Use and Abuse of Intelligence Testing," 18.

29. Monroe, *Educational Tests and Measurements*, 1924, 438, 439, 451. The revision was assisted by James DeVoss of San Jose, a former Terman student, which may help to explain the attention given to the proposal.

30. Freeman, "Sorting the Students," 169, 170.

31. Lyon, "The Submerged Tenth," 5.

32. Stenquist, "The Case for the Low I.Q.," 252.

33. Davis, "Some Problems Arising," 2–3, 13.

34. Ibid., 14, 15.

35. Reigner, "The Measurement Movement," 574–75.

36. Hargreaves, "Guidance: A Point of View," 10; Orr, "A Principal's Observations," 50.

37. Billet, "Another Principal's Views," 47.

38. Whipple, "The Intelligence Testing Program," 561, 562; Stark, "Scientific Mind," 80.

39. Counts, *School and Society in Chicago;* quoted in Counts, 185, 187.

40. Cf. Block and Dworkin, eds., *The IQ Controversy,* for a reprinting of the entire exchange between Terman and Lippmann, as well as Marks, "Testers," and Cronbach, "Five Decades"; see also Nicholas Pastore, "The Army Intelligence Tests," 316–27.

7. *National Patterns in the Use of Tests*

1. University of Illinois, Bureau of Educational Research, *Bulletin* (Urbana, Ill.: University of Illinois, 1920): no. 4, Holley, "Mental Tests for School Use"; no. 5, Monroe, "Report of Educational Tests for 1919–20"; no. 12, Odell, "The Use of Intelligence Tests"; no. 16, Charles W. Odell, "Conservation of Intelligence"; no. 42,

Monroe, "Ten Years of Educational Research"; and no. 43, Odell, "A Selected Annotated Bibliography."

2. U.S. Department of the Interior, Bureau of Education, *Bulletin* (Washington,
D.C.: Government Printing Office, 1913): no. 13, Strayer, "Report on Standards and
Tests"; no. 55, Doherty and MacLatchy, "Bibliography of Education."

3. Hildreth, *A Bibliography of Mental Tests*. Regarding the criteria for test selection,
Hildreth noted:

Tests standardized with reference to method of administration in the sense that they admit of
repetition by other examiners with other subjects, that were objective in character wholly or in part,
that were intended for repeated use in the measurement of mental characteristics primarily for
practical purposes or service functions, and tests that were generally available either from publishers
or tests distributors, or that were described adequately in professional journals were included, in
contrast to materials that were almost wholly subjective in character, were designed solely for use in
an isolated experiment, as for example, in the study of transfer of training, or mental fatigue, were
not standardized as to method of administration and were not available in satisfactory published
form. (11)

In 1933–1934 Oscar Buros at Rutgers began publishing a yearly listing of educational,
psychological, and personality tests which would eventually become the *Mental Measurements Yearbook*.

4. Although Hildreth used the term "mental test" to describe all types of ability,
aptitude, and achievement tests, in this and the following table, it is used to indicate
ability tests that were used for large-scale classification of schoolchildren; Hildreth also
occasionally listed a test under two categories. When this occurred, tabulation was made
for only the primary citation.

5. In developing this chart, the country of origin was estimated by noting the place
of publication, language, and professional journals cited as references. The headings for
the countries include places as follows:

Great Britain—includes several tests from other Commonwealth countries; Germany
—includes all references in German; Other European—includes Russia, Poland, Czech-
oslovakia, Sweden, Norway, the Netherlands, Italy, and Spanish-speaking countries;
Other—includes Japan, China, and Egypt.

6. The tests included in the previous two tables are represented here as the first four
items in category one. The category of miscellaneous indicates tests for which information is lacking and items identified too late for inclusion.

7. Other key test developers included: R. Pintner, W. A. McCall, W. F. Dearborn,
F. Kuhlman, F. N. Freeman, T. H. Haines, J. Wallin, S. D. Porteus, E. B. Huey,
H. H. Goddard, T. Baldwin, N. Bayley, A. I. Gates, A. Gesell, F. Goodenough,
G. Hildreth, R. Stutsman, and H. T. Woolley.

8. According to Hildreth, major test publishers were: World Book Co.; C. H. Stoelting Co.; Public School Publishing Co.; Warwick and York; Teachers College, Columbia
University; Educational Test Bureau, Minneapolis; Houghton Mifflin; Lippincott; Fol-
lett; Macmillan; and Dutton.

9. Monroe, "Ten Years of Educational Research."

10. The outpouring of textbooks on measurement can be seen in this partial listing:
Dearborn, *Intelligence Tests: Their Significance for School and Society* (1928): Freeman, *Mental
Tests: Their History, Principles, and Applications* (1926); Hines, *A Guide to Educational
Measurements* (1923); Kelley, *Interpretation of Educational Measurements* (1927); McCall,
How to Measure in Education (1922) and *How to Classify Pupils* (1928); Monroe, *An Introduc-*

tion to the Theory of Educational Measurements (1923); Pintner, *Intelligence Testing: Methods and Results* (1923); Pressey, *Introduction to the Use of Standardized Tests* (1922); Whipple, *Problems in Mental Testing* (1925); Ruch and Stoddard, Tests and Measurements in High School Instruction (1927); Thorndike, *Measurement of Intelligence* (1927).

11. Ayer, "Present Status of Promotional Plans," 37–39.

12. The programs entailed in the various "plans" are described below: Batavia Plan, decrease in recitation work and more individual assistance; North Denver Plan, special help for bright pupils and rapid progress; Pueblo Plan, individualized instruction; Elizabeth Plan, promotions regardless of time of year; Cambridge Plan, two parallel courses of study; Santa Barbara Plan, differentiated courses, parallel for first six grades, promotion by subject in last two; Platoon system, two groups of equal number classes, different coursework; opportunity classes, for bright pupils and rapid progress.

13. Ayer, "Present Status of Promotional Plans," 39.

14. Deffenbaugh, "Uses of Intelligence Tests."

15. Hebb, "Classification of Elementary School Pupils," 52, 148.

16. "Cities Reporting the Use of Homogeneous Grouping."

17. Henry J. Otto, "Administrative Practices Followed in the Organization of Elementary Schools," *American School Board Journal* 83 (Sept. 1931): 35.

18. Whipple, ed., "Intelligence Tests and Their Use," vii.

19. See, for example, Woolley, "The Use of Intelligence Tests," 257–60, and Alexander, "Presenting Educational Measurements," 345.

20. Layton, "The Group Intelligence Testing Program," 123–30.

21. Corson, "Classification of Pupils," 87; Paul C. Stetson, "Homogeneous Grouping," 353; Tildsley, "Possibilities of Intelligence Tests," 54.

22. Campbell, "Intelligence Tests," 46; Power, "The Effects of Grouping," 249; Feingold, "The Sectioning of High-School Classes."

23. Myers, "Teachers vs. Mental Tests," 300–303; Bliss, "How Much Mental Ability?" 40; Bell, "Educational Measurements and the Teacher," 289–90.

24. Bell, "Educational Measurements and the Classroom Teacher," 112; Buckingham and Monroe, "A Testing Program," 521.

25. Brooks, "Putting Standardized Tests to Practical Use," 392–97; Brooks, *Improving Schools by Standardized Tests*, 124, 125–26, 128.

26. Hobart Corning, *After Testing—What?* 186, 187; Madsen, "Participation in Testing Programs," 117.

27. Davis, "Classification by Intelligence Tests," 211; Myers, "Standard Tests in Rural Schools," 257; Brooks, "Some Uses for Intelligence Tests," 219; Price, "A Plan of Classifying Pupils," 341–48.

28. Buckingham, "The School as a Selective Agency," 139; Allen, "Some Neglected Problems," 353.

Conclusion

1. For a fascinating and provocative discussion of the way Americans viewed intelligence at an earlier time, see Calhoun, *The Intelligence of a People*.

2. For a good summary of legal and political challenges to testing and tracking see Jensen, *Bias in Mental Testing;* more detailed accounts of the *Hobson v. Hansen* case can be found in: "Recent Developments—*Hobson v. Hansen*," 1249–68; "Hobson v. Hansen: Judicial Supervision," 1511–27; Cohen, "Jurists and Educators," 233–50.

3. See for example: Jencks, "What Color is I.Q.?" 31–41; Lewontin, "Race and Intelligence," 1–17; Shockley, "Heredity, Environment, Race and I.Q." 297–312; and Shockley, "Negro I.Q. and Heredity," 127–28.

4. See, for instance: Rather, "The I.Q. Myth," and Edward B. Fiske, "Controversy Over Testing Flairs Again," *New York Times*, 1 May 1977, sec. 12, 1.

Appendix

1. Cronbach, *Essentials of Psychological Testing*, 26. Portions of the first two sections of the appendix rely upon Cronbach. Any errors of fact or interpretation, however, are entirely mine.

2. Terman, *Measurement*, 45.

3. Cronbach, *Essentials of Psychological Testing*, 109.

4. Ibid., 99.

Selected Bibliography

Like all historical studies this work has been defined by the nature of the evidence. Terman's role in the testing movement has been evaluated from several angles. His published works—which include ten books or major studies and several hundred articles—provided the central avenue for understanding his position in the movement. His unpublished papers in the Stanford Archives offered additional insight into the man and the tests; especially helpful was the professional correspondence that he carried on with other members of the testing community, philanthropic foundation officials, and publishers. Additional insight into Terman came from a variety of secondary interpretations written by both psychologists and historians.

The membership and links in the testing network were established through several sources. Numerous educational and professional journals—many founded during the period—provided a continual record of the development of testing and ability grouping. Addresses and proceedings of such national organizations as the National Education Association contained reports of municipal and city research bureaus. The bulletins of university bureaus of research also helped sketch the developing movement. Several important secondary studies of the network were also useful.

This study has been informed by the work of many scholars. The progressive period has been fertile ground for educational historians, and several key works describe the metamorphosis of the schools: David Tyack's *The One Best System*, Lawrence Cremin's *The Transfor-*

mation of the School, and Raymond Callahan's *Education and the Cult of Efficiency*. The reports of the U.S. Bureau of Education, especially those presenting the results of surveys, offered valuable primary sources on school practices. On the local level, the perspective of schools and the adoption of tests was documented through various city school publications, ranging from superintendents' reports to school board minutes.

No single source was adequate to describe the values of the progressive period, especially since historians have disagreed so vigorously about the true nature of the term "progressive." In the elusive search to find the core values of the time, however, two works were particularly valuable: Robert Wiebe's *The Search for Order* and David Kennedy's *Progressivism: The Critical Issues*.

Adler, Martha. "Mental Tests Used as a Basis for the Classification of School Children." *Journal of Educational Psychology* 5 (Jan. 1914): 22–28.

Alexander, Carter. "Presenting Educational Measurements so as to Influence the Public Favorably." *Journal of Educational Research* 3 (May 1921): 345.

Allen, Richard D. "Some Neglected Problems in Classifying High-School Pupils." *Journal of Educational Research* 11 (May 1925): 351–58.

——. "Use of Intelligence Tests in Educational Administration in the Providence Schools." *School and Society* 18 (Sept. 1923): 335–39.

Almack, John C., Bursch, James F., and DeVoss, James C. "Democracy, Determinism, and the I.Q." *School and Society* 18 (Sept. 1923): 292–95.

Ashbaugh, Ernest J. "Cooperative Work From a University Center." *Seventeenth Yearbook of the National Society for the Study of Education*, pt. 2, 57–70. Bloomington, Ill.: Public School Publishing, 1918.

——. "Homogeneous or Non-homogeneous Grouping." *Journal of Educational Research* 9 (Mar. 1924): 241–45.

Ayer, Fred C. "The Present Status of Promotional Plans in City Schools." *American School Board Journal* 66 (Apr. 1923): 37–39.

Ayres, Leonard P. "The Binet-Simon Measuring Scale for Intelligence: Some Criticisms and Suggestions." *Psychological Clinic* 5 (1911): 187–96.

——. "History and Present Status of Educational Measurements." *Seventeenth Yearbook of the National Society for the Study of Education*, pt. 2, 9–15. Bloomington, Ill.: Public School Publishing, 1918.

——. *Laggards in Our Schools: A Study of Retardation and Elimination in City School Systems*. New York: Charities Publication Committee, 1909.

Bachrodt, Walter L. *Annual Report of the Superintendent of Schools, 1921–22*. San Jose, Calif., 1922.

Bagley, William C. *Determinism in Education*. Baltimore: Warwick and York, 1925.

———. "Professor Terman's Determinism." *Journal of Educational Research* 6 (Dec. 1922): 376–85.

Ballou, Frank W. "General Organization of Measurement Work in City School Systems." *Seventeenth Yearbook of the National Society for the Study of Education*, pt. 2, 41–50. Bloomington, Ill.: Public School Publishing, 1918.

———. "Work of the Department of Educational Investigation and Measurement, Boston, Massachusetts." *Fifteenth Yearbook of the National Society for the Study of Education*, pt. 1, 61–68. Bloomington, Ill.: Public School Publishing, 1916.

Baritz, Loren. *The Servants of Power*. New York: John Wiley, 1965.

Barnard, Henry P. "Gradation of Public Schools, with Special Reference to Cities and Large Villages." *American Journal of Education* 2 (Dec. 1856): 455–64.

Barrows, Albert L. "A History of the National Research Council, 1919–1933." *National Research Council Reprint and Circular Services*, no. 106, 1933.

Beeson, M. F. "Certification of Teachers by Means of Mental and Standard Educational Tests." *Educational Administration and Supervision* 6 (1920): 471–75.

Bell, J. Carleton. "Editorial." *Journal of Educational Psychology* 9 (Sept. 1918): 400–401.

———. "Editorial." *Journal of Educational Psychology* 19 (Jan. 1919): 54–55.

———. "Educational Measurements and the Classroom Teacher." *Journal of Educational Psychology* 19 (Feb. 1919): 111–13.

———. "Educational Measurements and the Teacher." *Journal of Educational Psychology* 11 (May 1920): 289–90.

Bere, May. *A Comparative Study of the Mental Capacity of Children of Foreign Parentage*. Contributions to Education, no. 154. New York: Teachers College, Columbia University, 1924.

Berry, Charles S. "The Classification by Tests of Intelligence of Ten Thousand First-Grade Pupils." *Journal of Educational Research* 6 (Oct. 1922): 185–203.

Billet, Roy O. *The Administration and Supervision of Homogeneous Grouping*. Columbus, Ohio: Ohio State Univ. Press, 1932.

———. "Another Principal's Views on Intelligence Tests." *American School Board Journal* 74 (Feb. 1927): 47.

Binet, Alfred, and Henri, Victor. "On the Psychology of Individual Differences, 1895." In *A Source Book in the History of Psychology*, edited by Richard J. Herrnstein and Edwin G. Boring, 428–33. Cambridge, Mass.: Harvard Univ. Press, 1966.

Blau, Louis B. *A Special Study on the Incidence of Retardation*. Contributions to Education, no. 40. New York: Teachers College, Columbia University, 1911.

Bledstein, Burton. *The Culture of Professionalism*. New York: Norton, 1976.

Bliss, W. B. "How Much Mental Ability Does a Teacher Need?" *Journal of Educational Research* 6 (June 1922): 33–41.

Block, N. J., and Dworkin, Gerald, eds. *The IQ Controversy*. New York: Random House, 1976.

Boring, Edwin G. *A History of Experimental Psychology*. 2d ed. New York: Appleton-Century-Crofts, 1950.

——. "Lewis Madison Terman, 1877–1956." National Academy of Sciences. *Biographical Memoirs*, vol. 33. New York: Columbia Univ. Press, 1959.

——. "Measurement of Intelligence in the United States Army." In *Psychological Examining in the United States Army*, edited by Robert M. Yerkes, vol. 15, pt. 3, 553–875. National Academy of Sciences. Washington, D.C.: Government Printing Office, 1922.

Bowles, Samuel. "Unequal Education and the Reproduction of Social Division of Labor." *Review of Radical Political Economics* 3 (Fall/Winter 1971): 1–30.

Bowles, Samuel, and Gintis, Herbert. *Schooling in Capitalist America*. New York: Basic Books, 1976.

Bowman, George E., and Ryan, Nellie C., eds. *Who's Who in Education*. Greeley, Colo.: Tribune-Republican Publishing, 1927.

Boykin, J. C. "Class Intervals in City Public Schools." *Report of the United States Commissioner of Education*, vol. 2, 1891. 981–1009.

Breed, F. S. *Classroom Organization and Management*. Yonkers-on-Hudson, N.Y.: World Book, 1933.

Breed, F. S., and Breslich, E. R. "Intelligence Tests and the Classification of Pupils." *School Review* 30 (Jan. 1922): 51–66.

Brewer, John M. *History of Vocational Guidance*. New York: Harper, 1942.

——. *Mental Measurement in Educational and Vocational Guidance*. Cambridge, Mass.: Harvard Univ. Press, 1924.

Brigham, Carl C. *A Study of American Intelligence*. Princeton, N.J.: Princeton Univ. Press, 1923.

"Bright Children Upset Notions About Genius." *New York Times*, 19 July 1925, sec. 8, 14.

Brim, Orville. *American Beliefs and Attitudes About Intelligence*. New York: Russell Sage Foundation, 1969.

Brooks, Samuel S. "Getting Teachers to Feel the Need for Standardized Tests." *Journal of Educational Research* 2 (June 1920): 425–27.

——. *Improving Schools by Standardized Tests*. Boston: Houghton Mifflin, 1922.

——. "Putting Standardized Tests and Scales to Practical Use in the Rural Schools." *Journal of Educational Research* 1 (May 1920): 392–97.

——. "Some Uses for Intelligence Tests." *Journal of Educational Research* 5 (Mar. 1922): 217–38.

Bryner, Edna. "A Selected Bibliography of Certain Phases of Educational Measurement." *Seventeenth Yearbook of the National Society for the Study of Education*, pt. 2, 161–90. Bloomington, Ill.: Public School Publishing, 1918.

Buckingham, B. R. "The School as a Selective Agency." *Journal of Educational Research* 3 (Feb. 1921): 138–39.

Buckingham, B. R., and Monroe, W. S. "A Testing Program for Elementary

Schools." *Journal of Educational Research* 2 (Sept. 1920): 521–32.

Burnham, John C. "Psychology, Psychiatry, and the Progressive Movement." *American Quarterly* 12 (1960): 457–65.

Buros, Oscar K. "Educational, Psychological, and Personality Tests, of 1933, 1934, and 1935." Studies in Education, no. 9. *Rutgers University Bulletin*, vol. 13. 1936.

Butcher, H. J. *Human Intelligence: Its Nature and Assessment*. London: Methuen, 1968.

Caldwell, Otis W., and Courtis, Stuart A. *Then and Now in Education: 1845–1923*. Yonkers-on-Hudson, N.Y.: World Book, 1923.

Calhoun, Daniel, *The Intelligence of a People*. Princeton, N.J.: Princeton Univ. Press, 1973.

California, Palo Alto. Palo Alto Unified School District. Archives.

"California's Gifted Children Tested by Science." *San Francisco Examiner*, 12 April 1925.

Callahan, Raymond. *Education and the Cult of Efficiency*. Chicago: Univ. of Chicago Press, 1962.

Camfield, Thomas M. "The Professionalization of American Psychology, 1870–1917." *Journal of the History of the Behavioral Sciences* 9 (1973): 66–75.

Campbell, Cora. "Intelligence Tests as a Basis for Classification." National Education Association. *First Yearbook of the Department of Elementary School Principals*, 1922. 45–49.

Cardozo, F. L. "Tests and Measurements in Public Schools." *School and Society* 20 (1924): 797–98.

Carmichael, Leonard. "Robert M. Yerkes, 1876–1956." *Psychological Review* 64 (Jan. 1957): 1–7.

Carnoy, Martin. "Educational Reform and Social Control in the United States, 1830–1970." In *The Limits of Educational Reform*, edited by Martin Carnoy and Henry M. Levin, 115–155. New York: David McKay, 1976.

Caswell, Hollis L. *City School Surveys: An Interpretation and Appraisal*. Contributions to Education, no. 358. New York: Teachers College, Columbia University, 1929.

Cattell, J. McKeen. "Mental Tests and Measurements." *Mind* 15 (1890): 373–80.

——. "On Mental Tests." In *A Source Book in the History of Psychology*, edited by Richard Herrnstein and Edwin G. Boring, 423–27. Cambridge, Mass.: Harvard Univ. Press, 1966.

Chapman, Harold B. *Organized Research in Education*. Columbus, Ohio: Ohio State Univ. Press, 1927.

Church, Robert L. *Education in the United States*. New York: Free Press, 1976.

——. "Educational Psychology and Social Reform in the Progressive Era." *History of Education Quarterly* 11 (Winter 1971): 390–405.

"Cities Reporting the Use of Homogeneous Grouping and of the Winnetka Technique and the Dalton Plan." Department of the Interior, Bureau of

Education. City School Leaflet no. 22. Washington, D.C.: Government Printing Office, 1926.

Claxton, Philander P. "Army Psychologists for City Public School Work." *School and Society* 9 (Feb. 1919): 203–4.

Cogswell, Francis. "Promotions in the Grammar Schools of Cambridge, Mass." In "Classification and Promotion of Pupils." *Report of the United States Commissioner of Education*, vol. 1, 1898–99. 346–48.

Cohen, David K. "Jurists and Educators on Urban Schools: The Wright Decision and the Passow Report." *Teachers College Record* 70 (Dec. 1968): 233–50.

Committee of Ten. *Report.* New York: Published for the National Education Association by American Book, 1894.

Corning, Hobart M. *After Testing—What? The Practical Use of Test Results in One School System.* Chicago: Scott, Foresman, 1926.

Corson, David B. "Classification of Pupils." *Educational Administration and Supervision* 6 (1920): 86–91.

Counts, George. *School and Society in Chicago.* New York: Harcourt Brace, 1924.

———. *The Selective Character of American Secondary Education.* Chicago: Univ. of Chicago Press, 1922.

Courtis, S. A. "Training Courses in Educational Measurement." *Seventeenth Yearbook of the National Society for the Study of Education*, pt. 2, 133–38. Bloomington, Ill.: Public School Publishing, 1918.

Cox, E. Morris. "Report of Committee on Promotions and Rates of Progress." *Report of the Superintendent of Schools, Oakland, California, 1917–1918,* 77–79. Oakland, Calif.: Tribune Publishing, 1919.

———. "Survey of Nationalities." *Report of the Superintendent of Schools, Oakland, California, 1917–1918,* 34–38. Oakland, Calif.: Tribune Publishing, 1919.

Cravens, Hamilton. *The Triumph of Evolution: American Scientists and the Heredity-Environment Controversy, 1900–1941.* Philadelphia: Univ. of Pennsylvania Press, 1978.

Cremin, Lawrence. *The Transformation of the School: Progressivism in American Education, 1876–1957.* New York: Knopf, 1961.

Cronbach, Lee J. *Essentials of Psychological Testing.* 3d ed. New York: Harper & Row, 1970.

———. "Five Decades of Public Controversy Over Mental Testing." *American Psychologist* 30 (Jan. 1975): 1–14.

———. "Heredity, Environment, and Educational Policy." *Harvard Educational Review* 39 (Spring 1969): 190–99.

Crouse, James. "Does the SAT Make Better Selection Decisions?" *Harvard Educational Review* 55 (May 1985): 195–219.

Cubberley, Ellwood P. *Changing Conceptions of Education.* Boston: Houghton Mifflin, 1909.

———. *Public Education in the United States: A Study and Interpretation of American Educational History.* Boston: Houghton Mifflin, 1919.

———. *Public School Administration: A Statement of the Fundamental Principles Underlying the Organization and Administration of Public Education*. Boston: Houghton Mifflin, 1916.

———. *Report of a Survey of the Organization, Scope, and Finances of the Public School System of Oakland, California*. Oakland, Calif.: Oakland Public Schools, 1915.

Davis, Helen. "Classification by Intelligence Tests in Smaller Schools." National Education Association. *Second Yearbook of the Department of Elementary School Principals*, 1923. 211–19.

———. "Some Problems Arising in the Administration of a Department of Measurements." *Journal of Educational Research* 5 (Jan. 1922): 1–20.

Dearborn, Walter F. *Intelligence Tests: Their Significance for School and Society*. Boston: Houghton Mifflin, 1928.

Deffenbaugh, W. S. "Research Bureaus in City School Systems." Department of the Interior, Bureau of Education. City School Leaflet no. 5. Washington, D.C.: Government Printing Office, 1923.

———. "Uses of Intelligence and Achievement Tests in 215 Cities." Department of the Interior, Bureau of Education. City School Leaflet no. 20. Washington, D.C., 1925.

Dickson, Virgil E. "Classification of School Children According to Mental Ability." In *Intelligence Tests and School Reorganization*, edited by Lewis M. Terman, 32–52. Yonkers-on-Hudson, N.Y.: World Book, 1922.

———. "The Gifted Child." *Journal of Educational Research* 1 (Apr. 1920): 300–301.

———. *Mental Tests and the Classroom Teacher*. With an introduction by Lewis M. Terman. Yonkers-on-Hudson, N.Y.: World Book, 1923.

———. "The Need of a Counseling Program in Secondary Schools." *Journal of Educational Research* 11 (Jan. 1925): 12–16.

———. "The Relation of Mental Testing to School Administration." Ph.D. dissertation, Stanford University, 1919.

———. "The Relation of Mental Testing to School Administration, with Special Reference to Children Entering School." M.A. dissertation, Stanford University, 1917.

———. "Report of the Department of Research." *Report of the Superintendent of Schools, Oakland, California, 1917–1918*, 173–76. Oakland, Calif.: Tribune Publishing, 1919.

———. "Scientific Methods Applied to Vocational Guidance." *Report of the Superintendent of Schools, Oakland, California, 1917–1918*, 226–31. Oakland, Calif.: Tribune Publishing, 1919.

———. "The Test Controversy." *National Education Association Journal* 12 (May 1923): 176.

———. "The Treatment of Gifted Children in Oakland and in Berkeley." *Proceedings of the First Annual Conference on Educational Research and Guidance*, 26–28. San Jose State Teachers College, Sacramento, Calif.: State Printing Office, 1923.

———. "The Use of Mental Tests in the Guidance of Eighth-Grade and High

School Pupils." *Journal of Educational Research* 2 (Oct. 1920): 601–10.
——. "What First-Grade Children Can Do in School as Related to What Is Shown by Mental Tests." *Journal of Educational Research* 2 (June 1920): 475–80.

Dickson, Virgil E., and Martens, Elise E. "Training Teachers for Mental Testing in Oakland, California." *Journal of Educational Research* 8 (Feb. 1923): 100–108.

Dickson, Virgil E., and Norton, J. K. "The Otis Group Intelligence Scale Applied to the Elementary School Graduating Classes of Oakland, California." *Journal of Educational Research* 3 (Feb. 1921): 106–15.

Dockrell, W. B., ed. *On Intelligence: Contemporary Theories and Educational Implications: A Symposium, Toronto, 1969.* Toronto: Ontario Institute for Studies in Education, 1970.

Doherty, Margaret, and Joseph MacLatchy. "Bibliography of Education and Psychological Tests and Measurements." Department of the Interior, Bureau of Education. *Bulletin* no. 55. Washington, D.C.: Government Printing Office, 1923.

DuBois, Philip H. *A History of Psychological Testing.* Boston: Allyn and Bacon, 1970.

Dutton, S. T., and David Snedden. "Grading and Promotion." In *The Administration of Public Education in the United States*, 341–55. New York: Macmillan, 1908.

Echols, James P. "The Rise of the Evaluation Movement: 1920–1942." Ph.D. dissertation, Stanford University, 1973.

Eliot, Charles W. "Undesirable and Desirable Uniformity in Schools." In his *Educational Reform: Essays and Addresses*, 271–300. New York: Century, 1898.

Elliott, Richard M. "Robert M. Yerkes: 1876–1956." *American Journal of Psychology* 69 (Sept. 1956): 487–94.

Ensign, Forest. *Compulsory School Attendance and Child Labor.* Iowa City: Athens Press, 1921.

Evans, Brian, and Bernard Waites. *IQ and Mental Testing: An Unnatural Science and Its Social History.* Atlantic Highlands, N.J.: Humanities Press, 1981.

Fancher, Raymond E. *The Intelligence Men: Makers of the IQ Controversy.* New York: W. W. Norton, 1985.

Fass, Paula S. "The IQ: A Cultural and Historical Framework." *American Journal of Education* 88 (Aug. 1980): 431–58.

Feingold, Gustave A. "The Sectioning of High-School Classes on the Basis of Intelligence." *Educational Administration and Supervision* 9 (1923): 399–415.

Fenton, Norman. *Self-Direction and Adjustment.* Yonkers-on-Hudson, N.Y.: World Book, 1926.

Filene, Peter. "An Obituary for the 'Progressive Movement.'" *American Quarterly* 22 (Spring 1970): 24–43.

Findlay, Warren G., and Mirian M. Bryan. *Ability Grouping: Status, Impact and Alternatives, 1970.* Athens, Ga.: Univ. of Georgia, 1971.

Freeman, Frank N. *Mental Tests: Their History, Principles, and Applications.* Boston: Houghton Mifflin, 1926.

——. *Mental Tests: Their History, Principles, and Applications.* Rev. ed. Boston: Houghton Mifflin, 1939.

——. "Sorting the Students." *Educational Review* 63 (Nov. 1924): 169–74.

Garner, William, and Wigdor, Alexandra, eds. *Tests: Uses, Consequences, and Controversies.* Vols. 1 and 2. Washington, D.C.: National Academy of Sciences, 1982.

Gifford, Bernard R. "Testing, Politics, and the Allocation of Opportunities." *Journal of Negro Education* 55 (Summer 1986): 422–32.

Gilbert, Harry B. "On the IQ Ban." *Teachers College Record* 67 (Jan. 1966): 282–85.

Gill, Norman W. *Municipal Research Bureaus.* Washington, D.C.: American Council on Public Affairs, 1944.

Goddard, Henry H. "Two Thousand Children Tested by the Binet Measuring Scale for Intelligence." *Addresses and Proceedings of the National Educational Association* 49 (1911): 870–78.

Goodenough, Florence. *Measurement of Intelligence by Drawings.* Yonkers-on-Hudson, N.Y.: World Book, 1926.

Goslin, David A. "The Social Impact of Testing." *Personnel and Guidance Journal* 45 (Mar. 1967): 676–82.

Goslin, David A., and Glass, David C. "The Social Effects of Standardized Testing in American Elementary and Secondary Schools." *Sociology of Education* 40 (Spring 1967): 115–31.

Gould, Stephen Jay. *The Mismeasure of Man.* New York: W. W. Norton, 1981.

Grant, W. Vance, and Lind, C. George. *Digest of Education Statistics, 1977–78.* Washington, D.C.: Government Printing Office, 1978.

Graves, Frank Pierrepont. "The Use and Abuse of Intelligence Testing." *Ninth Annual Schoolmen's Week,* University of Pennsylvania (1922): 18–24.

Greenwell, W. M. "The Classification of Children in the Lincoln School." National Education Association. *Second Yearbook of the Department of Elementary School Principals,* 1923. 189–93.

Gross, Martin. *The Brain Watchers.* New York: Random House, 1962.

Haber, Samuel. *Efficiency and Uplift: Scientific Management in the Progressive Era.* Chicago: Univ. of Chicago Press, 1964.

Haggerty, Melvin E. "Recent Developments in Measuring Human Capacities." *Journal of Educational Research* 3 (Apr. 1921): 241.

——. "Specific Uses of Measurement in the Solution of School Problems." *Seventeenth Yearbook of the National Society for the Study of Education,* pt. 2, 25–40. Bloomington, Ill.: Public School Publishing, 1918.

Haller, Mark. *Eugenics: Hereditary Attitudes in American Thought.* New Brunswick, N.J.: Rutgers Univ. Press, 1963.

Haney, Walt. "Validity, Vaudeville, and Values: A Short History of Social Concerns Over Standardized Testing." *American Psychologist* 36 (October 1981): 1021–34.

Hanford, George H. "Yes, the SAT Does Help Colleges." *Harvard Educational Review* 55 (August 1985): 324–31.

Hargreaves, R. T. "Guidance: A Point of View." *Ninth Yearbook of the National Association of Secondary School Principals*, 1924. 9–18.

Harris, William T. "The Development of the Short-Interval System in St. Louis." In "Classification and Promotion of Pupils." *Report of the United States Commissioner of Education*, 1898–99. 303–30.

Hartwell, C. S. "The Grading and Promotion of Pupils." *Addresses and Proceedings of the National Education Association* 48 (1910): 294–306.

Hays, Samuel P. "The Politics of Reform in Municipal Government in the Progressive Era." *Pacific Northwest Quarterly* 55 (Oct. 1964): 157–69.

Hebb, Bertha Y. "The Classification of Elementary School Pupils into Homogeneous Groups." *American School Board Journal* 72 (May 1926): 52, 148.

Heberle, Rudolph, and Joseph R. Gusfield. "Social Movements." S.v. *International Encyclopedia of the Social Sciences*.

Herrnstein, Richard J. *I.Q. in the Meritocracy*. Boston: Little, Brown, 1971.

Hicks, Vinnie. "Report of the Work of the Child Study Laboratory in Reference to Subnormals." *Annual Report of the Republic Schools of Oakland, California, 1911–12*, 65–74. Oakland, Calif.: Oakland Enquirer Publishing, 1912.

Higham, John. *Strangers in the Land: Patterns of American Nativism, 1860–1925*. New Brunswick, N.J.: Rutgers Univ. Press, 1963; New York: Atheneum, 1970.

Hildreth, Gertrude A. *A Bibliography of Mental Tests and Rating Scales*. New York: Psychological Corporation, 1933.

Hilgard, Ernest R. "Lewis Madison Terman, 1877–1956." *American Journal of Psychology* 70 (1957): 472–79.

Hill, Andrew P., Jr. *Survey of the Palo Alto Public Schools*. Sacramento, Calif.: California State Printing Office, 1931.

Hines, Harlan C. *A Guide to Educational Measurements*. Boston: Houghton Mifflin, 1923.

——. "Measuring the Intelligence of School Pupils." *American School Board Journal* 64 (Apr. 1922): 35.

——. "What Los Angeles Is Doing with the Results of Testing." *Journal of Educational Research* 5 (Jan. 1922): 45–57.

"Hobson v. Hansen: Judicial Supervision of the Color-Blind School Board." *Harvard Law Review* 81 (1968): 1511–27.

Hoffmann, Banesh. *The Tyranny of Testing*. New York: Crowell-Collier Press, 1962.

Hofstadter, Richard. *Social Darwinism in American Thought*. Rev. ed. Philadelphia: Univ. of Pennsylvania Press, 1944; Boston: Beacon Press, 1955.

Holley, Charles E. "Mental Tests for School Use." University of Illinois, Bureau of Educational Research. *Bulletin* no. 4. Urbana, Ill.: Univ. of Illinois, 1920.

Holmes, William H. *School Organization and the Individual Child*. Worcester, Mass.: Davis Press, 1912.

Hull, Clark L. *Aptitude Testing*. Yonkers-on-Hudson, N.Y.: World Book, 1923.

Hunter, Frederick M. "The Principal and the Educational Expert." National Education Association. *Fourth Yearbook of the Department of Elementary School Principals*, 1925. 369–84.

———. *Superintendent's Bulletin, Special Edition*. Oakland, Calif.: Oakland Public Schools, Jan. 1926.

Jencks, Christopher. "What Color is I.Q.? Intelligence and Race." In *The Fallacy of I.Q.*, edited by Carl Senna, 31–41. New York: Third Press, 1973.

Jensen, Arthur R. *Bias in Mental Testing*. New York: Free Press, 1980.

———. "How Much Can We Boost IQ and Scholastic Achievement?" *Harvard Educational Review* 39 (Winter 1969): 1–123.

———. *Straight Talk About Mental Tests*. New York: Free Press, 1981.

Johnston, Nell B. "The Use of Standardized Educational Tests in School Surveys." *Educational Administration and Supervision* 2 (1925): 588–607.

Joncich, Geraldine. *Edward L. Thorndike: The Sane Positivist*. Middletown, Conn.: Wesleyan Univ. Press, 1968.

Jones, H. S., et al. "Report of the Committee on City School Systems: Pupils —Classification, Examination and Proportion." *Addresses and Proceedings of the National Education Association* 26 (1886): 276–84.

Jones, Maldwyn A. *American Immigration*. Chicago: Univ. of Chicago Press, 1960.

Judd, Charles H. "Educational Research and the American School Program." *Educational Record* 4 (Oct. 1923): 165–77.

Kamin, Leon J. "Heredity, Intelligence, Politics and Psychology." In *The IQ Controversy*, edited by N. J. Block and Gerald Dworkin, 374–82. New York: Random House, 1976.

———. *The Science and Politics of I.Q.* Potomac, Md.: Lawrence Erlbaum Associates, 1974.

Karier, Clarence J. *Man, Society, and Education: A History of American Educational Ideas*. Glenview, Ill.: Scott, Foresman, 1967.

———. "Testing for Order and Control in the Liberal Corporate State." In *The IQ Controversy*, edited by N. J. Block and Gerald Dworkin, 339–73. New York: Random House, 1976.

Karier, Clarence J., Spring, Joel, and Violas, Paul C. *Roots of Crisis: American Education in the Twentieth Century*. Chicago: Rand McNally, 1973.

Katz, Michael B. "The Emergence of Bureaucracy in Urban Education: The Boston Case, 1850–1884." In his *Class, Bureaucracy and Schools*, 56–104. New York: Praeger, 1972.

Kelley, Truman L. "Again: Educational Determinism." *Journal of Educational Research* 8 (June 1923): 10–19.

———. *Interpretation of Educational Measurements*. Yonkers-on-Hudson, N.Y.: World Book, 1927.

Kennedy, David. *Over Here: The First World War and American Society*. New York: Oxford Univ. Press, 1977.

——, ed. *Progressivism: The Critical Issues.* Boston: Little, Brown, 1971.

Kevles, Daniel. "Testing the Army's Intelligence: Psychologists and the Military in World War I." *Journal of American History* 55 (Dec. 1968): 565–81.

Keyes, Charles H. *Progress Through the Grades of City Schools: A Study of Acceleration and Arrest.* Contributions to Education, no. 42. New York: Teachers College, Columbia University, 1911.

Kingsley, Clarence D., chairman *Cardinal Principles of Secondary Education: A Report of the Commission on the Reorganization of Secondary Education.* Appointed by the National Education Association. Department of the Interior, Bureau of Education. *Bulletin* no. 35. Washington, D.C.: Government Printing Office, 1918.

Krug, Edward. *The Shaping of the High School, 1880–1920,* vol. 1. New York: Harper and Row, 1964.

——. *The Shaping of the High School, 1920–1941,* vol. 2. Madison, Wis.: Univ. of Wisconsin Press, 1972.

Lawler, James M. *IQ, Heritability and Racism.* New York: International Publishers, 1978.

Layton, Warren K. "The Group Intelligence Testing Program of the Detroit Public Schools." In "Intelligence Tests and Their Use," edited by Guy M. Whipple. *Twenty-First Yearbook of the National Society for the Study of Education,* pt. 2, 123–130. Urbana, Ill.: Public School Publishing, 1922.

——. "The Intelligence Testing Program of the Detroit Public Schools." *School and Society* 15 (Apr. 1922): 368–72.

Lazerson, Marvin. *Origins of the Urban School: Public Education in Massachusetts, 1870–1915.* Cambridge, Mass.: Harvard Univ. Press, 1971.

Lesser, Gerald S., and Fifer, Gordon. *Mental Abilities of Children from Different Social Class and Cultural Groups.* New York: Hunter College, 1964.

Lewontin, Richard C. "Race and Intelligence." In *The Fallacy of I.Q.,* edited by Carl Senna, 1–17. New York: Third Press, 1973.

Lincoln, Edward A. *Beginnings in Educational Measurement.* Philadelphia: Lippincott, 1924.

Lippmann, Walter. "A Future for the Tests." *New Republic,* 29 November 1922, 9–11.

——. "The Mental Age of Americans." *New Republic,* 25 October 1922, 213–15.

——. "Mr. Burt and the Intelligence Tests." *New Republic,* 2 May 1923, 263–64.

——. "The Mystery of the 'A' Men." *New Republic,* 1 November 1922, 246–48.

——. "The Reliability of Intelligence Tests." *New Republic,* 8 November 1922, 275–77.

——. "Tests of Hereditary Intelligence." *New Republic,* 22 November 1922, 328–30.

"The Lippmann-Terman Debate." In *The IQ Controversy,* edited by N. J.

Block and Gerald Dworkin, 4–44. New York: Random House, 1976.

Loretan, Joseph O. "The Decline and Fall of Group Intelligence Testing." *Teachers College Record* 67 (Oct. 1965): 10–17.

Lyon, Edmund D. "The Submerged Tenth." *Fifth Yearbook of the National Association of Secondary School Principals,* 1921. 1–7.

McCall, William A. *How to Classify Pupils.* New York: Teachers College, Columbia University, 1928.

———. *How to Measure in Education.* New York: Macmillan, 1922.

McDonald, Robert A. F. *Adjustment of School Organization to Various Population Groups.* Contributions to Education, no. 75. New York: Teachers College, Columbia University, 1915.

Madsen, I. N. "Participation in Testing Programs by the Classroom Teacher." *Educational Administration and Supervision* 15 (1929): 117.

Marks, Russell. "Lewis M. Terman: Individual Differences and the Construction of Social Reality." *Educational Theory* 24 (Fall 1974): 336–55.

———. "Testers, Trackers, and Trustees: The Ideology of the Intelligence Testing Movement in America, 1900–1954." Ph.D. dissertation, University of Illinois, 1972.

Martens, Elise H. "A High-School Counseling System in Operation." *Journal of Educational Research* 11 (Jan. 1925): 17–24.

———. "Organization of Research Bureaus in City School Systems." Department of the Interior, Bureau of Education. City School Leaflet no. 14. Washington, D.C.: Government Printing Office, Jan. 1924.

Mercer, Jane R. "I.Q.: The Lethal Label." *Education Digest* 38 (Jan. 1973): 17–20.

Minton, Henry L. "Lewis M. Terman and Mental Testing: In Search of the Democratic Ideal." In *Psychological Testing and American Society,* edited by Michael M. Sokal, 95–112. New Brunswick, N.J.: Rutgers Univ. Press, 1987.

Monroe, Walter S. *Educational Tests and Measurements.* Boston: Houghton Mifflin, 1917.

———. *Educational Tests and Measurements,* 1924. Rev. and enl. ed. Boston: Houghton Mifflin, 1924.

———. "Existing Tests and Standards." *Seventeenth Yearbook of the National Society for the Study of Education,* pt. 2, 71–104. Bloomington, Ill.: Public School Publishing, 1918.

———. *An Introduction to the Theory of Educational Measurements.* Boston: Houghton Mifflin, 1923.

———. "Report of Educational Tests for 1919–20." University of Illinois, Bureau of Educational Research. *Bulletin* no. 5. Urbana, Ill.: University of Illinois, 1921.

———. "Ten Years of Educational Research, 1918–1927." University of Illinois, Bureau of Educational Research. *Bulletin* no. 42. Urbana, Ill.: University of Illinois, 1928.

Myers, Charles E. "The Use of Standard Tests in Rural Schools." *Fourteenth Annual Schoolmen's Week*, University of Pennsylvania (1927): 257–61.

Myers, Garry C. "Teachers vs. Mental Tests as Prophets of School Progress." *School and Society* 16 (Sept. 1922): 300–303.

Nairn, Allan, and Associates. *The Reign of ETS, The Ralph Nader Report on the Educational Testing Service*. Washington, D.C.: Ralph Nader, 1980.

Nifenecker, Eugene A. "Bureaus of Research in City School Systems." *Seventeenth Yearbook of the National Society for the Study of Education*, pt. 2, 52–56. Bloomington, Ill.: Public School Publishing, 1918.

———. *Problems of School Maladjustments in New York City: Statistical Reference Data Showing Background Conditions, Factors, Trends and Problems, 1900–1934*, pt. 1. Bureau of Reference, Research and Statistics, Publication no. 27. Board of Education of the City of New York, Jan. 1936.

Oakland, California. *Annual Report of the Public Schools of the City of Oakland, 1903–1904*. Oakland, Calif.: Oakland Enquirer Publishing, 1904.

———. *Annual Report of the Public Schools of Oakland, California, 1911–12*. Oakland, Calif.: Oakland Enquirer Publishing, 1912.

Odell, Charles W. "An Annotated Bibliography Dealing with the Classification and Instruction of Pupils to Provide for Individual Differences." University of Illinois, Bureau of Educational Research. *Bulletin* no. 16. Urbana, Ill.: University of Illinois, 1923.

———. "Conservation of Intelligence in Illinois High Schools." University of Illinois, Bureau of Educational Research. *Bulletin* no. 22. Urbana, Ill.: University of Illinois, 1925.

———. "A Selected Annotated Bibliography Dealing with Examinations and School Marks." University of Illinois, Bureau of Educational Research. *Bulletin* no. 43. Urbana, Ill.: University of Illinois, 1929.

———. "The Use of Intelligence Tests as a Basis of School Organization and Instruction." University of Illinois, Bureau of Educational Research. *Bulletin* no. 12. Urbana, Ill.: University of Illinois, 1922.

———. "Who Have Contributed to the Educational Movement?" *School and Society* 29 (1929): 751–54.

O'Donnell, John M. *The Origins of Behaviorism: American Psychology, 1870–1920*. New York: New York Univ. Press, 1985.

Olson, Lynn. "National Panel on Testing Policy Planned." *Educational Week*, 17 December 1986, 4.

Orr, E. F. "A Principal's Observations on Intelligence Testing." *American School Board Journal* 70 (May 1925): 50, 136.

Otis, Arthur S. "Group Intelligence Tests: Their Value and Limitations." *Ninth Annual Schoolmen's Week*, University of Pennsylvania (1922): 55–67.

———. "Some Queer Misconceptions Regarding Intelligence Tests." *American School Board Journal* 75 (Nov. 1927): 42, 134.

———. *Statistical Method in Educational Measurement*. Yonkers-on-Hudson, N.Y.: World Book, 1925.

Owen, David. *None of the Above.* Boston: Houghton Mifflin, 1985.

Pastore, Nicholas. "The Army Intelligence Tests and Walter Lippmann." *Journal of the History of the Behavioral Sciences* 14 (1978): 316–27.

———. *The Nature-Nurture Controversy.* New York: Kings Crown Press, 1949.

Peterson, Joseph. *Early Conceptions and Tests of Intelligence.* Yonkers-on-Hudson, N.Y.: World Book, 1925.

Pintner, Rudolph. *Intelligence Testing: Methods and Results.* New York: Henry Holt, 1923.

———. "A Mental Survey of the School Population of a Village." *School and Society* 5 (May 1917): 597–600.

Power, Leonard. "The Effects of Grouping According to Intelligence in the Franklin School, Port Arthur, Texas." National Education Association. *Second Yearbook of the Department of Elementary School Principals,* 1923. 249–67.

Pressey, Sidney L. *Introduction to the Use of Standardized Tests.* Yonkers-on-Hudson, N.Y.: World Book, 1922.

Price, E. D. "A Plan of Classifying Pupils." *Journal of Educational Research* 12 (Dec. 1925): 341–58.

Proctor, William M. *Educational and Vocational Guidance.* Boston: Houghton Mifflin, 1925.

———. *Psychological Tests and Guidance of High School Pupils.* Bloomington, Ill.: Public School Publishing, 1921.

———. "Psychological Tests and the Probable School Success of High-School Pupils." *Journal of Educational Research* 1 (Apr. 1920): 258–70.

———. "The Use of Intelligence Tests in the Educational Guidance of High-School Pupils." *School and Society* 8 (Oct. 1918): 473–78, 502–9.

———. "The Use of Psychological Tests in the Educational Guidance of High-School Pupils." *Journal of Educational Research* 1 (May 1920): 369–81.

———. *The Use of Psychological Tests in the Educational and Vocational Guidance of High-School Pupils.* Bloomington, Ill.: Public School Publishing, 1923.

———. "The Use of Psychological Tests in the Vocational Guidance of High-School Pupils." *Journal of Educational Research* 2 (Sept. 1920): 533–46.

Rather, Dan. "The I.Q. Myth." CBS Special Report. 7 July 1975.

"Recent Developments—*Hobson v. Hansen:* The De Facto Limits on Judicial Power." *Stanford Law Review* 20 (June 1968): 1249–68.

Reed, James. "Robert M. Yerkes and the Mental Testing Movement." In *Psychological Testing and American Society,* edited by Michael M. Sokal, 75–94. New Brunswick, N.J.: Rutgers Univ. Press, 1987.

Reigner, Charles G. "The Measurement Movement—and the Man in the Street." *Education* 44 (May 1924): 571–75.

Resnick, Daniel P. "History of Educational Testing." In *Tests: Uses, Consequences, and Controversies,* vol. 2, edited by William Garner and Alexandra Wigdor, 173–94. Washington, D.C.: National Academy of Sciences, 1982.

Rice, Joseph Mayer. "A New Basis in Education." *Forum* (Jan.–Mar. 1904). Reprinted in his *Scientific Management in Education.* New York: Hinds, Nobel, and Eldredge, 1913.

———. "Obstacles to Rational Educational Reform." *Forum* (Dec. 1896). Reprinted in his *Scientific Management in Education*. New York: Hinds, Nobel, and Eldredge, 1913.

———. *The Public School System of the United States*. New York: Century, 1893.

Rist, Ray C. "Student Social Class and Teacher Expectations: The Self-Fulfilling Prophecy in Ghetto Education." *Harvard Educational Review* 40 (Aug. 1970): 411–50.

Richman, Julia. "A Successful Experiment in Promoting Pupils." *Education Review* 18 (June 1899): 23–29.

———. "What Can Be Done in a Graded School for the Backward Child." *Survey* 13 (Nov. 1905): 344–74.

Rosenthal, Robert, and Jacobsen, Lenore. *Pygmalion in the Classroom*. New York: Holt, Rinehart and Winston, 1968.

Ross, C. C. *Measurement in Today's Schools*. New York: Prentice-Hall, 1946.

Ross, Dorothy. *G. Stanley Hall: The Psychologist as Prophet*. Chicago: Univ. of Chicago Press, 1972.

Ruch, Giles M., and Stoddard, George D. *Tests and Measurements in High School Instruction*. Yonkers-on-Hudson, N.Y.: World Book, 1927.

Rudy, Willis. *Schools in an Age of Mass Culture*. Englewood Cliffs, N.J.: Prentice-Hall, 1965.

Samelson, Franz. "Putting Psychology on the Map: Ideology and Intelligence Testing." In *Psychology in Social Context*, edited by Allan Buss, 103–68. New York: Irvington, 1979.

———. "Was Early Mental Testing: (a) Racist Inspired, (b) Objective Science, (c) A Technology for Democracy, (d) The Origin of the Multiple-Choice Exams, (e) None of the Above? (Mark the RIGHT Answer)." In *Psychological Testing and American Society*, edited by Michael M. Sokal, 113–27. New Brunswick, N.J.: Rutgers Univ. Press, 1987.

Schwegler, R. A., and Winn, Edith. "A Comparative Study of the Intelligence of White and Colored Children." *Journal of Educational Research* 2 (Dec. 1920): 838–47.

Seagoe, May V. *Terman and the Gifted*. Los Altos, Calif.: William Kaufmann, 1975.

Sears, Jesse B. *The School Survey: A Textbook on the Use of School Surveying in the Administration of Public Schooling*. New York: Houghton Mifflin, 1925.

———. *Spelling Efficiency in the Oakland Schools*. Bureau of Information, Statistics, and Educational Research, *Publication* no. 1. Oakland, Calif.: Oakland Public Schools, 1915.

Sears, Robert R. "L. M. Terman, Pioneer in Mental Measurement." *Science* 125 (1957): 978.

Senna, Carl, ed. *The Fallacy of I.Q.* New York: Third Press, 1973.

Sharp, Evelyn. *The IQ Cult*. New York: Coward, McCann and Geoghegan, 1972.

Shearer, William J. *The Grading of Schools*. New York: H. P. Smith, 1898.

Sheldon, William H. "The Intelligence of Mexican Children." *School and Society* 19 (Feb. 1924): 139–42.

Shockley, William. "Heredity, Environment, Race, and I.Q." *Phi Delta Kappan* 53 (Jan. 1972): 297–312.

——. "Negro I.Q. and Heredity." *School and Society* 96 (Mar. 1968): 127–28.

Sizer, Theodore R. *Secondary Schools at the Turn of the Century.* New Haven, Conn.: Yale Univ. Press, 1964.

——. "Testing: Americans' Comfortable Panacea." *Report for 1970 Invitational Conference on Educational Testing.* Princeton, N.J.: Educational Testing Service, 1970.

Snyderman, Mark, and Rothman, Stanley. "Science, Politics, and the IQ Controversy." *Public Interest* 83 (Spring 1986): 79–97.

Sokal, Michael M. "Approaches to the History of Psychological Testing." *History of Education Quarterly* 24 (1984): 419–30.

——. "James McKeen Cattell and Mental Anthropometry: Nineteenth-Century Science and Reform and the Origins of Psychological Testing." In *Psychological Testing and American Society,* edited by Michael M. Sokal, 21–45. New Brunswick, N.J.: Rutgers Univ. Press, 1987.

——. "The Origins of the Psychological Corporation." *Journal of the History of the Behavioral Sciences* 17 (1981): 54–67.

——. "Psychological Testing and Historical Scholarship—Questions, Contrasts, and Context." In *Psychological Testing and American Society,* edited by Michael M. Sokal, 1–20. New Brunswick, N.J.: Rutgers Univ. Press, 1987.

——, ed. *Psychological Testing and American Society.* New Brunswick, N.J.: Rutgers Univ. Press, 1987.

Spring, Joel H. *Education and the Rise of the Corporate Order.* Boston: Beacon Press, 1972.

——. "Psychologists and the War: The Meaning of Intelligence in the Alpha and Beta Tests." *History of Education Quarterly* 12 (Spring 1972): 3–15.

Starch, Daniel. "Standard Tests as Aids in the Classification and Promotion of Pupils." *Fifteenth Yearbook of the National Society for the Study of Education,* pt. 1, 143–48. Bloomington, Ill.: Public School Publishing, 1916.

Stark, William E. "When the Scientific Mind Meets Popular Prejudice." *Journal of Educational Research* 11 (Feb. 1925): 79–84.

Stedman, Louise. *Education of Gifted Children.* Yonkers-on-Hudson, N.Y.: World Book, 1924.

Stenquist, John L. "The Case for the Low I.Q." *Journal of Educational Research* 4 (Nov. 1921): 241–54.

Stetson, Paul C. "Homogeneous Grouping in The First Year of a Five-Year High School." *School Review* 29 (May 1921): 351–65.

Strayer, George D. "Report of the Committee of the National Council of Education on Standards and Tests for Measuring the Efficiency of Schools or Systems of Schools." Department of the Interior, Bureau of Education. *Bulletin* no. 13. Washington, D.C.: Government Printing Office, 1913.

Strayer, George D., et al. "Standards and Tests for the Measurement of the Efficiency of Schools and School Systems." *Fifteenth Yearbook of the National Society for the Study of Education*, pts. 1, 2. Bloomington, Ill.: Public School Publishing, 1916.

"The Study of Gifted Children." *School and Society* 13 (June 1921): 694–95.

Terman, Lewis M. "The American Psychological Association." *Science* 59 (June 1924): 546–48.

——. "The Binet Scale and the Diagnosis of Feeble-Mindedness." *Journal of American Institute of Criminal Law and Criminology* 7 (Nov. 1916): 530–43.

——. "The Binet Scale and the Diagnosis of Feeble-Mindedness." *National Education Association Journal* 1 (1916): 874–79.

——. "The Binet-Simon Scale for Measuring Intelligence." *Psychological Clinic* 5 (Dec. 1911): 199–206.

——. "The Conservation of Talent." *School and Society* 19 (Mar. 1924): 363.

——. "Feebleminded Children in the Public Schools of California." *School and Society* 5 (1917): 161–65.

——. "Genius and Stupidity: A Study of Some of the Intellectual Processes of Seven 'Bright' and Seven 'Stupid' Boys." *Pedagogical Seminary* 13 (Sept. 1906): 307–73.

——. "The Great Conspiracy; or the Impulse Imperious of Intelligence Testers Psychoanalyzed and Exposed by Mr. Lippmann." *New Republic*, 27 December 1922, 1–15.

——. *The Hygiene of the School Child.* Boston: Houghton Mifflin, 1914.

——. "The Influence of Nature and Nurture Upon Intelligence Scores: An Evaluation of the Evidence in Part I of the 1928 Yearbook of the National Society for the Study of Education." *Journal of Educational Psychology* 19 (Sept. 1928): 362–73.

——. "Intelligence in a Changing Universe." *School and Society* 51 (Apr. 1940): 465–70.

——. *The Intelligence of School Children: How Children Differ in Ability, the Use of Mental Tests in School Grading and the Proper Education of Exceptional Children.* Boston: Houghton Mifflin, 1919.

——. Introduction to "Nature and Nurture; Their Influence Upon Intelligence." *Twenty-Seventy Yearbook of the National Society for the Study of Education*, pt. 1, 1–7. Bloomington, Ill.: Public School Publishing, 1928.

——. *The Measurement of Intelligence.* Boston: Houghton Mifflin, 1916.

——. "Medical Inspection of Schools in California." *Psychological Clinic* 5 (May 1911): 57–62.

——. "Mental Growth and the I.Q." *Journal of Educational Psychology* 12 (1921): 325–41, 401–7.

——. "The Mental Hygiene of Exceptional Children." *Pedagogical Seminary*, 22 (Dec. 1915): 529–37.

——. "The Mental Test as a Psychological Method." *Psychological Review* 31 (Mar. 1924): 93–117.

——. "Methods of Examining: History, Development and Preliminary Results." In *Psychological Examining in the United States Army*, edited by Robert M. Yerkes, 299–546. Mem. Nat. Acad. Sci., vol. 15, pt. 2. Washington, D.C.: Government Printing Office, 1921.

——. *National Intelligence Tests, Manual*. Yonkers-on-Hudson, N.Y.: World Book, 1923.

——. "The 1927 Yearbook of the National Society for the Study of Education, on the Possibilities and Limitations of Training." *School and Society* (Mar. 1926): 404–6.

——. "The Possibilities and Limitations of Training." *Journal of Educational Research* 10 (Dec. 1924): 335–43.

——. Papers. Stanford University Archives. Cecil H. Green Library. Stanford University. Stanford, Calif.

——. "A Preliminary Study in the Psychology and Pedagogy of Leadership." *Pedagogical Seminary* 11 (Dec. 1904): 413–51.

——. "The Psychological Determinist, or Democracy and the IQ." *Journal of Educational Research* 6 (June 1922): 57–62; reprint ed., 2–7.

——. "Recent Literature of Juvenile Suicide." *Journal of Abnormal Psychology* 9 (Apr.–May 1914): 61–66.

——. "The Relation of the Manual Arts to Health." *Popular Science Monthly* 78 (June 1911): 602–9.

——. "A Report of the Buffalo Conference on the Binet-Simon Test of Intelligence." *Pedagogical Seminary* 20 (Dec. 1913): 549–54.

——. *Report of the Survey of the Public School System of Salt Lake City, Utah*. Salt Lake City, Utah: Grocer Printing, 1915.

——. "School Clinics for Free Medical and Dental Treatment." *Psychological Clinic* 5 (Feb. 1912): 271–78.

——. "The Significance of Intelligence Tests for Mental Hygiene." *Journal of Psycho-Asthenics* 18 (Mar. 1914): 119–27.

——. "Social Hygiene: The Real Conservation Problem." *North American Review* 198 (1913): 404–12.

——. *The Stanford Revision of the Binet-Simon Tests*. Boston: Houghton Mifflin, 1916.

——. "The Stanford Revisions and Extension of the Binet-Simon Scale for Measuring Intelligence." *Educational Psychology Monograph* no. 18. Baltimore: Warwick and York, 1917.

——. "The Status of Applied Psychology in the United States." *Journal of Applied Psychology* 5 (Mar. 1921): 1–4.

——. "A Study in Precocity and Prematuration." *American Journal of Psychology* 16 (Apr. 1905): 145–83.

——. "Survey of Mentally Defective Children in the Schools of San Luis Obispo." *Psychological Clinic* 6 (Oct. 1912): 131–39.

——. *The Teacher's Health: A Study in the Hygiene of an Occupation*. Boston: Houghton Mifflin, 1913.

———. "A Tentative Revision and Extension of the Binet-Simon Measuring Scale of Intelligence." *Journal of Educational Psychology* 3 (Feb.–May 1912): 61–74, 133–43, 198–208, 277–89.

———. *Terman Group Test of Mental Ability.* Yonkers-on-Hudson, N.Y.: World Book, 1920.

———. "Tests of General Intelligence." *Psychological Bulletin* 15 (May 1918): 160–67.

———. "Trails to Psychology." In *A History of Psychology in Autobiography*, edited by Carl Murchison, 4 vols., 297–331. Worcester, Mass.: Clark Univ. Press, 1930–1952.

———. "The Ultimate Influence of Standard Tests." *Journal of Educational Research* 17 (Jan. 1928): 57–59.

———. "The Use of Intelligence Tests in the Army." *Psychological Bulletin* 15 (June 1918): 177–87.

———. "The Use of Intelligence Tests in the Grading of School Children." *Journal of Educational Research* 1 (Jan. 1920): 20–32.

———, ed. *Genetic Studies of Genius.* Vol. 1, *Mental and Physical Traits of a Thousand Gifted Children*, by Lewis Terman. Vol. 2, *The Early Mental Traits of Three Hundred Geniuses*, by Catherine M. Cox. Stanford, Calif.: Stanford Univ. Press, 1925.

———. *Intelligence Tests and School Reorganization.* Yonkers-on-Hudson, N.Y.: World Book, 1922.

Terman, Lewis M., and Chase, J. M. "The Psychology, Biology and Pedagogy of Genius." *Psychological Bulletin* 17 (1920): 397–409.

Terman, Lewis M., and Cubberley, Ellwood P. "To Help Backward School Children." *Stanford Alumnus* (Apr. 1914): 1–4.

Terman, Lewis M., and DeVoss, J. C. "The Educational Achievements of Gifted Children." *Twenty-Third Yearbook of the National Society for the Study of Education*, pt. 1, 169–84. Bloomington, Ill.: Public School Publishing, 1924.

Terman, Lewis M., Dickson, Virgil, and Howard, Lowry. "Backward and Feeble-minded Children in the Public Schools of 'X' County, California." *Surveys in Mental Deviation in Prisons, Public Schools, and Orphanages in California*, 19–45. Sacramento, Calif.: California State Board of Charities and Corrections, 1918.

Terman, Lewis M., et al. "Intelligence and Its Measurement: A Symposium." *Journal of Educational Psychology* 12 (Mar., Apr., May 1921): 123–47, 195–216, 271–75.

———. *National Intelligence Tests, with Manual of Directions.* Yonkers-on-Hudson, N.Y.: World Book, 1920.

———. "The Stanford Revision of the Binet-Simon Scale and Some Results from Its Application to 1000 Non-Selected Children." *Journal of Educational Psychology* 6 (Nov. 1915): 551–62.

———. *Surveys in Mental Deviation in Prisons, Public Schools, and Orphanages in California.* Sacramento, Calif.: State Board of Charities and Corrections, 1918.

———. "A Trial of Mental and Pedagogical Tests in a Civil Service Examination of Policemen and Firemen." *Journal of Applied Psychology* 1 (1917): 17–29.

Terman, Lewis M., and Hoag, Ernest B. *Health Work in the Schools.* Boston: Houghton Mifflin, 1914.

Terman, Lewis M., and Kelley, Truman L. "Dr. Ruml's Criticism of Mental Test Methods." *Journal of Philosophy, Psychology and Scientific Methods* 18 (Aug. 1921): 459–65.

Terman, Lewis M., and Whitmore, Ethel D. "Age and Grade Norms for the National Intelligence Tests, Scales A and B." *Journal of Educational Research* 3 (Feb. 1921): 124–32.

Theisen, W. W. "Operation of Bureaus of Educational Research." *Journal of Educational Research* 1 (May 1920): 383–91.

Thelen, David P. "Social Tensions and the Origins of Progressivism." *Journal of American History* 56 (1969): 323–41.

Thorndike, Edward L. *An Introduction to the Theory of Mental and Social Measurements.* New York: Teachers College, Columbia University, 1904.

———. *Measurement of Intelligence.* New York: Teachers College, Columbia University, 1927.

———. "The Nature, Purposes and General Methods of Measurement of Educational Products." *Seventeenth Yearbook of the National Society for the Study of Education,* pt. 2, 16–24. Bloomington, Ill.: Public School Publishing, 1918.

Tildsley, John L. "Some Possibilities Arising from the Use of Intelligence Tests." *Fifth Yearbook of the National Association of Secondary School Principals,* 1921. 45–54.

Trabue, M. R. "Some Pitfalls in the Administrative Use of Intelligence Tests." *Journal of Educational Research* 6 (June 1922): 1–11.

Tyack, David B. *The One Best System: A History of American Urban Education.* Cambridge, Mass.: Harvard Univ. Press, 1974.

U.S. Bureau of the Census. *The Statistical History of the United States, From Colonial Times to the Present.* New York: Basic Books, 1976.

Van Denburg, Joseph K. *Causes of the Elimination of Students in Public Secondary Schools of New York City.* Contributions to Education, no. 47. New York: Teachers College, Columbia University, 1911.

Van Sickle, James H. "Plan of the North-Side Schools of Denver." In "Classification and Promotion of Pupils." *Report of the United States Commissioner of Education,* vol. 1, 1898–99. 341–346.

Van Sickle, J. H., Witmer, Lightner, and Ayres, Leonard P. "Provisions for Exceptional Children in City School Systems." Department of the Interior, Bureau of Education. *Bulletin* no. 14. Washington, D.C.: Government Printing Office, 1911.

Volkmar, Hilda, and Noble, Isabel. "Retardation as Indicated by One Hundred City School Reports." *Psychological Clinic* 8 (May 1914): 75.

Von Mayrhauser, Richard T. "The Manager, the Medic, and the Mediator: The Clash of Professional Psychological Styles and the Wartime Origins of Group Mental Testing." In *Psychological Testing and American Society,* edited by Michael M. Sokal, 128–57. New Brunswick, N.J.: Rutgers Univ. Press, 1987.

Wallin, J. E. Wallace *The Mental Health of the School Child*. New Haven, Conn.: Yale Univ. Press, 1914.

——. "A Practical Guide for the Administration of the Binet-Simon Scale for Measuring Intelligence." *Psychological Clinic* 5 (1912): 217–38.

——. *The Problems of Subnormality*. Yonkers-on-Hudson, N.Y.: World Book, 1917.

Wells, Frederick L. *Mental Tests in Clinical Practice*. Yonkers-on-Hudson, N.Y.: World Book, 1927.

Whipple, Guy M. "Educational Determinism: A Discussion of Professor Bagley's Address at Chicago." *School and Society* 15 (June 1922): 599–602.

——. "The Intelligence Testing Program and Its Objectors—Conscientious and Otherwise." *School and Society* 17 (May 1923): 561–64.

——. *Problems in Mental Testing*. Bloomington, Ill.: Public School Publishing, 1925.

——. "The Use of Mental Tests in the School." *Fifteenth Yearbook of the National Society for the Study of Education*, pt. 2, 149–60. Bloomington, Ill.: Public School Publishing, 1916.

——. ed. "The Grouping of Pupils." *Thirty-Fifth Yearbook of the National Society for the Study of Education*, pt. 1, Bloomington, Ill.: Public School Publishing, 1936.

——. "Intelligence: Its Nature and Nurture." *Thirty-Ninth Yearbook of the National Society for the Study of Education*, pt. 1. Bloomington, Ill.: Public School Publishing, 1940.

——. "Intelligence Tests and Their Use." *Twenty-First Yearbook of the National Society for the Study of Education*, pt. 1 and pt. 2, Bloomington, Ill.: Public School Publishing, 1922.

——. "The Measurement of Educational Products." *Seventeenth Yearbook of the National Society for the Study of Education*, pt. 2, Bloomington, Ill.: Public School Publishing, 1918.

——. "Nature and Nurture: Their Influence Upon Intelligence and Their Influence Upon Achievement." *Twenty-Seventh Yearbook of the National Society for the Study of Education*, pt. 1 and pt. 2, Bloomington, Ill.: Public School Publishing, 1928.

Who's Who and Why in After-War Education. New York: Institute for Public Service, 1921.

Wiebe, Robert. *The Search for Order, 1877–1920*. New York: Hill and Wang, 1967.

Wigdor, Alexandra K. "Ability Testing: Uses, Consequences, and Controversies." *Educational Measurement: Issues and Practice* 1 (Fall 1982): 6–8, 26.

Wolf, Theta H. *Alfred Binet*. Chicago: Univ. of Chicago Press, 1973.

Wolfle, Helen M., ed. *American Psychological Association, Directory, 1948*. Washington, D.C.: American Psychological Association, 1948.

Wood, Ben D. *Measurement in Higher Education.* Yonkers-on-Hudson, N.Y.: World Book, 1923.

Woody, Clifford. "Tests and Measures in the Schoolroom and Their Value to the Teachers." *School and Society* 6 (July 1917): 61–66.

Woolley, Helen T. "The Use of Intelligence Tests in the Public Schools." *Seventh Annual Schoolmen's Week,* University of Pennsylvania (1920): 257–60.

Yerkes, Robert M. "Autobiography." In *A History of Psychology in Autobiography,* vol. 2, edited by Carl Murchison, 381–89. 4 vols. Worcester, Mass., Clark Univ. Press, 1930–1952.

——. "History and Organization of Psychological Examining and the Materials of Examination." In *Psychological Examining in the United States Army,* vol. 15, pt. 1, edited by Robert M. Yerkes, 1–292. Washington, D.C.: Government Printing Office, 1921.

——. "Psychology in Relation to the War." *Psychological Review* 25 (Mar. 1918): 85–115.

——. "Report of the Psychology Committee of the National Research Council." *Psychological Review* 26 (Mar. 1919): 83–149.

Yerkes, Robert M., and Yoakum, Clarence S., eds. *Army Mental Tests.* New York: Henry Holt, 1920.

Young, Kimball. "The History of Mental Tests." *Pedagogical Seminary* 31 (1924): 1–48.

——. *Mental Differences in Certain Immigrant Groups; Psychological Tests of South Europeans in Typical California Schools with Bearing on the Educational Policy and on the Problems of Racial Contacts in this Country.* Eugene, Oreg.: University of Oregon, 1922.

Zehm, Stanley J. "Educational Misfits: A Study of Poor Performers in the English Class, 1825–1925." Ph.D. dissertation, Stanford University, 1973.

Zunderland, Leila. "The Debate Over Diagnosis: Henry Herbert Goddard and the Medical Acceptance of Intelligence Testing." In *Psychological Testing and American Society,* edited by Michael M. Sokal, 46–74. New Brunswick, N.J.: Rutgers Univ. Press, 1987.

Index